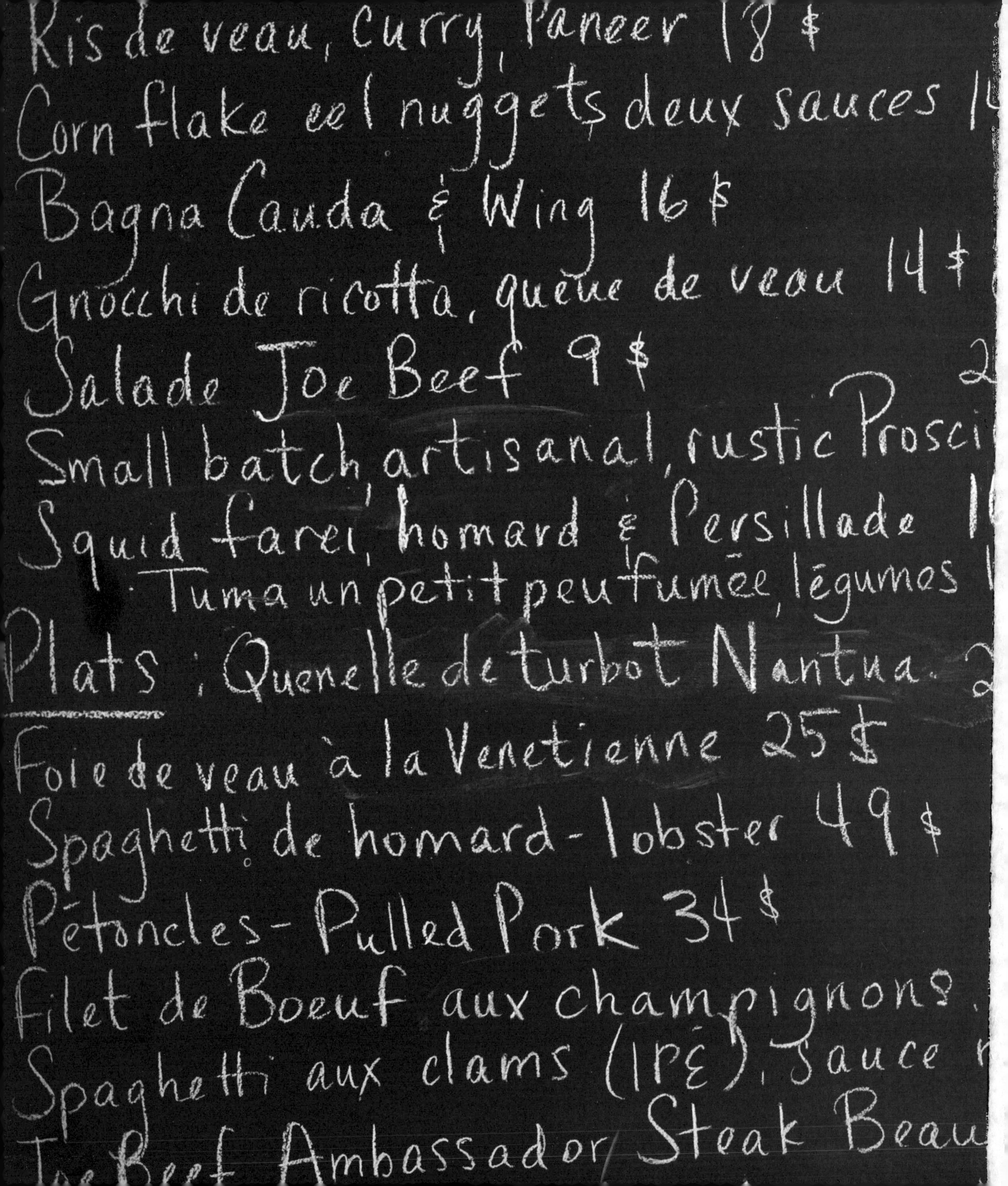

Ris de veau, curry, Paneer 18 $

Corn flake eel nuggets deux sauces 1

Bagna Cauda & Wing 16 $

Gnocchi de ricotta, queue de veau 14 $

Salade Joe Beef 9 $ 2

Small batch, artisanal, rustic Prosci

Squid farci, homard & Persillade 1

Tuma un petit peu fumée, légumes 1

Plats ; Quenelle de turbot Nantua. 2

Foie de veau à la Venetienne 25 $

Spaghetti de homard - lobster 49 $

Pétoncles - Pulled Pork 34 $

Filet de Boeuf aux champignons

Spaghetti aux clams (Irε), Sauce

Joe Beef Ambassador Steak Beau

THE ART OF LIVING ACCORDING TO JOE ✤ BEEF

THE ART OF LIVING

according to

JOE ✦ BEEF

✦ A COOKBOOK OF SORTS ✦

FRÉDÉRIC MORIN, DAVID McMILLAN & MEREDITH ERICKSON

Photographs by Jennifer May

TEN SPEED PRESS
Berkeley

CONTENTS

People ask me all the time what my favorite restaurant in the world is, and I always give them the wrong answer. My favorite restaurant in the world is Joe Beef.

The first time I went to Montreal, I reported immediately to the bar at Martin Picard's iconic Au Pied de Cochon (PDC). During my dinner, everybody kept asking me, "Have you been to Joe Beef yet?"

FOREWORD

by David Chang

The name Joe Beef sounded terrible to me. I was thinking, like, "What the fuck is Joe Beef? Do they serve Sloppy Joes?" I kept seeing images of Sloppy Joes, of ground meat in ketchup, and of hairnets. Or, even worse, could it be one of those red velvet and dark wood steak houses? I imagined it was something really poorly done, but then who doesn't like to see a train wreck?

When I finally got to Joe Beef, it felt like it was on the outskirts of Montreal, certainly not the city center, and certainly not any place chic or hip.

I sat down at the bar where a big, burly guy was opening oysters, and the place had this really amazing vibe. It reminded me of a couple of important New York restaurants, like a male version of Prune or of 71 Clinton Fresh Food back when Wylie Dufresne was cooking. I loved the wine list and the menu. Both are only available in chalk on the wall, and if you can't read them, they'll probably just tell you you're old. The décor had a rustic, lived-in feel—the kind that makes you never want to leave.

It had personality. It was alive. Those are rare and typically fleeting qualities in a restaurant.

I ordered a ridiculous amount of food because it all sounded amazing. I asked the bruiser in the Expos hat behind the bar for a gin and tonic and a dozen oysters. At the time—I feel this is important to note, because I look like a desk jockey now—I still had cooking scars on my hands and arms and all that.

I put in a classic "Hey, I'm a restaurant person, too" order with Dave McMillan, who looked at me and asked, with real malice in his voice, "Are you a narc?"

At the time I didn't know who he was. Joe Beef had been open about a year, and I didn't know anything about Montreal restaurants except for PDC. And this guy was questioning what I was doing. It was weird and unsettling. His tone escalated, "Who the fuck are you?"

I am a big guy, but Dave could kill a bear with his hands. I was totally taken aback. What did I do? He's like, "Are you a cook? Who are you? What restaurant do you work at? Are you that fucking guy David Chang?"

At that point, I didn't know up from down, and as I am beginning to let out an apologetic "uhhh-hhh," a drink is suddenly put down in front of me and Dave is shucking an egregious excess of oysters that I will clearly be eating and at the same time talking to himself out loud: "Chang doesn't know shit. Like in Montreal, we don't fucking know what's going on in New York." Then he turns to me and says, "I'm in New York every year, I go to your restaurant, I love it. You come in, try to sneak in and order food without even fucking telling us?"

We start talking and I start eating a torrent of oysters. A white-wine glass appears next to my cocktail, and Dave and I are splitting a bottle

of wine. I know the night's gonna be good because he's outdrinking me.

Once I'm convinced he's the genius behind the place, he says, "You know what? This restaurant's not about me, it's about Fred. He's doing the cooking. I just shuck oysters. That's all I do." I met Fred that night, too, and he immediately starting giving me shit, so I immediately liked him. He introduced me to his kitchen crew—an amazing group.

I got so many beautiful plates of food that I had to ask where everything was coming from, so Fred took me out back and showed me the garden. He also showed me some stuff that obviously can't make the book, like where the wormwood is growing. My mind was blown.

The next day, I go in for dinner again and I'm ordering oysters and Fred comes out. "You like bavette of beef?" he asks. I reply in the affirmative. "You get bavette of beef then."

It's massive, it's perfect, it's just so fucking spot on. I eat the whole thing, and fast. He comes back out and makes a little conversation. "You like lamb? I think you like lamb." I'm bursting at the seams, in obvious discomfort. He's like, "I'm gonna cook you some lamb."

I'm expecting a chop or two, a couple ounces at most, and what lands in front of me? A whole fucking rack! I am thinking, what's going on here? But it was perfect and I ate it. We drank until I felt hungry again, and then I found myself with Fred and his crew cooking Brussels

sprouts in the kitchen. Nights at Joe Beef can be like that: nonlinear.

And that cemented my love for the place. It's hard to eat anywhere else in Montreal. It didn't hurt that they had the hottest waitstaff of all time, though now Fred's married to one of them (Hi, Allison) and another is the coauthor of this book (Hi, Meredith). Everybody was having a good time, but also being crazy professional and awesome at what they did. It was impossible. It was a dream restaurant.

After I left Montreal, I learned Dave and Fred were joined at the hip. They were incredibly well versed in French food and wine. They were the hottest duo in town. They owned Montreal. That fascinated me because they had decided to get the hell out of the spotlight and open this place that was totally them, where they could be jerks—or just be themselves, if they wanted—and close whenever they wanted and that was fine. They live the high life, you know. Yet here they are trying to do something low-key, trying to work as little as possible, and it's still an amazing place. That is an impossible balancing act.

Now they have McKiernan's, now they have Liverpool House. When I was there, Fred was talking like Rain Man about building Liverpool House. He had this vision of the place and kept telling me about all these beautiful-sounding things he was going to do in the backyards of these buildings that looked like the

ghetto to me. I couldn't see it at the time, but what they've built since then is amazing.

Everything they do is amazing. It almost seems like they're trying not to try, but they make it work. They're so talented that it works. And they're trying to work the bare minimum. Dave's like, "I'm so fucking pissed when I have to work four fucking days . . . so pissed. I wanna work just three days. Is that so wrong?" Money, all of it, all the things that as a New York restaurant owner, as a New York chef, I know they have defied—they have defied what it is to be in the business. From the beginning, they have had a totally different agenda. It isn't about anything other than, "You know what? Let's have a good time. If it ever gets to the point where it's not, we'll just stop the whole thing."

A lot of people like to talk like that, but very few people can

actually do it, and no place on the planet I know does it half as well as Joe Beef. That's why it's so special to me.

As far as this book: I don't think anyone can replicate what these guys do. But it's worth trying. The food, sure, learn it. Learn to love trains, learn to weld, learn to make your own smoker, learn anything you can from these guys. I think there's some kind of Montreal black magic to it, that it might only work up there with all those crazy French Canadians. But after checking out how many good recipes, how much secret knowledge, how much humor, and how many good stories they've stuck between these two covers, I am ready to be proven wrong.

David Chang
New York City
January 2011

I never imagined when I agreed to wait tables part-time at Joe Beef that five years later I would end up writing the restaurant's cookbook. But that's exactly what happened.

INTRODUCTION
by Meredith Erickson

I met Frédéric Morin in 2004, when I began working at a restaurant where he was the chef de cuisine. Maybe it was his inquisitiveness, his obsessive hobbies, or his quirky sense of humor (many of the Joe Beef staff have fallen victim to Fred's signature cocktail, the codtini), but I liked him right away. I didn't know David McMillan well, though I had heard plenty of stories about him, so I was surprised to see his number pop up on my phone in the summer of 2005. "Come down to Saint Henri. Fred and I want to talk to you," he said. I couldn't imagine what they were dreaming up.

When I pulled up in front of 2491 Rue Notre Dame West, I saw a big man sitting on a small chair outside of a café that had brown paper covering the windows. He was drinking an espresso, pinkie up, and reading *Modern Painters*; CBC news was playing loudly in the background. Surely this wasn't the David McMillan who was rumored to throw busboys into dumpsters, drink magnums of Chablis nightly, and, in general, either terrify or completely charm everyone around him?

We exchanged pleasantries and David gave me a tour of the "restaurant." As we walked through what would become Joe Beef, David and Fred spoke about their plans and I saw the restaurant unfold in front of me: the four banquettes would go here, the giant fish would be mounted behind the bar in the corner over there, and the wine would go in the walk-in closet (because that was the only space for it). A giant blackboard listing all the food and wine would cover one entire wall, and on the adjacent wall, twelve to fifteen small Peter Hoffer paintings would be hung. And speaking of Peter, David explained, he was coming by in ten minutes with said paintings, so let's move on to the gist of this get-together: "We want you to scrounge up some information on Charles McKiernan (see page 6). He was a man of the people who had a canteen in the Old Port district in the 1870s. His patrons were hookers, wharf rats, and sailors; he was a brute who scared the shit out of everyone and his nickname was Joe Beef. That's what we're thinking of naming the restaurant: Joe Beef. We want you to write a nice paragraph about Joe Beef for the back of our [large] business card . . . oh, and do you want to work here?"

By this time we were leaning against David's truck in the garbage-ridden backyard and Allison, the third partner in the restaurant and Fred's girlfriend (now wife), had walked outside to meet me. She was organized, calm, quiet, financially sharp, and clean. In other words, she wasn't covered with sawdust, paint, coffee grinds, and baked beans. She would be in charge of the front-of-the-house staffing and all of the accounting (not an enviable position). She was, and is, one of the unsung heroes of this whole operation and was in the middle of telling me the kind of service she expected when Fred piped in, "This is where the garden will be." We all had lunch and some laughs at what was then Bonnys and is now McKiernan, and I agreed to work at Joe Beef two or three nights each week (or whatever my day job of editing would allow).

I started at Joe Beef as a waitress on opening day and stayed for nearly five years. I loved the people I worked with; the French food we served; the conversations I had with David about art, books, and rap music; and how he would allow me to say "Maybe this restaurant's not for

you" to certain disdainful customers who were giving the staff a hard time. Five years is much longer than the industry standard of time spent at one restaurant; it's really not normal at all. But ask anyone and they'll tell you, there is nothing normal about Joe Beef.

The vibe at Joe Beef and its sister restaurants is a cross between a food temple and *Pee-wee's Playhouse*. From 2:00 P.M. to 2:00 A.M. five days a week, cooks bounce among the restaurants speaking a mix of English and French. At any given time the staff could be potting ferns, smoking baloney, or sewing muslin sausage bags. When the restaurant opened, there was nothing in Little Burgundy but a burger joint and a few

quiet antique stores. Indeed, there were times when we expected to look out the front windows and see tumbleweeds rolling past the local degenerates in the doorways of the abandoned storefronts. Fast forward to today and you'll see that *we* are the local degenerates. You'll also see an extremely busy restaurant putting out inventive French market cuisine. You will also see Liverpool House, our tavern, and McKiernan, our luncheonette, straddling Joe Beef on the same block.

I like to describe Fred and David as fruitful sophists; that is, they have a multitude of interests in which they both excel, and all of those interests affect the success of their restaurants. Joe Beef is a

This shot of the decrepit little space wedged between McKiernan and the store next door is a fitting visual metaphor for our little restaurant: Our vision was to create something large in something small. As Fred says, it's like building a large boat inside an apartment just for the joy of it, knowing that the boat will never fit through the door and embracing the process anyway.

A NOTE ON THE SCALE FROM FRED

I WISH I HAD ANTHONY ROBBINS'S VERVE so that I could convince you to buy a nifty, twenty-dollar metric scale. I don't own shares in any scale corporation, and all of the recipes in this book include the standard U.S. volume and weight measures. But the only way to achieve accuracy is to weigh ingredients in grams on a reliable scale.

I'm not on a crusade for metric measurement. I love the inches and their fractions when I work with wood or metal. I run five miles, and that's fine, too. But grams make so much sense. The whole ounce, liquid, solid, pound thing gets me confused. With grams, everything is simple and precise. Why do you think the drug dealers went with grams?

In our days of foodism, where we all own (or wished we did) Damascus steel knives, a stand mixer, and a wax bean splicer, the scale is stigmatized. But it's neither expensive nor complicated. A cookbook is expensive; driving a car through a roundabout is complicated.

Go for an electronic model. One was on sale for eleven dollars in the big store near my house. I bought it, and it is as precise as my truffle-peddler friend's jeweler's scale.

Weigh stuff on a sheet of printer paper. It is easy to transfer. And don't forget to tare (zero) your scale and wipe it clean after every use.

---

universe unto itself. And the chapters of this book could be seen as planets spinning in the Joe Beef orbit. Each chapter represents a facet of the restaurant, whether it is a physical attribute, such as the garden or the smoker, or one of Fred's or David's obsessions, such as Chapter 2: The Builders, the Brewers, the Bankers, and the Gangsters: A Brief History of Eating in Montreal (David; see page 45) or Chapter 3: Trains! (Fred; see page 81).

When speaking about Fred, David says, "Fred makes the food I always want to eat, even when I don't know it yet." I have that same feeling when I walk into one of the restaurants and look at the chalkboard menu. It has been changing weekly since the beginning, always with five or six completely new dishes. When deciding which recipes should go in these pages, Fred, David, and I reviewed old menu drafts from the past five years, reminiscing along the way. From a list of (I would guess) nearly two thousand items, we chose the 135 recipes that we thought people would enjoy. It was also a good opportunity to get all of these recipes on paper for the first time. Because the operation is small and has a consistent staff, we had never bothered to write down any of our recipes (other than a handful that have been printed in newspapers and magazines or shown on television). It was a huge challenge to record the recipes and to test them for home cooks.

This cookbook has truly been a group effort. Fred and David each narrated half of the chapters, and I did my best to capture their larger-than-life personalities in writing. The recipes were developed by both Fred and David, but in the end, in every chapter, it's all Joe Beef. Each recipe fits within its chapter for a reason. For example, in Chapter 3: Trains!, you'll find the Dining Car Calf Liver recipe (page 95) that Fred developed after enjoying a similar dish on an Old Canadian National Railway menu. The behemoth Smorgasbord (insert) belongs to Chapter 4: The Seaway Snack Bar. And the Spaghetti Homard-Lobster (page 27) is found in Chapter 1: Building a Tiny Restaurant in the Middle of Nowhere, because that's where we put all of the Joe Beef classics.

You'll also find some neurotic stuff in here that you don't usually see in a cookbook. Tall Tales, Taste, and a Few Theories (page 166) is a roguish section full of equations, conjectures, and offenses and of the Joe Beef "parts" that make up the whole. These are the mother-ship recipes that we use again and again: mayonnaise (page 175), chicken skin jus (page 174), hollandaise (page 177), and the like. You'll also find a lot of how-tos inspired by our parents' copies of *Reader's Digest* and *Harrowsmith*. These are recipes for people who will never step foot in a kitchen: how to build a smoker (page 146) and how to (theoretically, of course) make your own absinthe (page 234). And for those of you who live on parallel latitude lines (or in destitute neighborhoods), there is Chapter 6: Building a Garden in a Crack Den.

Each chapter could have been a whole book in and of itself. This is not, for instance, the definitive book on Canadian train routes, Quebec cuisine, or the complete guide to Burgundy wines. *The Art of Living According to Joe Beef* is our take on food, wine, and spirits; a description of some of our unique experiences; and a collection of the recipes we love to cook and eat. We've tried to represent our tiny restaurant with all of its style, ambience, and humor. This is our hard guide to the easy life. It's not a straightforward cookbook. It's an art.

JOE BEEF OF MONTREAL

Working Class Culture and the Tavern: 1869–1889*

PETER DELOTTINVILLE

CHARLES MCKIERNAN WAS BORN on 4 December 1835, into a Catholic family in Cavan County, Ireland. At a young age, he entered the British Army and, after training at the Woolwich gunnery school, was assigned to the 10th Brigade of the Royal Artillery. In the Crimean War, McKiernan's talent for providing food and shelter earned him the nickname "Joe Beef," which would stay with him for the rest of his life. In 1864, McKiernan's Brigade was sent to Canada to reinforce the British forces at Quebec. By then a sergeant, McKiernan was put in charge of the military canteens at the Quebec barracks and later on St. Helens Island. If army life had seemed an alternative to his Irish future, then McKiernan saw better opportunities in North America. In 1868, McKiernan bought his discharge from the Army and with his wife and children settled in Montreal, opening the Crown and Sceptre Tavern on Saint Claude Street.

By settling in Montreal, McKiernan joined an established Irish community which accounted for 20 percent of the total population. Centred in

Griffintown, the largely working-class Irish had their own churches, national and charitable societies, political leaders, and businessmen. And as a tavern owner, McKiernan entered a popular profession in a city with a liquor license for every 150 inhabitants. The increasing number of taverns caused one temperance advocate to lament that if trends continued Montreal was destined to become "the most drunken city on the continent." The Crown and Sceptre, commonly known as "Joe Beef's Canteen," had a central location with Griffintown and the Lachine Canal to the east and the

extensive dockyards stretching out on either side. Business was good for Charles McKiernan.

In spite of the large numbers of taverns, Joe Beef's Canteen had an atmosphere, and a reputation, which was unique. Located in the waterfront warehouse district and at night identified only by a dim light outside the door, the Canteen housed a fantastic assortment of the exotic and the commonplace. One visitor described it as, "a museum, a saw mill and gin mill jumbled together by an earthquake; all was in confusion. The bar-room was crudely furnished with wooden tables and chairs, sawdust covering the floor to make the cleaning easier. At one end of the bar, great piles of bread, cheese and beef supplied the customers with a simple meal. Behind the bar a large mirror reflected a general assortment of bottles, cigar boxes, and curios. One bottle preserved for public display a bit of beef which lodged fatally in the windpipe of an unfortunate diner. The quick-witted McKiernan served his patrons with an easy manner. An imposing figure with a military bearing and fierce temper, the owner had few problems with rowdyism.

Joe Beef's Canteen had a special type of patron, and McKiernan aptly referred to his establishment as the "Great House of Vulgar People." His clientele was mostly working class. Canal labourers, long shoreman, sailors, and ex-army men like McKiernan himself were the mainstays of the business. Along with these waterfront workers, Joe Beef's Canteen attracted the floating population along the Atlantic coast. W.H. Davies, in his *Autobiography of a Super Tramp*, remarked that, "not a tramp throughout the length and breadth of the North American continent . . . had not heard of [Joe Beef's Canteen] and a goodly number had at one time or another patronized his establishment." McKiernan's tavern was also a well-known *rendezvous* for the "sunfish" or "wharf-rats" of the harbour who lived a life of casual employment and poverty. Newspaper reporters often dropped into the tavern to check on petty criminals who mingled with the crowd. Unemployed labourers visited the Canteen in the early morning

JOE BEEF

OF MONTREAL

The friend of the working man.

to look for a day's labour and often remained there throughout the day in the hope of something turning up. In all it was not a respectable crowd and, no doubt, was shunned by the more self-respecting artisans of the neighbourhood.

For working-class Montreal, the tavern held attractions beyond the simple comforts of food and drink. With no public parks in the immediate area, and only occasional celebrations by national societies and church groups, their daily recreational activities were centred around places like Joe Beef's Canteen. McKiernan's tavern was exceptionally rich in popular recreations. A menagerie of monkeys, parrots and wild cats of various kinds were from time to time exhibited in the Canteen, but it was McKiernan's bears which brought in the crowds. Joe Beef's first bear, named Jenny and billed as the "sole captive" of the

"courageous" 1869 expedition to the North West, never retired sober during the last three years of her life. One of her cubs inherited the family weakness. Tom, who had a daily consumption of 20 pints of beer, was often as "drunk as a coal heaver" by closing. Indeed, Tom was one of the regulars, usually sitting on his hind quarters and taking his pint between his paws, downing it without spilling a drop. Local temperance men had always pointed out that drink turned men into animals but in observing Tom's habits Joe Beef could point out this curious reversal of behaviour which the Canteen produced. Other bears were kept in the tavern's cellar and viewed by customers through a trap door in the bar-room floor. Occasionally, McKiernan brought up the bears to fight with some of his dogs or play a game of billiards with the proprietor. . . .

Although lacking formal education, Charles McKiernan considered himself a man of learning and regularly read the *New York Journal*, the *Irish American*, the *Irish World*, and local newspapers. He employed a musician (which was illegal under the terms of his license) to entertain his customers. Regular patrons played the piano in the tavern. McKiernan, however, led much of the entertainment. Drawing on personal experience and varied readings, McKiernan eagerly debated topics of the day, or amused patrons with humourous poems of his own composition. He had a remarkable ability to ramble on for hours in rhyming couplets. Sometimes to achieve his end, he distorted the accepted English pronunciation beyond recognition. This disgusted some middle-class visitors to the Canteen, but regular customers clearly enjoyed these feats of rhetoric. Behind the bar, two skeletons were hung from the wall and served as props for McKiernan's tales. From time to time, the skeletons represented the mortal remains of McKiernan's first wife, his relatives in Ireland, or the last of an unfortunate temperance lecturer who mistakenly strayed into Joe Beef's Canteen one night.

*Reprinted from *Labour/Le Travailleur*, 8/9 (Autumn/Spring 1981–1982), 9–40.

Joe Beef's Death

Fifty years ago, The Gazette reported a great loss to the city of Montreal. "Joe Beef," who had fed and housed more down-and-outers than he could count, and to whose establishment many men alive today, were taken by their fathers to see the bears (while the fathers enjoyed themselves in other ways), was a Montreal character, whose fame extended far beyond the limits of the Dominion. His waterfront saloon was patronized by bums, as he openly termed many of his patrons, as well as other more or less respectable drinkers of his day. In addition to the bottles and the beer barrels which graced his establishment, bread was piled up on the bar and there was soup and other provender.

"Joe" was a powerful man who would stand little nonsense at the expense of himself and his house, but he had a kindly feeling for the unfortunate and seldom denied food to a man down-and-out. In a pit in the centre of his taproom was a big bear, chained to a pole, up which it was wont to climb for the amusement of spectators. Visitors from the United States, other parts of Canada and Great Britain frequently went down to the wharf to see "Joe Beef's." Indulgent Montreal fathers would take their small boys to see the bear and gaze in awe upon the frowsy customers, who were always present. On one occasion the bear, which was as independent as the proprietor, jabbed at a child and scratched its fingers. "Joe" brought Bruin back to reason with a shot from a blunderbuss, into the ground of the pit, of course. The roar of the firing-piece was louder than the answering roars of the bear, and was effective, for the indignant animal settled down to its customary task of dancing on its hind feet and climbing the pole for the benefit of the visiting onlookers. After "Joe's" death, the tavern became the Salvation Army Lighthouse. One of his sons is living in Montreal today, a blacksmith on Vitre street.

The Gazette of January 16, 1889, reported Joe Beef's death as follows:

"JOE BEEF" DEAD.

A City Character Gone to His Rest.

Yesterday evening Mr. Charles McKiernan, proprietor of "Joe Beef's Canteen," died suddenly from what is thought to have been heart disease. The deceased was formerly in the Imperial Artillery and saw service in the Crimea. It was there that he received the name of Joe Beef. He made a capital forager and could find beef when no one else could; hence the name. Twenty-five years ago, when the Royal Artillery came to Canada, he accompanied them, and was canteen sergeant on St. Helen's island for about two years. He then procured his discharge and opened a restaurant named the Crown and Sceptre on Claude street. When the street was widened he removed to his present quarters on Nos. 4, 5 and 6 Common street.

Two Days I[n]
His[tory]

Janua[ry]
1840—Death at [
land, of Rt. [
Macdonell, Rom[an
Bishop of Kings[ton
1876—Halifax [
sued.
1879—Hon. J. [
transferred from [
Ontario to Supr[eme
Canada.
1898—Hon. Fra[
appointed Judg[e
Court of Quebec[
1902—Death of [
Prowse, senator [
ward Island.
1902—Supreme [
ada upheld pro[
Prince Edward I[
1907—E. W. P[
appointed judge [
Court, Montreal. [
1921—Death of [
Gage, Toronto, [
upon tuberculosi[s
1929—Death o[
Warburton, Pre[mier
Edward Island, [
1930— Hon. A[
judge of Appeal, [
ferred to Supr[eme
Canada.
1932 — Premie[r
Manitoba propos[
three central pro[
1936—Levy of [
Ontario announc[
1936—Hon. Th[
sworn as Premier[
ward Island.
1938—J. L. Ba[
M.P. for Champl[
Legislative Coun[cil

Janua[ry]
1808—Sir Geor[ge
pointed Lieuten[ant
Nova Scotia.
1832 — Tracy [
Montreal editors, [
islative Council [
ada.
1838—Militia oc[
land and Macken[
was no more.
1852—Trinity C[
opened by Bisho[p
1896—Dominion [
stituted; A. R. [
Minister of Ju[stice
Charles Hibber[t
Charles Tupper [
retary of State; [
ter, Finance; H[
Trade and Com[
G. Haggart, Post[
Hon. W. H. Mo[
ture; and Alpho[
Militia.
1896 — Genera[l
Manitoba; Green[
istry sustained.
1899—Death o[
Chiniquy, tempe[
1901 — Manito[
took over North[
ways in provinc[
1902—Hon. Ja[
sworn as Minist[er
Fisheries.
1904—Hon. H.[
sworn as Minist[er
and Canals.
1907—Hon. Joh[
Dan. Gillmor (N[
Hon. George W. [
Beith (Ontario), [
eau (Nova Sco[tia
Senate.
1910— Acade[

CHARLES M'KIERNAN
BETTER KNOWN AS
"JOE BEEF"
BORN IN CO CAVAN IRELAND
DEC 4, 18[ ]
[DIED IN] MONTREAL JAN 16, 1889.

*L*ittle Burgundy was a refuge. To escape our prior workplace, Fred and I would go for drives around Montreal, stopping at hardware stores, food markets, Chinatown, old corner restaurants. Sometimes we would browse junk shops or raid the downtown Salvation Army. Maybe we were already starting to build a restaurant in our minds, or maybe we just needed to get away from the supper-club scene on Boulevard Saint Laurent, where we worked. Either way, we were always on the lookout for old plates, oyster forks, live king crabs, shitty chairs, medicine cabinets, or the ultimate baloney sandwich. All roads led to Little Burgundy.

CHAPTER 1

BUILDING A TINY RESTAURANT IN THE MIDDLE OF NOWHERE

Little Burgundy is an area in southwest Montreal bordering the Lachine Canal. In the mid-1700s, French colonists named it La Petite-Bourgogne because of its resemblance to its namesake in France. It sits on a plateau, south of Mount Royal and just north of the Saint Lawrence River. Home to the Canadian National Railway yards and the Canadian Steel plant, Little Burgundy was, and remains, a working-class neighborhood. For the past ten years, it has been featured in every local magazine's "next up-and-coming neighborhood" article, but for reasons both obvious and obscure, it has been slow to reach its supposed potential.

Notre Dame is Little Burgundy's main north-to-south thoroughfare, a street full of inimitable characters, historical edifices, and appealing old boutiques, among

them the amazing Grand Central antiques, the eclectic and now sadly defunct Arcadia, the Irish lady junk shop, and the All Things Vintage store. Nearby is antique purveyor Madame Cash, who earned her nickname in the 1960s from cashing government checks for residents in the surrounding row houses. Across the street stands the majestic Corona Theatre. Ella and Oliver Jones played there; so did Oscar Peterson, who was born in Little Burgundy. Around the corner is the ever-abiding Atwater Market. This neighborhood has everything going for it.

Among all this stood Café Miguel, a diamond in the (very) rough located at 2491 Rue Notre Dame West owned by a wildly passive-aggressive troll of a man. He made six killer sandwiches and espresso as strong as it was good. And while his ambition to open a small restaurant was good, he soon

ran into trouble—trolls, alas, don't make good restaurant owners. His trouble was our opportunity, and Allison, Fred, and I got to thinking. We knew we could cook, we knew what the restaurant should look like, and we knew intuitively that we could get people to come to Little Burgundy. But it would take work.

For one thing, the café was a bit of a dump, like a dirty pig that wears a dress, too many accessories, and perfume. It had a solid, yet filthy shell and was furnished with IKEA tables, school chairs, and a blackboard with sandwich listings full of spelling mistakes. There was a six-burner stove, a deep fryer, a ventilation hood, an espresso machine, and a working chimney. We would essentially be acquiring the bare bones of a restaurant, which might make it workable, since we had very little money to start.

The backyard was full of graffiti, cigarette butts, beer bottles, tiny plastic bags, and what Fred believed was industrial waste. The clientele consisted of local furniture refinishers and antique dealers—basically guys with yellow fingers who stunk of lacquer thinner. Allison, Fred, and I held meetings in my truck in the backyard, during which we brainstormed on what our restaurant might look like, what food we would serve, and who we would harass—or terrorize—for favors to get it off the ground. We had anxiety about putting it all together, and for good reason: we don't have the organizational skills to do anything. Ask anyone and they'll tell you that we essentially have the attention spans of ferrets on speed. At least Fred and I do. Allison is the voice of reason.

So we met with three friends who also happen to be financial guys, Ronnie Steinberg, Jeff Baikowitz, and David Lisbona, to see if our idea could become a financial reality. We don't remember much of the meeting except that it was boring, it was held in a boardroom, and after five minutes I was wearing a baseball helmet I picked off a nearby shelf and Fred was chasing me around with no shirt on. The obvious conclusion is that Ronnie, Jeff, and David convinced us it could work (if we did it on the cheap), and they agreed to partner in for 10 percent. Jeff tells us now that when we left the room, he told Ronnie and David to give whatever amount they would feel comfortable never seeing again.

We are still partners with these three, and if it weren't for them, none of this would be possible. If you walk into David Lisbona's office today, you'll see seventy-five laminated newspaper clippings about Joe Beef alongside one picture of his kids. Their faith and pride in us are astounding.

BUILDING JOE BEEF

It took two months to build. We scrounged quickly to make it work. The restaurant came together with love, about twenty packs of wainscoting, and unlimited generosity and interest from friends. Mathieu Gaudet, a Montreal sculptor, friend, and Saint Henri local, built, among other things, our tables. On first glance, they look like they are ebony and mahogany, but they are actually MDF (medium-density fiberboard) combined with that really bad Masonite pressboard and many shiny coats of oil finish. He also built the bar from an old farmhouse floor that probably had fifteen coats of lead paint on it. (Don't worry, it's sealed; you can't go crazy from eating at the Joe Beef bar.)

The beautiful old tavern chairs we found by chance. We spotted them when we were driving around one day and pulled over and asked

the guy what he wanted for them. He said twenty bucks—not per chair, but for the lot.

Our friend Peter Hoffer did a beautiful installation of paintings: about twenty small abstracts and landscapes on one wall. We have always liked Peter's aesthetic, whether it is of Quebec trees or girls without shirts. His art fits our rustic environment and feels like it has always been there.

The eccentric and kooky Joe Battat, another one of our friends and favorite customers, showed up one day in the dining room with a giant bison head. It looks real and is about half the size of a Honda Civic. We zapped it onto the wall of the bathroom, and it has been scaring young kids ever since.

A couple of years back, one of our customers, Howie Levine, gave Fred a fart machine with a remote control. Fred immediately hid it in an ear of the bison, so whenever

someone walked into the bathroom and closed the door, Fred would go crazy on the remote and wait for the customer to emerge in a daze of confused humiliation.

The bathroom also boasts old photos taken at Bob Dylan and Neil Young concerts by Joe Battat and the door is covered with old Canadian license plates, fishing permits, and Quebec signage. Serendipitously, all the crazy elements seem to come together.

People still show up with old nostalgia-laden items that somehow fit the spirit of Joe Beef—things they've found at yard sales, in their grandma's attic, at the back of the garage. We have a barracuda caught by a Quebec politico, Viking candelabras, bear heads, a grand notice of the beatification of the now good brother Saint Andre, whale bones, trophies (Best Eater: Kevin), pictures of Uncle Jack fishing for salmon in British Columbia, and glasses shaped like naked women.

In other words, ambience is a big part of Joe Beef. The lighting, the music, and what's on the walls matter a great deal to us. Wine and food are not the only story. A true restaurateur has to be a jack of many trades. You see it all the time in restaurants: the food is good and the wine list is awesome, but the chairs suck, the art on the wall is revolting, and a Café Del Mar CD is playing continuously on the sound system. You can be a good cook or even a great chef, but it doesn't make you a restaurateur. You

have to have other interests, and you have to actually read.

Thankfully, Fred, Allison, and I geek out over the same classic stuff: a perfect Adirondack chair, a red vinyl banquette with brass nails, a pretty oyster-bar counter, old enameled cast-iron sinks, industrial lamps, a banged-up Rancilio coffee machine. We like wood, old paint, and a simple touch of cottage. This is why we love Maine, the Gaspé, and Kamouraska. I had so many bad experiences with Montreal's "hottest" designers, who simply couldn't design a proper service station, that I ended up buying an old medicine cabinet for Joe Beef. Its shelves, drawers, and glass bottles that once held swabs now hold knives. It works and it looks like it is where it should be. As Joe Beef came together, that's how it felt in general: like it had always been there.

The restaurant group we worked with prior to Joe Beef never understood our cooking, but the customers did. We are thankful for the experience; it just wasn't for us. We wanted our next project to be different from anything we had done before. We wanted to open a small, simple bistro, not unlike what Sam Hayward was doing with beautiful country food at Fore Street in Portland, Maine.

We imagined we would walk to the market and buy our produce every day. I was going to cook the meats, Fred was going to do the appetizers and vegetables, and then we were going to do the dishes . . . together. Allison would run the dining room, and John Bil would tend bar and shuck the occasional oyster. We would be open for lunch. Seventy bucks would be our top-end wine. Fred would put one lobster item on the menu, but more for him than for anyone else. We figured we might

move one or two lobster spaghettis per day but not much more. We just wanted to sell a few oysters, a bit of fish, and a bit of steak.

On opening day, the restaurant was packed. It went well. The only crazy thing was that Fred and I shelled fava beans in the backyard for three hours, and we believed that it was going to be that way every day. On the second day of business, we realized we needed to get a proper dishwasher. We also realized at 4:00 P.M. that we had been there since 9:00 A.M. and we wanted to go home. One lunchtime highlight was watching a country gentleman named Mr. Barber eat Dungeness and drink Meursault while wearing classic hunting apparel. Hence, the Grand Opening and prompt Grand Closing of lunch service at Joe Beef.

When we first opened, we thought we would be catering primarily to the antique dealers and other locals who lived on the Lachine Canal. But people actually followed us from our previous workplace, and we were getting customers who wanted to pay for two-pound lobsters, small-farm beef, and small-grower Champagnes and premier cru Burgundies. Fred was thrilled to come up with these dishes, and I was more than willing to work with private wine agents who wouldn't have dealt with us on Saint Laurent. We had the opportunity to work with modest-sized purveyors because we were working in a different context. All of a sudden, these smaller sources were not only willing to sell to Joe Beef, they were also coming to the restaurant to eat and visit!

We have never experimented with the concept of the food at Joe Beef. It has evolved in some ways, of course, but the food has always been the food we wanted to do since day one. We serve true Bocusian-Lyonnaise *cuisine du marché* (French market cuisine), which enables us to roll with the market in a way that wouldn't be possible with a printed menu. Although some complained that our food "lacks presentation" or is "too simplistic," we started getting good reviews and earning acclaim soon after opening. Chefs from every corner of the United States started showing up at our door.

One night, Fred noticed a ragged-looking Korean American guy ordering everything on the menu. Lo and behold, it was David Chang, owner of New York's Momofuku. This was right before David was ordered to

THE ART OF LIVING ACCORDING TO JOE BEEF

rest by his doctor. He had boarded a plane for Montreal, landed at Trudeau International Airport, and was at the Joe Beef bar a couple of nights later. The week was, of course, a complete haze of food, wine, and long nights, and David has been a good friend and Joe Beef supporter ever since. The props he gave us were a game changer for us, and now we seem to be part of the North American Food Itinerary. We're baffled and utterly appreciative. But more important, we are truly happy coming to work every day.

LIVERPOOL HOUSE

Six months after Joe Beef opened, we were booking one month in advance. You may think it is a dream to be that busy, but when you're small, reservations can be a nightmare to manage. Each day you pick up the phone and say no to all the people who were there with you from the beginning, including your mom.

So two years later, when our landlord and friend, Danny Lavy, told us that the restaurant space he owned two doors down was coming up for rent, we jumped at the chance to expand. "More tables and more room for all of our shit in the basement," we thought.

The building at 2501 Rue Notre Dame West is a beautiful Victorian. It has a double entrance and, from the outside, looks like two side-by-side soda-pop shops. When we took over the lease, the inside was a complete disaster. Electrical wiring was covered by floral wallpaper, and chicken wire was posing as some sort of modern installation on the ceiling. We took four truckloads of garbage out of there in the first week, and soon after painted the walls and floors the original Canadian National Railway green. We worked steadily for five or six weeks, and with the exception of Pelo (one of the earliest cooks at Joe Beef) falling through the floor into the basement, there was little drama.

From the beginning, Liverpool House had a more feminine aesthetic than the decidedly masculine Joe Beef. What was not feminine, however, was the smell. It took us a few weeks to find out we had a dead skunk under the storage room. When a skunk dies, it, like most animals, decomposes quickly. The scent sack, on the other hand, doesn't. Each time a customer walked in the front door, we prayed he or she wouldn't notice. But, of course, everyone noticed. It stunk! So we called Monsieur Caron, a murder grow-op cleanup guy who did skunks on the side. He and his wife (who also calls him Monsieur Caron) showed up, and after a couple of minutes said, "The good news is you don't have a live skunk. The bad news is you have a dead one." He tried everything from a perfume that smelled like patchouli to an oxidizing compound. Nothing worked. Finally, he brought in the big gun, an ozone generator that we had to turn on each night after service (and walk away quickly because it was toxic). It took about six months for the smell to disappear completely.

Other than the persistent scent sack, we had no real issues opening Liverpool . . . well, except maybe for the Italian thing. We had the idea to open an Italian version of Joe Beef, but we all knew that the idea was mostly tongue-in-cheek, since neither Fred nor I has a drop of Italian blood. We didn't want to mess with Joe Beef. We loved it the way it was, and our plan was that Liverpool would complement it and vice versa. That said, we wanted to serve Italian food that you might get in London, à la River Café, not what you would get in Rome. If you could order mushrooms with a poached egg and mimolette cheese at Joe Beef, then you could get mushrooms with a poached egg and shaved Parmesan at Liverpool, and all of a sudden it seemed Italian. We wanted to order basket-clad Chianti; hang heavy, purple velvet curtains; and get someone really rich to lend us a Caravaggio ("Don't worry about it, we're in the worst part of town, it will be fine.")

We stuck with the Italian idea for about six months and then phased it out. Few people asked any questions. Liverpool House now is like Joe Beef's bistro,

or Joe Beef lite. It's for the everyday, and we gladly serve many locals. A TV is tucked away in one corner for watching *nos glorieux* Canadiens de Montréal play, and luckily for us, it's a favorite after-game destination for the Habs players. It's got a bustling bar, and I would say four of the eight stools are almost always taken by restaurant people. Liverpool is the kind of place you can drop in after work for a dozen Carr's Family Malpeque oysters, a couple glasses of Muscadet, and a piece of fish, and have a conversation with the bartender or watch the game and go home.

McKIERNAN LUNCHEONETTE

Named after Montreal's venerable tavern owner Charles McKiernan (see the excerpt by Peter DeLottinville, page 6), our luncheonette sits on the other side of Joe Beef, right next door. The two share one backyard, which serves as the McKiernan lunch terrace and the Joe Beef dinner terrace in the summer. The space used to be a great little vegetarian spot called Bonnys, which we happily took over when Bonny moved down the street. It's about the size of a large walk-in closet and seats eighteen people all day, max.

The idea for the luncheonette was pretty straightforward: a lunch spot that we were always looking for but could never find. The method of Fred locking himself into Liverpool House with a pile of tools and a couple of minions, with me feeding them pizza through a crack in the door, worked well, so we decided to do the same with McKiernan. I did my usual collage of old and inspiring French and Canadian home magazines. Allison opened new accounts, and Fred began building. It was ready in two months.

Brunch at McKiernan consists of dishes like a half lobster with poached eggs and baloney, smorgasbords, and breakfast sandwiches made with homemade sausage. For lunch, we serve classic soups, sandwiches, and salads for women with sensible shoes. At night, McKiernan is almost like a Joe Beef private room for parties. But when it's not rented, it acts as the local quiet spot with a new menu nightly. One unique aspect of McKiernan is that Fred's woodworking shop, complete with drafts and train calendars, lies directly below, in the basement. It is also rumored to have a tunnel that connects the three restaurants: a mythical mine shaft or "tunnel of pleasure."

Now, five years later, we're on "the compound," sharing what seems

like a massive backyard, with cooks running between the three restaurants, speaking Frenglish, and finishing service with a drink under the lights of the baseball field in the back. The "we" has gone from a staff of six at the beginning to thirty-five as we write this book.

The idea of having three restaurants next to one another on the same street may seem weird to some people. The restaurants rose from a desire for something different and all our own. Everything else happened from that. We wanted more room, so we built Liverpool House. We wanted to smoke everything ourselves, so we built a smoker in the backyard. Fred wanted Joe Beef to have its own vegetables, so we built (and continually care for) a garden. The idea of a greenhouse came up, and within a week, we (along with John Bil on his "vacation") had finished it.

Joe Beef was created with nostalgia in mind, with the sense that the original paint is probably better than what is covering it and that the classic *L'art culinaire français* has almost more use than any cooking manual that's come after it. We're inspired by the traditions of Quebec and what's in our own backyard. The following recipes are the Joe Beef classics. —**DM**

FOIE GRAS PARFAIT with MADEIRA JELLY

Makes 10 to 12 ramekins

This dish, which calls for a whole fresh duck foie gras, has been on our menu since day one. We like it with a thin layer of our Madeira Jelly poured on top, but almost any compote, jam, or jelly can be served alongside.

1 whole fresh duck foie gras, about 18 ounces (500 g)

4 cups (1 liter) milk

1½ cups (375 ml) whipping cream (35 percent butterfat)

1 tablespoon brandy

1 teaspoon sugar

Salt and pepper

6 egg yolks

2 whole eggs

Boiling water, as needed

Black truffle shavings for topping (optional)

Madeira Jelly (recipe follows)

Toasted brioche or *pain de campagne* (country bread) for serving

1. Place the liver in a large bowl, and pour the milk over it. Cover and set aside at room temperature for 1½ to 2 hours. You want the liver to soften and to look and feel like a giant piece of Silly Putty. When you have that consistency, take the liver out of the bowl, put it on paper towels, and pat it dry. Throw out the milk.

2. Preheat the oven to 325°F (165°C). Put the cream in a small saucepan and place it over high heat.

3. Now, here's the weird part: Using a table knife, split the liver in half lengthwise. There will be veins and nerves and bile ducts. Basically, anything you see that is red or green should be taken out. It's not a big deal if you don't remove it all. Just get what you can. Pat both halves dry.

4. Cut the liver into cubes. The smaller they are, the easier on your blender or food processor. Put the cubes in a large, wide bowl; add the brandy, sugar, and a healthy sprinkle each of salt and pepper; and turn the cubes gently to coat them on all sides.

5. Put the cubes in a blender or food processor and pulse until the cubes are all gone and you are left with a creamy consistency. Add the egg yolks and whole eggs. The cream will be at a boil by now, so take it off the burner. You want to pulse for about 10 seconds, add some cream, pulse for 10 seconds more, add a little more cream, and then pulse again. Continue like this until all the hot cream is added and the liver is smooth and creamy, like a frothy McDonald's milk shake.

6. Pour the liquid liver through a coarse-mesh sieve into a bowl with a spout or a large measuring pitcher. You need to strain out any nasty bits you may have missed before. Divide the mixture evenly among 10 to 12 ramekins or jam jars, ½ cup (125 ml) each. Select a baking dish just large enough to hold the ramekins without touching (you may need to use 2 baking dishes or bake the parfaits in batches), and line the bottom with a double layer of paper towels. Place the ramekins in the baking dish.

continued

7. Pull out the oven rack, put the baking dish on it, pour the boiling water into the baking dish to reach about halfway up the sides of the ramekins, and push in the oven rack. Bake for 25 minutes, then pull out the oven rack and lightly shake the ramekins. If the liver wobbles stiffly, you're ready. If not, push in the rack and bake for another 5 to 8 minutes, then test again.

8. When the parfaits are ready, remove them from the baking dish and let them cool to room temperature. If you are using the truffle shavings, arrange some on top of each parfait. Cover the parfaits and refrigerate until chilled. Top with the jelly as directed, then re-cover and return to the refrigerator as directed. The parfaits will keep for up to 4 days. Remove from the refrigerator about 10 minutes before serving with the toasted brioche.

MADEIRA JELLY

Makes 1 cup (250 ml)

6 sheets gelatin
1 cup (250 ml) Madeira wine
6 1/2 tablespoons (100 ml) water
2 tablespoons maple syrup
1 teaspoon white wine vinegar

1. Bloom the gelatin sheets in a bowl of cool water to cover for 5 to 10 minutes, or until they soften and swell.

2. In a small pot, combine the wine, water, maple syrup, and vinegar over medium heat. When hot, remove from the heat. Gently squeeze the gelatin sheets, add to the wine mixture, and whisk until completely dissolved.

3. If using for the parfaits, spoon a thin layer of the warm liquid over each chilled parfait and refrigerate for 15 minutes to set the jelly. The layer should be 1/8 inch (3 mm) thick. If not using for the parfaits, pour the warm liquid into a jar with a tight-fitting lid and refrigerate. It will keep for up to 7 days. When serving this jelly on a plate, we press it through a ricer to give it a mound of kryptonite appearance.

MARROWBONES CULTIVATEUR

Serves 2 for dinner (2 bones per person)
or 4 for lunch (1 bone per person)

Nowadays, every restaurant seems to have marrow on the menu. But for decades, the after-work evenings of local chefs have usually ended up (drunkenly) in the same place, L'Express, with its infamous three large trunks of marrowbone, *sel gris*, and rounds of cabbage. There is something about hot marrow in a cold climate; it's the kind of thing you want to eat when snow is melting off your boots.

Essentially a thick French peasant (*cultivateur*) vegetable soup with marrow, this recipe is a Joe Beef winter standard. Marrowbones are always from the hind legs of the animal. You want them crosscut, which reveals a long tube of marrow. If you have purchased them frozen, thaw them in the fridge first.

4 crosscut marrowbones, each about 6 inches (15 cm) long

Salt and pepper

3 tablespoons unsalted butter

½ cup (45 g) or 6 slices diced bacon

⅓ cup (50 g) diced onion

⅓ cup (55 g) diced, peeled potatoes (Yukon Gold or fingerling)

⅓ cup (55 g) diced carrots

⅓ cup (25 g) diced cabbage

⅓ cup (45 g) tiny cauliflower florets

⅓ cup (25 g) chopped leek, white part only

⅓ cup (55 g) diced white turnip

⅓ cup (45 g) diced zucchini

6 sugar snap peas, thinly sliced on the diagonal

2 sprigs thyme

2 cups (500 ml) chicken stock

1 teaspoon cider vinegar

1 tablespoon Dijon mustard, plus more for serving

Canola oil for searing

1 clove garlic, smashed

Fresh flat-leaf parsley leaves for garnish

Italian bread, as much as you want

Sea salt for serving

1. When you get the marrowbones home, put them in a big bowl with water to cover and 2 tablespoons salt. They should sit refrigerated for a minimum of 4 hours or as long as overnight.

2. To prepare the vegetables, place a cast-iron pot over medium heat and add 2 tablespoons of the butter. Once it starts to bubble, add the bacon. Let the bacon crisp up for 2 minutes, and then add the onion. Let the onion cook for a couple of minutes, stirring now and again, and then bomb the rest of the vegetables in except for the zucchini and snap peas. Cook the vegetables for about 5 minutes, stirring occasionally. Base the cooking on the potatoes, as they will taste the worst if they are not cooked through. In the last minute of cooking, add the zucchini and snap peas.

continued

3. Add 1 teaspoon salt, 1 thyme sprig, and a pinch of pepper to the pot, then pour in the stock and bring to a boil. Cook for 2 minutes and add the vinegar. At the last minute, add the remaining tablespoon of butter and the mustard, mixing well. Season with salt and pepper and set aside over very low heat.

4. Now for the bones. Preheat the oven to 425°F (220°C). Drain the bones and pat them dry. Put a large ovenproof pan over high heat. Pour in a thin film of canola oil, and add the garlic and the remaining 1 thyme sprig. Cook, stirring, for 1 minute. Add the bones, marrow side down, and sear for 2 minutes. You are not looking for color, just a bit of heat penetration. Flip the bones marrow side up and put the pan into the oven. Roast for 12 minutes. We suggest using a thermometer to check the core of the marrow for doneness. It should register 140°F (60°C). A knife should penetrate the marrow easily. If the bones wobble and tip over, loosely crumble a sheet of foil and nestle them for sturdiness.

5. Take the bones out of the oven and place 1 or 2 bones, cut end up, in each shallow soup bowl. Divide the vegetable mixture among the bowls. Garnish with the parsley. Serve with the bread, mustard, and sea salt.

SPAGHETTI HOMARD-LOBSTER

Serves 2

We take this name from an old *Iron Chef* episode when the host declared "Battle Homard Lobster!" Yes, *homard* and lobster mean the same thing (like "minestrone soup").

Among other things that don't make any sense: this is probably the most popular Joe Beef dish.

8 quarts (8 liters) plus 2 cups (500 ml) water

Salt and pepper

1 live lobster, weighing about 2½ pounds (1.2 kg)

2 portions spaghetti

1 tablespoon olive oil

2 cups (500 ml) whipping cream (35 percent butterfat)

1 teaspoon unsalted butter

2 tablespoons brandy

1 sprig tarragon

1 clove garlic, smashed

3 slices slab bacon, cut into matchsticks and crisped in a pan

Fresh parsley, julienned, for garnish

1. Start by dividing the 8 quarts water evenly between 2 pots. Add 2 tablespoons salt to each pot, and bring both pots to a rolling boil. (One is for the lobster, and the other one is for the spaghetti.)

Lobsters live in the sea, and the best lobster you'll ever eat will be when you are on a ship or near the shore and the lobster is boiled in seawater. So, before you add the lobster, salt the water. When it is as salty as the sea, slide in the live lobster. You need to cook a lobster for about 5 minutes per pound (455 g), which is about 12 minutes for this lobster. If you don't want to look at the live lobster as it boils, you are probably someone who likes to have sex with the light off. That's okay.

2. Measure the spaghetti. To do that, make the size of a quarter with your thumb and index finger; 1 portion of pasta is what fits into that "hole." Measure 2 portions and add them to the second pot of boiling water. Cook the pasta according to the instructions on the package. We don't make our own spaghetti, so we don't expect you to, either. Drain it, then disregard the "canons of pasta" and go ahead and rinse it under cold running water. Toss it with the olive oil so it doesn't stick together and keep it at room temperature nearby.

3. The lobster will be cooked by now. With your trusty long tongs, take it out of the water and put it in a bowl. Let it cool down until you can touch it with your hands, then remove the claws and the knuckles. Crack the claws with a knife or with a cracker, whichever you feel most comfortable using. Take the tail off the torso and crack it in two. (See the diagram on page 28 to see how to cut the lobster.) Everything is still in the shell, and you want to leave it like that. Put the claws, knuckles, and tail pieces in a bowl and put the bowl aside.

continued

4. Now you will be left with the torso. Hack it into 4 or 5 rough chunks with a cleaver. If that's too dramatic, use a large knife. Keep them separate from the other pieces.

5. Next comes the sauce: In a large stockpot, combine the torso pieces, cream, butter, brandy, tarragon, garlic, and the remaining 2 cups water. Place over medium heat until the mixture starts to bubble. Reduce the heat to very low and simmer gently for 30 minutes, making sure it doesn't reduce too much. You need about 1 cup (250 ml) liquid left.

6. Filter out all the parts, toss them away, and keep just the cream. You don't want the cream runny; instead, it should nicely coat the back of a spoon. Season with salt and pepper.

7. In a large, shallow pan, warm together the lobster cream and the lobster pieces over medium heat. Add the spaghetti and bacon and twirl all the ingredients around with a wooden spoon for 3 to 4 minutes to heat through. Garnish with the parsley and serve family style (turn on the TV and start arguing).

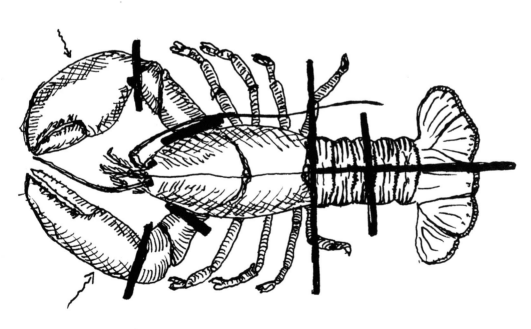

LA DÉCOUPE DU HOMARD

OEUFS EN POT

Serves 2

The great thing about this recipe is that even if you mess it up (which is tough to do), you still have a delicious mushroom and bacon cream that you can pour on toast and call it a day. This is a classic coddled egg but with much more garnish.

8 ounces (225 g) chanterelle or morel mushrooms

3 tablespoons unsalted butter

1 French shallot, thinly diced

6 slices bacon, diced (about 1⅔ ounces/50 g)

Salt and pepper

½ cup (125 ml) whipping cream (35 percent butterfat)

½ cup (125 ml) Chicken Skin Jus (page 174), Beef Shank Stock (page 249), or chicken stock, reduced to ¼ cup (60 ml)

1 tablespoon *vin jaune* or dry sherry (optional)

2 eggs

Buttered toasted bread wedges for serving

1. In a frying pan, sweat the mushrooms with the butter over medium heat for about 2 minutes, or until the mushrooms have released their water. Add the shallot, bacon, and a pinch each of salt and pepper and simmer for 5 minutes.

2. Meanwhile, ready a bain-marie: place 2 ramekins, each about ⅔ cup (160 ml), in a small pan. Fill the pan with water to reach about halfway up the sides of the ramekins. Take the ramekins out and put the pan of water on to boil.

3. Meanwhile, add the cream, stock, and *vin jaune* to the mushrooms and cook over medium heat, stirring occasionally, for 5 to 7 minutes, or until the cream has reduced by one-third.

4. Fill each ramekin two-thirds full with the cream mixture. Crack 1 egg onto each ramekin, nesting it on top of the cream mixture.

5. The water should now be boiling: using tongs, carefully place each ramekin into the pan of boiling water and cover the pan immediately. Cook for 5 minutes, or until the egg whites are cooked but the yolks are still slightly runny.

6. Remove the ramekins from the pan and serve at once with the buttery toast soldiers.

SCALLOPS with PULLED PORK

Serves 4

At Joe Beef, we serve this dish with East Coast scallops, about 5 or 6 per person, with a few tablespoons of hollandaise and a nice spoonful of pulled pork on top. Such a portion is a food-cost disaster and intimidating to some*, but the scallops go down easily and they're better topped with pork than some foamy composition. To make this dish, you are going to work on the pulled pork first, then the hollandaise, and lastly the scallops, as they take only minutes. You will end up with an excessive amount of meat, which you can use to make some pulled pork sandwiches (page 151).

PULLED PORK

2 tablespoons paprika

1 tablespoon salt

1 tablespoon pepper

1 tablespoon sugar

1 Boston butt (shoulder), 4 to
    5 pounds (about 2 kg)

¼ cup (60 ml) yellow mustard

½ cup (125 ml) water

BBQ Sauce (page 176)

Hollandaise sauce (page 177)

16 to 20 sea scallops (U10 size),
    4 or 5 per person

Canola oil for frying

Sea salt and pepper

A Note on Pork: Boston butt (échine in French and coppa di spalla in Italian) comes from the upper part of the shoulder. It lends itself to both braising and smoking. It is a good idea to test your oven with a thermometer before attempting the long cooking called for here. You would be surprised how much effect just fifteen degrees of difference can have to a long cooking time. Put the thermometer in the oven, turn on the oven to the specified temperature, and then wait for it to preheat. Check the thermometer and adjust the oven setting accordingly.

1. To make the pulled pork, preheat the oven to 275°F (135°C). In a small bowl, stir together the paprika, salt, pepper, and sugar. Rub the meat all over with the mustard and then with the paprika mixture.

2. Put the pork in a large roasting pan and add the water to the pan. Place the pork in the oven and roast for up to 9 hours. Check the pork after 5 hours and every hour after that to make sure it isn't burning or drying out. If the meat starts to dry out or feel like cardboard, cover it with foil. Remove the pork from the oven at 9 hours and verify that it shreds easily with a fork. The best way is to press it against the side of the pan. If it is not shredding easily, put it back in the oven for another 10 to 15 minutes. When it's ready, remove the pork and let it cool for 10 minutes.

3. While the pork is still warm, shred it by hand or with a fork and place in a bowl. Mix the pork with as much BBQ sauce as you like and keep the bowl warm until you are ready to serve.

4. Make the hollandaise and reserve, then immediately set to work on the scallops. Pat the scallops dry with paper towels. Do not season them at this point. Outfit yourself with long sleeves and long tongs. Heat a cast-iron or nonstick frying pan over high heat. When the pan is hot, pour in the oil to a depth of ⅛ to ¼ inch (3 to 6 mm). When the oil is almost smoking, *carefully* place the scallops in the pan, spacing them 1 inch (2.5 cm) apart. After 1 minute, wiggle each scallop ever so gently with your tongs. After another 2 minutes, flip 'em away from you ("away" is important, so you don't propel vast amounts of scalding oil toward you if you drop a scallop!). Remove from the heat and season the scallops with sea salt and pepper.

5. To serve, divide the scallops evenly among 4 plates. Top each serving of scallops with a few spoons of the hollandaise and then a big spoonful of the pork. Serve right away.

* This is true for most people, except for our friend Dan "The Automator" Nakamura, who we have seen eat four Joe Beef main courses, followed by a "snack" of Big Ed burgers, poutine (fries, gravy, and cheese curds), and hot dogs four hours later at Montreal's Moe's diner. By himself, he can decimate the food reserves of a small nation, bringing famine upon its inhabitants. Sir, we tip our hat to you.

ARCTIC CHAR FOR TWO with GULF OF ST. LAWRENCE SNOW CRAB

Serves (you guessed it) 2

Some chefs have decided cedar-planked fish is out of fashion, but we are still making it into the 2000s for two reasons: because it's delicious and because our friend Mathieu, who is an amazing sculptor, will sometimes show up with some pretty radical cedar boards.

Before starting this recipe, it's a good idea to fill up the sink and soak your cedar board in cold water for as long as you can. This prevents a fire and makes the board a perfect steam generator for cooking the fish.

12 ounces (340 g) Gulf of St. Lawrence snow or Jonah crabmeat (frozen is good as long as you drain it), flaked and checked for bits of shell and cartilage

2 tablespoons minced fresh chives

2 tablespoons minced fresh dill

1 egg

1 slice white bread, cut into small cubes

1 tablespoon Dijon mustard

2 tablespoons chopped capers

Salt and pepper

1 artic char (rainbow trout works too), 2 to 2½ pounds (about 1 kg), boned from inside by the fish guy (butterflied and pin boned)

1 or 2 slices bacon

3 bay leaves

3 tablespoons canola oil

Wax Beans and Clams for garnish (recipe follows), optional

1. Preheat the oven to 400°F (200°C).

2. To make the crab stuffing, in a bowl, combine the crab, chives, dill, egg, bread, mustard, and capers and mix gently. Season lightly with salt and about 6 turns of pepper.

3. Stuff the crab mixture into the fish cavity and cover the opening with the bacon slices—like a bacon fence—to hold the stuffing in place. Tie with kitchen twine in 4 or 5 spots down the fish to hold everything in place. Sneak those bay leaves under the twine. Drizzle the oil over the fish, and season again lightly with salt and pepper.

4. Bake for 35 to 40 minutes, or until a metal skewer inserted in the thickest part of the fish and then withdrawn is hot when you touch it to your chin. If you have an instant-read thermometer, that's about 140°F (60°C).

5. Remove the fish from the oven, transfer it to a platter, and snip the twine. Using a serrated knife, slice the fish along the twine grooves. Bring the whole fish on the platter to the table and serve each piece of fish with a heaping spoonful of beans and clams on the side.

WAX BEANS AND CLAMS

Serves 4

¹/₄ cup (55 g) unsalted butter

24 small clams such as little-necks, savoury (aka varnish), or manila, well scrubbed and free of sand

1 pound (455 g) yellow wax beans, trimmed and cut in half crosswise

¹/₄ cup (60 ml) dry white wine

1 teaspoon chopped garlic

¹/₂ teaspoon chopped fresh chile

1 teaspoon smoked paprika

¹/₄ cup (40 g) whole roasted almonds

1 tablespoon chopped green onion

Salt and pepper

1. In a large frying pan or sauté pan, melt half of the butter over medium-high heat. Add the clams, beans, wine, garlic, chile, and smoked paprika. Cover and cook for about 5 minutes, or until the clams open. Lift the lid and peek occasionally to make sure the pan doesn't go dry. If it does, add a little water.

2. Uncover and pick out and discard any clams that failed to open. Add the remaining butter, the almonds, and the green onion and toss to mix evenly and melt the butter. Season with salt and pepper and serve right away.

FOIE GRAS BREAKFAST SANDWICH

Makes 1 sandwich

When we opened Joe Beef, we made all kinds of promises, oaths of sorts: no cranberry juice, we would wash dishes ourselves, we would stay open on Monday nights. We also said we would always have (at least) one breakfast item on the dinner menu. Of course, we are closed Mondays and never do the dishes ourselves, but we do always have one breakfast item on the menu. Oh, and we still don't serve cranberry juice.

We see foie gras the same way we see skateboarding: we had a phase, like most everyone. But then it stopped, and now it's here and there and we enjoy it in small doses. If you come to town and want to feast on foie gras everything, make a pit stop at Au Pied de Cochon; they are good friends and do it better than anyone.

Our favorite way to serve foie gras is with a breakfast-sausage patty or with peameal bacon, a well-peppered over-easy egg, and an English muffin. Add a dash of maple mustard and you're happy, whether it's 7:00 A.M. or 7:00 P.M. (You'll have plenty of mustard left over, but that's okay. It's good with everything from salmon to corn dogs.) Remember, when you sear foie gras, be generous with salt, use a good pan, and most important, be prepared for a smoke show. Work fast and have a tray and tongs at hand before you start.

MAPLE MUSTARD
¾ cup (230 g) maple syrup
½ cup (125 ml) Dijon mustard
1 tablespoon mustard seeds
½ teaspoon pepper

2 thin slices Canadian back bacon or Peameal Bacon (page 100)
1 egg
1 English muffin, split
2 tablespoons canola oil
4-ounce (115-g) piece fresh duck or goose foie gras, ¾ inch (2 cm) thick
Salt and pepper

1. To make the maple mustard, bring the maple syrup to a boil in a heavy saucepan over medium-high heat and boil for about 6 minutes, or until the bubbles increase in size. Remove from the heat, let cool for about 3 minutes, then whisk in the prepared mustard, the mustard seeds, and the pepper. Let cool completely before using. Maple mustard stores well in a tight-capped container in the fridge for at least a couple of weeks.

2. The best thing to have for this operation is one of those plug-in flat, nonstick griddles, the kind the tasting ladies have in the grocery store. You can cook your egg, bacon, and muffin on the griddle while you blast the liver on the stove top. Preheat the oven to 350°F (180°C); this is to keep the bacon warm after cooking or to blast the foie if need be. Turn on the griddle and set to medium-high heat. When the griddle is ready, cook the bacon until the edges are golden brown and lightly crispy, fry the egg over easy, and toast the cut sides of the muffin.

3. Heat the oil in a frying pan over high heat. When the frying pan is superhot, add the liver and cook, turning once, until nicely colored. You want a good color on the foie gras, kind of like the skin of a roasted chicken. This will take only a minute or two total in a very hot pan. Remember to flip the liver away from you so you don't splash your belly. Carefully transfer the liver to a baking sheet. If the liver is still hard to the touch, put it in the oven for a minute or two. The fat that collects in the baking sheet (but not the fat from the frying pan) is good to drizzle on the muffin.

4. Now build your sandwich: start with a muffin half, cut side up, and top it with the bacon, the egg, and the foie. Drizzle the stack with a little mustard, sprinkle with salt and pepper to taste, and top with the other muffin half.

SCHNITZEL OF PORK

Serves 4

Not long ago, restaurants were just fun places to eat out—not the foodist temples of today. And they were often an ode to the owner's homeland, hobby, or previous livelihood: a ski or fishing lodge, a Bahamian beach hut, a Chinese pagoda. At the top of our list is the *stube*, the Austrian ski shack with crossed skis hung over the mantel, beer steins, pretzel buns as bread, schnapps, and *kabinnet*. The menus here would invariably feature sides of mustard in glass jars, parsleyed potatoes, krauts and wursts of all kinds, and, ultimately, the schnitzel—crisp and hot and overlapping the plate like Dom DeLuise on a bar stool.

We include schnitzel on the Joe Beef menu twice a year: in the spring with peas, cream, and morels, and in the fall with chanterelles, eggs, and anchovies (of course). Ask your butcher for 4 large, pounded schnitzels. Sizewise, default to your biggest pan. You can top the schnitzel with Oeufs en Pot (page 29), or with a plain fried egg with a lemon wedge alongside.

3 cups (385 g) all-purpose flour

Salt and pepper

4 eggs

1 cup (250 ml) sour cream

¼ teaspoon freshly grated nutmeg

4 cups (170 g) *panko* (Japanese bread crumbs), pulsed for a few seconds in a food processor until the texture of regular bread crumbs

1 cup (115 g) grated sbrinz or grana padano cheese

4 large pork schnitzels (loin cutlets), pounded by the butcher to ¼ inch (6 mm) thick

¼ cup (60 ml) canola oil or more if needed

1. Prepare 3 flat containers, each big enough to contain 1 schnitzel at a time. Put the flour and a good pinch each of salt and pepper in the first container. In the second container, whisk together the eggs, sour cream, nutmeg, and another good pinch each of salt and pepper. In the third container, mix together the processed *panko* and the cheese.

2. Dip a schnitzel in the flour and shake off the excess; drop it in the egg mixture and drain off the excess; and lay it in the third container with the *panko* mixture and coat it well. Shake off the excess crumbs and put it on a platter. Repeat with the remaining schnitzels, then put the platter, uncovered, in the fridge, and leave it to dry a little.

3. Heat the oil in a big frying pan over medium-high heat. Do not wait until the oil smokes, but it should be hot enough so that a pinch of crumbs sizzles on contact. Place 1 schnitzel in the pan. Remember to lay it down away from you, so you don't splash yourself. Cook, turning once, for 3 minutes on each side, or until golden brown. You want to maintain a steady sizzle the whole time the schnitzel cooks, but you don't want it to overcolor. Transfer to paper towels to absorb the excess oil, and season with salt and pepper. Repeat with the remaining schnitzels, adding more oil to the pan if needed.

4. Serve the schnitzels one at a time as they are ready, or leave them on the paper towels and place in a low oven until serving.

POJARSKY DE VEAU

Serves 2

This is one of our favorite dishes from the old classic French reper-toire, essentially a big moist meatball served on a bone. According to legend, Pojarsky (or Pojarski), a favored innkeeper of Czar Nicholas, was made famous by his killer meatballs re-formed on a veal chop bone. Serve with a frond of blanched fennel.

4 large pats unsalted butter

¼ cup (8 g) dried porcini mushrooms, hydrated in warm water to cover, drained, and chopped

1 shallot, finely chopped

1 clove garlic, finely chopped

1 pound (455 g) ground veal

Leaves from 1 sprig thyme

¼ cup (15 g) day-old white bread crumbs in ¼-inch pieces soaked in ¼ cup (60 ml) milk for 15 minutes

1 egg, lightly beaten

1 teaspoon salt

1 ball (size of a fist) caul fat, thawed in the refrigerator if frozen and soaked in cold water until it can be gently stretched flat

2 veal chop bones or lamb chop bones obtained from a butcher (optional, but without the bones, you have lonely meatballs)

Fennel for garnish

1. Preheat the oven to 450°F (230°C).

2. In a frying pan, melt 2 pats of butter over medium heat. Add the mushrooms, shallot, and garlic and sweat for 4 or 5 minutes, or until soft. Let cool for 5 minutes.

3. In a large bowl, combine the veal, porcini mixture, thyme, soaked bread, egg, and salt. Mix together with your hands. It's wise to have a little hot pan on a burner, so you can cook and test a spoonful for flavor, then adjust the seasoning if needed.

4. Divide the mixture in half, and shape each half into a ball. Flatten the balls a bit and then shape each one to look like a large chop. With a sharp knife, cut the caul fat in half, and wrap half around each "chop." Finally, poke a hole at one end of each "chop," and stick a bone into each hole.

5. Drop the remaining 2 pats of butter onto the bottom of a large cocotte or other heavy ovenproof pot. Carefully lay the "chops" side by side in the pot. Place in the oven and cook for 30 to 40 minutes, basting with the butter every 4 or 5 minutes, until sizzling and fragrant, and the caul fat has melted down.

6. In the meantime, bring a small pot of water to a boil over medium-high heat. Add the fennel and blanch for 2 minutes.

7. When the veal is ready, toss the fennel in the cooking fat. Bring the cocotte to the table and serve at once.

LIÈVRE À LA ROYALE

Serves 6 to 8

In Quebec, only two real game meats can be legally sold, caribou from the great north and hare snared in the winter. The taste of these meats is surprising at first, the incarnation of the word "gamey," but like truffles or blue cheese, it becomes what you crave.

Many little classic Parisian restaurants offer this dish in season, and there are as many ways to cook it as there are chefs. The basics are wild hare (*lièvre*), red wine, shallots, thyme, and garlic. The rest can vary. At Joe Beef, we use both hare and rabbit. D'Artagnan (www.dartagnan.com) ships in-season Scottish game hare that we have tried. It's gamey all right, but it's the real McCoy. If you can't find a hare, you can use all rabbit. Count on two days to prepare this recipe. It should yield six to eight portions, and it freezes well.

FIRST DAY

1 small rabbit, 2 to 2½ pounds (about 1 kg), quartered

1 hare, about 1¾ pounds (800 g), quartered and the blood collected if possible and kept in the fridge

1 chunk bacon, about 9 ounces (250 g)

1 veal trotter (ideally) or 2 pig's trotters (not the leg, just the foot, about 8 inches/20 cm long)

2 large carrots, peeled

2 celery stalks

1 bouquet garni of 1 sprig each parsley, thyme, bay leaf, and peppercorn

1 (750 ml) bottle sturdy red wine such as Merlot or Cabernet

¼ cup (60 ml) brandy

Salt and pepper

SECOND DAY

SAUCE

¼ cup (25 g) finely chopped French shallots

3 tablespoons unsalted butter

Leaves from 4 sprigs thyme

1 bay leaf

4 juniper berries

1 clove garlic, minced

6 tablespoons (90 ml) brandy

2 cups (500 ml) sturdy red wine such as Merlot or Cabernet

1 tablespoon cocoa powder

3 cups (750 ml) reserved cooking jus from first day

MATIGNON

10 French shallots, finely diced

3 cloves garlic, minced

¼ cup (55 g) unsalted butter

2 tablespoons chopped fresh flat-leaf parsley

Salt and pepper

TO BUILD

6 to 8 slices fresh duck or goose foie gras, each about 3½ ounces (100 g) and ¾ to 1 inch (2 to 2.5 cm) thick

Salt and pepper

12 ounces (340 g) caul fat, thawed in the refrigerator if frozen and soaked in cold water until it can be gently stretched flat

1 or 2 fresh or canned black truffles, thinly sliced (optional)

Unsalted butter for baking dish

FINISHING SAUCE À LA ROYALE

1 (750 ml) bottle sturdy red wine such as Merlot or Cabernet

Reserved cooking jus from first day

1 tablespoon whipping cream (35 percent butterfat)

1 tablespoon red wine vinegar

1 tablespoon brandy

Salt and pepper

¼ cup (55 g) unsalted butter, cut into 1-inch pieces

2 egg yolks

The reserved blood (optional, if you have it)

Purée de Pommes de Terre (page 180)

FIRST DAY

1. Preheat the oven to 275°F (135°C). In a big, enameled cast-iron pot, combine the rabbit, hare, bacon, veal trotter, carrots, celery, bouquet garni, wine, and brandy. Season with salt and pepper and add water to reach 1 inch (2.5 cm) below the top of the meats.

2. Cover the pot, place in the oven, and bake for 9 hours, or until the meats begin to fall apart. Check the water level every now and again and add more water if it begins to drop.

3. Remove the pot from the oven and carefully transfer the meats and the trotter to a rimmed baking sheet and let cool. Strain the liquid into a clean bowl and discard the solids. Cover the bowl and refrigerate.

4. Shred the meat away from the hare and rabbit bones, keeping it in big chunks. Be careful as you work, as both meats are notorious for their tiny bones, which can pose a choking risk. Remove the meat from the trotter; discard the gelatin, skin, and bones; and chop the meat finely. Shred the bacon. Cover and refrigerate all of the meats.

continued

SECOND DAY

1. To make the sauce, in a 2-quart (2-liter) saucepan, sweat the shallots in the butter over low heat for 4 or 5 minutes, or until fragrant and translucent. Add the thyme, bay leaf, juniper berries, and garlic, and sweat for 2 minutes more. Add the brandy to deglaze the pan.

2. Turn the heat to medium. Add the wine and cocoa powder, stir, and then cook for 15 to 20 minutes, until the sauce turns syrupy.

3. Add 3 cups of the reserved cooking jus and cook for 20 to 25 minutes, until the sauce is reduced by half. Remove the pan from the heat and strain the sauce through a fine sieve, pressing on the shallots to extract the pulp.

4. To make the *matignon*, in a sauté pan, sweat together the shallots and garlic in the butter over medium heat for 4 to 6 minutes, or until fragrant and translucent. Stir in the parsley and season with salt and pepper. Set aside.

5. To build the dish, season the foie gras slices on both sides with salt and pepper. Place a large frying pan or sauté pan over medium-high heat. When the pan is hot, add the foie gras and sear for 1 minute on each side. Transfer to a plate and let rest. Reserve the fat that collected in the pan for adding to the meat mix or the sauce.

6. In a bowl, combine the meat mixture, the *matignon*, and enough of the sauce to moisten the dish. Season with salt and generously with pepper, then give the mixture a once-over again for bones.

7. Preheat the oven to 400°F (200°C). Cut 6 to 8 pieces of caul fat each the size of a legal letter, and fold each piece in half. Shape the meat mixture into 12 to 16 patties each the size of a pack of American cigarettes. Place 1 slice of foie gras between 2 patties, then arrange a line of truffle slices on the top. Wrap the stack in a folded sheet of caul fat, cutting away the excess and tucking the ends under. The truffle slices will be visible through the caul fat layer.

8. Butter a baking dish just large enough to hold the wrapped stacks side by side, and arrange the stacks in it. Place in the oven and bake for 35 minutes, or until slightly golden.

9. Just before the stacks are ready to come out of the oven, make the finishing sauce. In a saucepan, reduce the wine to half over medium heat. Add the remaining reserved cooking jus and cook until reduced to 2 cups (500 ml). Add the cream, vinegar, and brandy; mix well and season with salt and pepper. Bring to a boil, whisk in the butter, a piece at a time, and remove from the heat. In a bowl, whisk together the yolks and the blood, add to the sauce, and buzz the sauce with a hand blender until smooth. (At this point, you cannot reheat the sauce above about 180°F/84°C or it will separate.)

10. For each serving, place a spoonful of the potatoes on a warmed plate, and put a portion of *lièvre* on each mound of potatoes Break an opening in the top of each portion, and spoon some sauce inside. Keep the rest of the sauce handy. Serve at once. You will find it is necessary to drink un grand Bourgogne with this dish.

LAMB PALOISE

Serves 2

Occasionally we refer to *Le Repertoire de la Cuisine*, the little brown book of classic French recipes, to find inspiration for the Joe Beef menu. It's a gold mine of forgotten culinary knowledge, including the sauce *paloise*, a classic variation on sauce béarnaise that uses mint instead of tarragon. You decide on the meat. If you freak on kidneys, use kidneys. We like it on a mutton chop, one chop per person.

PALOISE SAUCE

½ cup (50 g) diced French shallots
½ cup (125 ml) white wine vinegar
2 tablespoons dried mint
2 tablespoons cracked peppercorns
6 egg yolks
1 cup (225 g) unsalted butter, melted
Salt and pepper
Leaves from 4 sprigs mint, chopped

SAUSAGE

8 ounces (225 g) ground pork
8 ounces (225 g) ground lamb
1¼ teaspoons salt
1 teaspoon wild dill or fennel seeds
1 clove garlic, finely chopped
1 teaspoon Sriracha sauce
½ teaspoon pepper
1 tablespoon cold water

Watercress for serving
Apple Vinny for serving (page 196)

1. To make the sauce, in a nonreactive saucepan, combine the shallots, vinegar, dried mint, and peppercorns over high heat. Cook, stirring occasionally just to keep the sides of the pan clean, until reduced by half. Strain the reduction. This is the beginning of your *paloise*. Discard the solids.

2. In a saucepan, whisk together the yolks and the reduction. Now, create a double boiler—a small pan (or a heatproof bowl) above a larger pan—which is a good way to whisk your delicate sauce over high heat: Pour water to a depth of about 2 inches (5 cm) into a large pan, bring to a boil over high heat, and rest the small pan holding the egg yolk mixture over (not touching) the water in the large pan. Start whisking continuously.

3. Now is a good time to whip out an instant-read thermometer. You don't want the mixture to go above 183°F (85°C) or the eggs will curdle. As the eggs start heating up, start slowly pouring in the butter while continuing to whisk constantly. After all of the butter is in, add a couple

tablespoons of hot water to loosen up the sauce a bit, then add a pinch or two of salt and pepper. Keep the sauce in a warm spot but not on a burner. Have the fresh mint on hand.

4. To make the sausage, turn on the broiler or light a charcoal or gas grill. In a bowl, combine the pork, lamb, salt, dill, garlic, Sriracha sauce, pepper, and cold water. Mix together well with your hands. Shape the mixture into small torpedo-shaped sausages about 2 inches (5 cm) long.

5. Place the sausages on a rimmed baking sheet and slip the sheet under the broiler, or place on a grill rack. Cook, turning as needed, for 4 to 5 minutes, or until browned on all sides.

6. Put the sausages on a platter and immediately turn to the *paloise*. Add in the fresh mint and stir well. Serve the sausages with the *paloise*—from a nice old sauce tray, if possible—with the watercress dressed with Apple Vinny on the side.

A good Montreal restaurateur has to be a cultural chameleon, moving from table to table, switching from English to French, and generally feeling at ease in all company. David embodies that. He doesn't sit down with diners and have intimate conversations; he holds court. At the beginning, he was the bartender at Joe Beef, evoking a similar presence to what I imagine the real Joe Beef was like (if the real Joe Beef was tyrannical about iPod playlists and not making Caesars after 10:00 P.M.). David would sit with the bar diners, aka the "audience," and tell tales of Old Montreal, Winslow Homer in Quebec, his canoeing trips in Kamouraska, and his daughters, Dylan and Lola.

CHAPTER 2

THE BUILDERS, THE BREWERS, THE BANKERS, AND THE GANGSTERS:

A Brief History of Eating in Montreal

After breaking free of his shucking shackles and bartending duties, David is now mostly at Liverpool, standing at the bar in grand French Canadian storytelling fashion, drinking a magnum of Brocard Chablis premier cru Montmains (what he calls his "story lubricant"), and probably saying something like "Yes, I'm sure there is an amazing Bordeaux list at Restaurant X in Miami. You know who else had a good Bordeaux list? Samuel de Champlain, on his boat, over 350 years ago . . ."). David is a history buff and Montreal dining is the favored topic. —**ME**

Montrealers of all classes seem to have an inherent knowledge of dining. We prepare rabbit at Joe Beef. Customers ask about cheese in lieu of dessert. Kids eat oysters and terrines on a baguette and know how to sit still for a two-hour dinner; it's expected. Parents say, "Our kids eat what we eat," and it's a source of unspoken pride as their kids slurp down a Malpeque oyster or chew on Matane shrimp heads.

The real oyster eater is a devilish beast, and when I say "real oyster eater," I mean someone who eats them for dinner, as a main, thirty-six or forty-eight, perhaps with some raw clams mixed in. The equally committed clam eater can consume two pounds (900 g) of steamers at a sitting, but only when they're at their best. There is something primal about eating a lot of bivalves while quietly watching hockey alone with a beer or glass of Muscadet.

We see these types a lot at Joe Beef: intelligent, quiet purists with piercing eyes. These friends are the ones who truly understand the essence of food, as they chuckle and slurp another bivalve with a dash of Tabasco. Whether he or she is business, working, or street class, each is a force to be reckoned with. But watch out, they're sly and a lot of them know old family black magic. I know this, I am one!

The Old Port, the southernmost section of Montreal harboring the

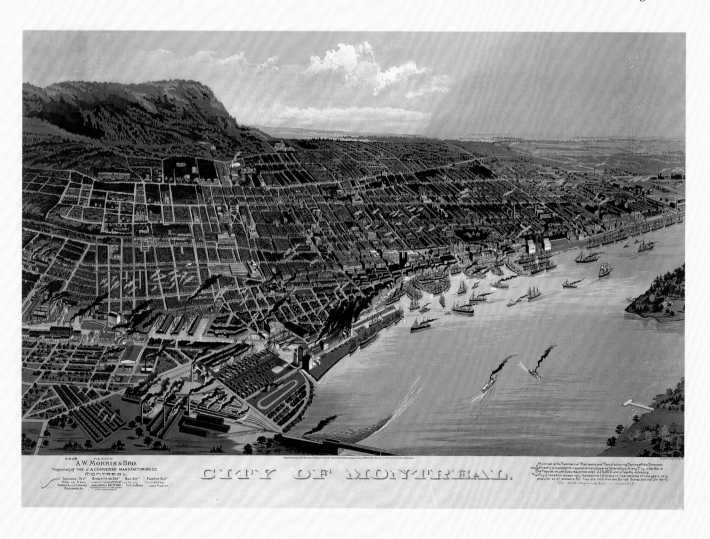

A.W. MORRIS & BRO.
Proprietors of THE J.A. CONVERSE MANUFACTURING CO.
MONTREAL

CITY OF MONTREAL.

mouth of the Saint Lawrence River and the Lachine Canal, was built by men who ate oysters by the barrel, a trait that was passed down through the old families of the builders, brewers, bankers, and gangsters. Indeed, something about oysters and gangsters has always existed. Al Capone, a famed patron of Montreal, was part owner of an oyster-serving burlesque club, where the Lion D'Or now sits. And Charles "Joe Beef" McKiernan ran the old port of Montreal like the fictionalized Bill the Butcher ran the Five Points in *Gangs of New York*.

We've been eating well in this province for the last three centuries. And although the United States has Thomas Keller and Michelin-starred restaurants now, can anyone say what was going on foodwise in Las Vegas or Miami twenty-five or thirty years ago? Don't get me wrong, I'm excited about the American food revolution and how we're all turning to a more healthful way of eating. But for me, Montreal's traditions of eating, drinking wine, and

speaking French sound like history in a candlelit dining room, that is, the French language evokes a historical sentiment. (Please forgive any embellishments. They seem quite natural when accompanied by dramatic hand waving and swearing: I'm a bar storyteller, remember?). The food culture of Montreal, in my opinion, is influenced by four major things: the early seigniorial system, the *casse-croûte* tradition, the immigration wave after World War II, and Expo 67.

THE SEIGNIORIAL SYSTEM

Quebec was settled by the French, the English, the Scots, and the Irish—yet the food at its core has always been French based, absolutely. The classic dishes are remnants of Quebec farmhouse cooking: leftovers of a system (with the exception of a few states in the American South) that was specific to the building of Nouvelle-France. When Quebec was being settled, the land

along the Saint Lawrence River was divided into strips. The Crown of France owned all of the land, but each strip had a designated, appointed landlord known as a *seigneur*, who provided a mill, a well, and a bread oven on his tract of land. The *seigneur* (though he was only himself, in theory, a renter) would lease out land to farmers, who would in turn raise animals, make cheese, grind flour, and catch fish. Ultimately, co-ops were born, and the first towns of Quebec rose along the shores of the Saint Lawrence River.

My cottage in Kamouraska is next door to the *seigneuriale* home of the Taché family, from which come the writers of the *Je me souviens* (I remember) phrase on Quebec license plates. The property is amazing: It is a large clapboard home with ten bedrooms and a stone foundation. It has a large *cuisine d'été* (summer kitchen) with a fireplace spit big enough to roast a whole cow and a cast-iron cauldron in which you could confit two hundred duck legs, one hundred whole geese, or make soup for the entire town. The house also sports a huge old outdoor bread oven and fortified covered well. The wells were reportedly covered and fortified to protect the water from being poisoned by the enemies of the *seigneur.*

This period in Quebec history gave us many of our traditional foods and our inherent knowledge of things like bread and cheese making. When taxes are increased in Quebec, there is some (but little) protest. But if our raw milk and cheese are threatened with government interference, Quebecers protest loudly. To continue to enjoy real cheese, we are ready to fight with petitions and public demonstrations. We have even halted the Quebec National Assembly over cheese! Indeed, Quebec is the only place on the planet that has banned butter-colored margarine.

The larder of Quebec is wildly impressive, even to our French friends. Visiting chefs always mention that our markets are set up differently than elsewhere: basically, they make it possible for everyone to cook restaurant-quality food at home. Montreal has two major central public markets, Jean-Talon in the north and Atwater in the south, both opened in 1933. You can get tripe, Cornish hens, stuffed rabbits, rabbit kidneys, horse, any cheek of meat you want, foie gras in all of its forms, and produce of every type. Atwater alone has three cheese

shops. (For a list of the province's larder and our go-to shops, see page 280.) Unfortunately, gone are the days of the *restaurant du coin* (corner restaurant), a place where you could meet your friends for lunch; have hot bread, bacon and eggs, rotisserie chicken, or plain ham and Cheddar sandwiches; and then buy all of your groceries for the week. You can still see the remnants, though: the old absinthe-green lead paint, L-shaped counters, and wooden beer fridges. And of course, there are still places like Wilensky's in Mile End and the Green Spot diner near Joe Beef. I promise one day we will open something similar, with the necessary evils of smokes, lottery tickets, Popsicle fridges, wine, and odds and ends that make good neighborhood living: hot lasagna every Wednesday at 5:00 P.M. and hockey cards picked through to feature only Habs players.

It is rare to find traditional Quebec dishes served in restaurants anymore. Things like *jambon à l'érable* (ham in maple syrup), *chiard de porc* (pork hash), and *pets de soeurs* (nuns' farts) are endangered and disappearing slowly. Our dear friend Martin Picard and his team at Au Pied de Cochon (PDC) are basically Quebec food preservationists and thank god for that. PDC's Sugar Shack, which is open only four months of the year and is bursting with customers each of those days, is like a Quebec monument, and everyone at Joe Beef always enjoys

seeing what will come out of Martin's twisted head next. Quebecois youth no longer mimic the star chefs of France (or the Food Network). They mimic Martin. If you come to our city during the late winter or early spring, you must go to Au Pied de Cochon (see itinerary, page 278).

THE CASSE-CROÛTE TRADITION

In my youth, I paid no real attention to another great Quebec tradition, the *casse-croûte,* or snack bar. But now I see what treasures they are, as fast-food chains and clone malls slowly homogenize everything. A lot of these *casse-croûtes* (*casser la croûte* literally means to "break the crust") are put together from old buses or milk trucks or are simply slapped-together buildings made of junk. Amazingly, you can

La Plage
MOTEL
RESTAURANT

DEJEUNER
PATES - PIZZA
GRILLADES
FRUITS DE MER

Patate Mallette

GLACÉE

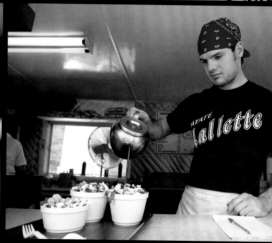

PEPSI
CASSE-CROÛTE
CHEZ OSCAR

MOINEAU DU CAPITAINE
3,50

Menu

	Petite	Moyenne	Grosse	
...es	1.75	2.25	4.50	Pogo
...es sauce	2.70	3.40	4.50	Rondelles
...tine	4.25	5.40	7.50	Hamburger
...ine italienne	4.50	5.50	8.00	Hamburger fromage
				Hamburger poulet
				Hamburger super garni
...n chaud vapeur	1.25			Pépites poulet (6)
...n chaud rôti	1.35			Pépites poulet (12)
...n chaud fromage	1.50	50 ANS		Doigts de poulet repas
...gan	2.00			
...patate	1.10			
...lle	1.10			Extra bacon
...outine	2.25			piment
				cornichon

JOE BEEF AND THE HABS: RIAD'S SWEET HOMECOMING

I HADN'T BEEN BACK TO MONTREAL in far too long. The Habs were playing two games in three nights, so I booked my flight home and bought scalped tickets for both games. The 2007–2008 Habs had a magic run. Indeed, it started to feel like 1993, as the Habs were poised for a legit run for the Stanley Cup. Though the Bruins pushed us to seven games, we pushed back harder and next up was the big bad Flyers. In game one, Kovy scored with the goalie pulled and Kosty won it in overtime . . . Ole Ole Ole! The next night, I dropped in to visit "Les Boys" on Notre Dame Ouest.

I parked it at the Joe Beef bar, in front of John Bil—oyster-shucking master. I tried to keep up with him. "Beausoleils aren't as fat, sweet, or briny as this in NYC," I told him. Fred was making a Civet when I popped my head in the kitchen. He looked like he had seen a ghost, and up until that moment, that's exactly what I had been. "Welcome home," he said. We hugged and I felt a lump in my throat.

The Cotat Sancerre ran dry and we moved on to Lapierre Morgon. Our old friends Martin Picard and Normand Laprise showed up—I hadn't seen them since our days at Toqué! More tall tales, backslapping, reminiscing, and of course, drinking, ensued. Fred mercifully roasted a Côte de Boeuf with Marrowbones and Gyromites. We needed it to soak up all of that good juice. We ate with our hands and I kept one eye closed so I could see straight.

Later in the backyard, Fred and I talked about the gardens he was planting and David spoke of the smoker they had plans to build. Someone showed up with tobacco and we drained another magnum. "Welcome Home" someone cheered again. I returned home and I found my center that night. John Bil gave me a ride to my hotel in his minivan and I was sick on the way, but I wore a smile and was never more proud to be a Montrealer.

—**Riad Nasr, executive chef, Minetta Tavern**

find a few in really beautiful settings along the Saint Lawrence River on old Route 132 between Quebec City and Rivière-du-Loup or on Route 148 near the Château Montebello Hotel. Usually the backlit sign shows their soft-drink colors of choice, and they are turning out to be great fodder for photographers and for burger and *poutine* bloggers. You've got your homemade hot dogs, hamburgers, fries, and *poutines*, and some specialties like hot gravy–soaked hamburgers and all-dress hot dogs (with the works) dipped in batter and fried. I've had a Ti-Gus burger, which is an all-dressed burger on a plate, with a ladle of Kraft Thousand Island dressing poured over the top.

The best part of a *casse-croûte* is the name. It's fun to try and name your own. It usually goes one of four ways: Casse-croûte Joe Beef, Casse-croûte chez Joe Beef, Patate Joe Beef, or Pataterie Joe Beef. Our favorite Quebec *casse-croûtes* to visit are Cantine Ben la Bédaine (Belly Ben), Patate Mallette (Mallette's Potatoes), La Patate à Serge (Serge and his Spud), Casse-croûte chez Ti-Gus (Small Gus Snack Bar), Casse-croûte chez Miss Patate (Miss Potatoes Snack Bar), Au Royaume de la Patate (Potato Kingdom), Pataterie "Guy la patate" (Potato Shop "Guy the Potato"), Le King de la Patate (The King of Potatoes), and Patate d'Or, Marcelle (Marcelle, The Golden Spud).

Depending on where the *casse-croûtes* are located in the province, items may vary, and a lot of them have their own eclectic toppings for *poutines*. We've seen chopped wieners, peas, chicken, meat sauce, Nordic shrimp, venison stew, a few slices of country pâté terrine, and eggs sunny-side up. I've also had hot dogs and hamburgers with raw green tomatoes, eggs, *cappocollo* (spicy ham), and creamed corn. And when I asked the person behind the counter, "Why creamed corn?", he looked at me like everyone serves creamed corn on their hot dogs, and maybe I should just go back to where I came from.

THE IMMIGRATION WAVE

In our twenties, Fred, Allison, and I worked on The Main, the strip of Boulevard Saint Laurent that runs from the tip of Chinatown up to Little Italy. It was during this amazing and inspirational time that we cut our purveyor chops, so to speak. We were lucky to meet all of the butchers, shop owners, Euro-grocers, and fishmongers doing business in the area. In my early days, at least ten butcher shops manned by old nitrite-soaked, red-faced butchers with hands like baseball mitts were operating between Sherbrooke and Pine streets. When we left the street ten years later, only one was left. Johnny Bottle Service restaurants, seedy bars, and pizza slice and souvlaki shops had taken over.

Remnants still exist, though, places like Slovenia, Boucherie Fairmount, La Vieille Europe, and Schwartz's, and great Portuguese spots like Portus Calle, Coco Rico, Romados, and Chicken Portugalia. There is also Moishes, a Montreal institution. Owned by the Lighter brothers, the steak house was opened by their father, Moishes Luchterman, in 1938. His son, our friend Lenny Lighter, told us that his father came to Montreal with nothing at the age of fifteen in 1925. He worked his way from the bottom up on The Main at a restaurant

called Saffrin, and it's rumored that he won the restaurant in a card game. Speaking to someone like Lenny about the history of his family's restaurant is something I could do for hours. There are many people like Lenny in Montreal—people who have helped shaped Montreal's current foodscape.

Like what happened in many cities, the end of World War II brought new immigrants and new food traditions to Montreal. French, Scottish, and Irish were in the first wave, followed by Italians, Greeks, Ukranians, Hungarians, and Poles, all of them helping to shape the city. Mordecai Richler's 1969 short-story collection *The Street* paints a vivid picture of the core neighborhoods around Boulevard Saint Laurent and Rue Saint Urbain, filled with Jewish delis and Portuguese rotisseries. You still find quality eats and mouthwatering smells today. Quebec continues to receive forty-five thousand immigrants annually. We welcome Chinese, South Asians, Haitians, and Latinos, and their tasty food, with relish and open arms. They come together in new neighborhoods and the food just gets better and better.

EXPO 67

Another less serious, yet notable event that changed the city's food scene was Expo 67. Its restaurants and pavilions attracted many of the world's chefs to Montreal, and lucky for us, many of them stayed. Of these chefs, the majority were French. They came for the food and stayed for the forests, rivers, lakes, and the women (hey, it was the summer of love!). Over the next thirty years, the French reigned in Quebec City and Montreal. It was the age of restaurants like Les Halles, La Mère Michel, Chez Alexandre, Le Paris, Le Mas des Oliviers, Chez Gauthier, L'Express, Le Béarn, Claude Postel, Bonaparte, L'Actuel, Au Petit Extra, Le Witloof, and Maison Serge Bruyère. The chefs of these restaurants are the great mentors and teachers of many of our peers, and although some restaurants of the era have closed, many are still around.

Anytime I get the chance to eat at Le Mas des Oliviers, it's a treat. I ask to sit at Mordecai Richler's table, and I daydream about what the hell could have gone on in this corner. This is where he held court by day, and had dinner with his family by night. It's also a famous haunt for politicos, but anytime I ask what kind of deals are going down, the staff remains annoyingly tight-lipped. Among other great chefs, restaurateurs, and mentors of note are Jean-Paul Grappe, Marcel Kretz, Daniel Schandelmayer, Rene Pankala, Moreno DiMarchi, the Creton brothers, Peppino Perri, André Besson, and Jacques Muller. These are the pillars of Montreal cuisine. This group of European expatriates nurtured a whole generation of Quebec chefs, and most of today's chefs have been to France to work in great restaurants on their recommendations.

Montreal has always boasted a strong French tradition. But Expo 67 brought new Hungarian, Alsatian, and Parisian chefs to the city. It also delayed the arrival of ready-made foods like margarine, and curbed Montrealers' appetites for abominations like canned meat and processed cheese, at least for a little while. Raise your glass to Expo 67 and the French expats, here, here!

THE SHOCK OF THE NEW: NORMAND LAPRISE AND THE MOTHERSHIP CONNECTION

Another small yet widely felt shift in Montreal's food scene was the arrival of another chef. . . .

Everything was peachy and French cooking ruled until Normand Laprise opened Citrus in 1989. It was like an alien spaceship had landed: vertically stacked presentations, pinks and oranges, little butter or cream. He fried things you weren't supposed to fry, upsetting the natural order of food. He moved to Rue Saint Denis a few years later and opened Toqué!, with a kitchen right in the window. It was so fresh, new, and cool: everyone wanted to work there. And a lot of us did: Martin Picard, Riad Nasr, and Fred, to name a few. Normand is the great bond in this city; if it weren't for him, Fred and I may not have met. Toqué! was a meeting place for chefs young and old. It was like the Bohemian movement in Paris, a powerhouse of great talent. Today it sits proudly on the edge of the old port, watching over us, keeping us sage.

Of course, French isn't the only game in town. As we compiled our list of restaurants for the itinerary (page 278), we were bombarded by friends and colleagues with endorsements for the city's best Haitian, Somalian, Ethiopian, Armenian, Greek, Japanese, Indian, and Jamaican food. That's the thing about this city. If you have not been to their favorite spots, people get mad: "What do you mean you haven't been to Meli Melo for Haitian? What's wrong with you?" And it's a Greek guy who's telling me this. It makes me think sadly about the lava pockets (patties) from the now-defunct Mom's Caribbean Heaven. Those delicious, liquid molten chicken or beef Jamaican patties are responsible for countless second-degree burns on my chin, lips, tongue, chest, and arms. Everybody in Notre Dame de Grace, a neighborhood on Montreal's west side, has similar burn stories from those patties.

The value of any neighborhood in this city is determined by its coffee shops, bakeries, and restaurants. Without these establishments, a neighborhood's value plummets. I love this city. And with the exception of perhaps Kamouraska or of Maine in the summer, there is no other place I would rather be. Even after working in the restaurant business here for so long, I am still completely enamored with the history and the people of Quebec. Now, if we could just do something about the damn snow.

The following recipes, for us, reflect the character of our city's culinary traditions. —DM

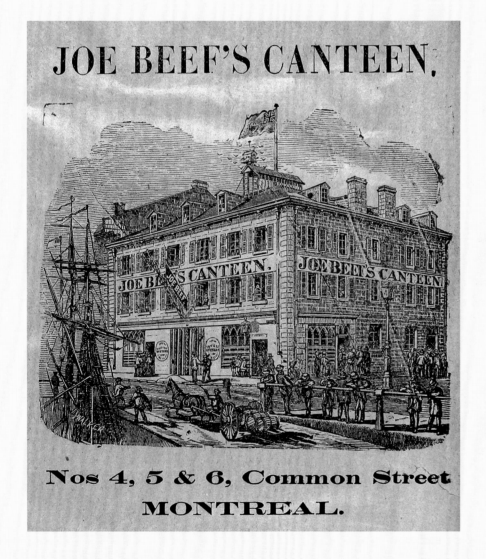

JOE BEEF'S CANTEEN.

Nos 4, 5 & 6, Common Street
MONTREAL.

LAMB SHOULDER FOR TWO, CONDI*MINT*

Serves 2

Mint is a classic accompaniment for lamb. And it wasn't until Jennifer May shot this classic braised lamb recipe with its mint condiment that we really appreciated its beauty. It's something we imagine on the Sunday table of Mayor Drapeau, who brought Expo 67 and the '76 Olympics to Montreal (and chased away the hookers and the gangsters—albeit temporarily).

2 pounds (about 1 kg) boneless lamb shoulder, trimmed, rolled, and tied

Salt and pepper

3 tablespoons neutral oil

1 onion, quartered

1 carrot, peeled and chopped into chunks

1 cup (140 g) frozen or very fresh shelled peas

10 cloves garlic

10 sprigs thyme

1 cup (250 ml) dry white wine

CONDIMENT

1 cup (170 g) pitted dates

½ cup (125 ml) water

½ cup (100 g) packed brown sugar

1 cup (250 ml) cider vinegar

Pinch of cayenne pepper

½ cup (55 g) grated fresh horseradish

3 heaping tablespoons dried peppermint, stems removed

1 tablespoon Worcestershire sauce

Cider Turnips (page 196)

1. Preheat the oven to 375°F (190°C). Season the lamb on all sides with salt and pepper.

2. Heat the oil in a large ovenproof sauté pan over high heat. Add the lamb and sear for 3 or 4 minutes on each side, or until you get a nice golden crust. Transfer to a plate.

3. Reduce the heat to medium, throw in the onion, carrot, peas (thawed, if using frozen) and garlic, and cook, stirring occasionally, for about 4 minutes, or until nicely browned. Add the thyme, nestle the lamb on top of the vegetables, and pour in the wine.

4. Cover the pan with aluminum foil, place in the oven, and braise for 4 hours. Every 30 minutes, baste the top of the lamb with the pan juices. If the pan begins to dry out, add some water.

5. While the lamb is cooking, make the condiment. In a small pot, combine the dates and water, bring to a boil over high heat, and boil for about 10 minutes, or until soft. Reduce the heat to medium, add the sugar, vinegar, and cayenne, and stir well. Cook, stirring occasionally, for 10 minutes, or until the sugar is dissolved and the condiment has the consistency of jam.

6. Remove from the heat, add the horseradish, mint, and Worcestershire sauce, and buzz with a hand blender or whisk in. Let cool completely before serving. (Leftover condiment can be stored in a tightly capped jar in the refrigerator for up to 1 month.)

7. When the lamb is ready, transfer it to a warmed platter with the vegetables. Snip the strings and serve *à la cuillère*, with a spoon. Serve the condiment and the turnips on the side.

OEUFS EN GELÉE

Serves 6

Fred used to offer this dish to girls at the restaurant L'Express because it was cheap and quirky. But in the end, that's how he came across: cheap and quirky! Although it is no longer offered at L'Express, we sometimes make it at Joe Beef both for old time's sake and because it's just very good. You should count on two days to make this recipe, the first for filtering and chilling the consommé and the second for assembling the aspics. The classic version includes cooked ham, tarragon leaves, and egg whites cut and assembled in the shape of lilies. Now we do it with Spam, lobster, fava beans, crab, or anything we suspect will be delicious in a set consommé.

You can purchase *oeufs en gelée* molds online, or you can use standard muffin tins made of silicone.

CONSOMMÉ

½ cup (70 g) diced celery (about ¼-inch/6-mm chunks)

½ cup (70 g) diced, peeled carrot (about ¼-inch/6-mm chunks)

½ cup (60 g) diced onion (about ¼-inch/6-mm chunks)

1 pound (455 g) lean ground beef

1 pound (455 g) ground turkey

1 bay leaf

2 tablespoons chopped parsley

1 tablespoon peppercorns

1 clove garlic

3 quarts (3 liters) ice water

6 sheets gelatin

1 teaspoon sherry vinegar

¼ cup (60 ml) Madeira

Salt

EGGS

8 cups (2 liters) water

1 tablespoon salt, plus more for serving

6 to 8 medium eggs (or the smallest you can find), at room temperature

Any of the following: sliced premium cooked ham; sliced fresh, flash-frozen, or jarred black truffle; shelled and peeled fresh fava beans; crabmeat chunks; lobster tail silvers; sliced Spam; sliced smoked salmon; fresh tarragon leaves; jambon persillé (chopped ham and parsley tightly packed in a mustard-meat jelly); gold leaf (if you're feeling sprightly)

Toasted country bread for serving

Ground black pepper and flake salt for serving

1. To make the consommé, in a heavy stockpot, whisk together the celery, carrot, onion, beef, turkey, bay leaf, parsley, peppercorns, garlic, and ice water. Place over low heat and stir until the consommé begins to simmer. Stop stirring; the meats and vegetables will rise to the top, forming a "raft." Now, leave it alone (do not stir) and allow it to simmer gently for 2 hours. Do not let it come to a boil.

continued

2. To strain the consommé, line a sieve with muslin cloth or several layers of cheesecloth and place it over a large bowl. Carefully create a hole in the top of the consommé. Plunge a ladle through the hole, being careful not to sink the raft, and ladle the liquid through the sieve. The consommé shouldn't look cloudy; rather, it should be a pristine "meat tea" of sorts. Cover the bowl and refrigerate long enough for the fat to separate and congeal on top: overnight is a good option.

3. The next day, bloom the gelatin sheets in a bowl of cool water to cover for 5 to 10 minutes, or until they soften and swell. Meanwhile, remove the consommé from the refrigerator and lift off and discard the fat. Transfer 2 cups (500 ml) of the consommé to a small pot and place over high heat. (Freeze the rest of the consommé for soup. It will keep for up to 3 months.) When the consommé starts to boil, add the vinegar and Madeira and season with salt. Gently squeeze the gelatin sheets, add to the consommé, and stir for 2 or 3 minutes, or until fully dissolved. Remove from the heat and keep the consommé at room temperature.

4. Place six (3½-ounce/100-g) molds on a small, flat tray. Pour the consommé to a depth of ¼ inch (6 mm) into each mold. Place in the fridge to set (about 20 minutes). This layer is really important as it prevents the egg from poking through.

5. To prepare the eggs, in a large pot, bring the water and salt to a boil over medium-high heat. Carefully add the eggs and boil for exactly 4½ minutes. Use a timer here, as the consistency of the eggs matters! Transfer the eggs to a bowl of ice water to cover and chill for about 10 minutes. Peel each egg carefully underwater; they are soft boiled and could easily break, which is why we suggest that you make two extra eggs, just in case.

6. Now for the fun part, creating your *gelée* (aspic). You can get creative here, one rule withstanding: everything you mix with your egg has to have a somewhat soft texture. For instance, adding raw carrots or celery would give you more of a 1960s jellied salad and would ruin the whole aesthetic. Also, keep in mind the bottom of the mold is actually the top of the *gelée*. That is, it is what everyone will see. If you want, you can artistically arrange a black truffle slice or tiny pieces of ham, peas, or slivers of lobster in the bottom of each mold (on the set layer of jelly) before you add the egg. Carefully place an egg in each mold. Once the egg is in, surround it with your choice of ingredients. Your consommé will come in handy for holding and suspending the pieces in place, so wield its power. When you have all of your ingredients in, make the sure the mold is filled evenly, using the consommé to top it off. Carefully transfer the molds back to the fridge for at least 2 hours to set before serving. (They will keep for up to 2 days maximum.)

7. To unmold the aspics, pour hot water to a depth of 1 inch (2.5 cm) into a wide, shallow pan. Carefully place the bottom of each mold into the water and let it sit for 30 seconds. Invert the mold onto the serving plate; the aspic should slip right out. If it doesn't, release the vacuum between the aspic and the mold by inserting the tip of a blade and twisting lightly. Classic decorum dictates that you serve the aspics with toast, black pepper, and salt for the yolk.

A PLEA FOR THIN CHOPS

WE WANT TO SIT AT A NICE TABLE, order a bottle of wine, have a dozen oysters each, and then eat a great plate of chops. Unpretentious thin chops, nicely browned, hot and salty, a heaping plate of them, in the middle of the table. Lamb chops, pork chops, veal chops, thin rib steaks—all cooked medium, and the meat around the bone perfect. A dozen assorted chops each, then a few cigarillos and some Calvados to aim us down the wrong road. Of course, you can cook this at home easily: just pull out the great big pan, turn on the hood fan, and fry them away, two to three minutes on each side.

DUCK STEAK au POIVRE

Serves 2

This is the kind of dish that used to be prepared tableside in Montreal chophouses. A few restaurants still do tableside crêpes Suzette, steak tartare, and specialty coffees. We get excited like kids on Halloween when we see that cart rolling toward us. It's tough to do ourselves because of the size of Joe Beef, but we hope it comes back in a big way (and not in the "lavender and tomato essential oils being pumped over my table from a Provençal print balloon as we eat lamb and the waiter tickles our nose and ears with said lamb's tail" way).

1 large duck breast half, about 15 ounces (420 g)

1 tablespoon black or green peppercorns, crushed in a mortar until somewhere between whole and powder

Salt

2 tablespoons canola oil

2 tablespoons unsalted butter

1 tablespoon chopped French shallot

2 tablespoons Dijon mustard

1 tablespoon brined green peppercorns, drained and patted dry

2 tablespoons Cognac

½ cup (125 ml) Beef Shank Stock (page 249)

¼ cup (60 ml) whipping cream (35 percent butterfat)

Good Fries (page 154) or pont-neufs (fries cut ⅜ inch by ⅜ inch by 2¾ inches/1 cm by 1 cm by 7 cm)

1. Remove the silver skin from the duck breast by running a sharp knife between the skin and the meat, lifting the skin away from the meat with your fingers. This is a detailed, annoying task, similar to unwrapping a new dishwasher. When you've separated the two, you can set the skin aside to use for a confit.

2. Cover the meat with plastic wrap and pound it with a rolling pin or the side of a giant cleaver until it is flattened by about 20 percent. Lightly score the meat to prevent retracting. Rub one side of the duck steak with the black peppercorns to season it, and salt the other side.

3. Heat a nice (you're serving tableside, remember?) pan over medium-high heat. Let it get quite hot, add the oil, and when it is hot, add the steak. Cook, turning once, for 1½ minutes on each side.

4. Take the steak to a plate and set aside. Pour off any fat from the pan, and then wipe it clean.

5. Put the pan over medium heat, add the butter, and sweat the shallots for 4 or 5 minutes, until translucent. Add the mustard, green peppercorns, and Cognac, and mix for 30 seconds. Add the stock and reduce until almost syrupy, about 2 minutes. Add the cream and mix well, taste and adjust the seasoning, then reduce for a full 2 minutes. If you reduce the sauce too much, add stock or water, not cream.

6. Return the steak to the pan and toss it in the sauce for a few seconds on each side. Serve on a silver tray with the sauce and fries on the side.

VARIATION

You could also tie 2 small duck breasts together, flesh to flesh, and roast them in the pan for 3 minutes per side, then finish in a 425°F (220°C) oven for 4 minutes (see photo opposite).

PÂTÉ EN CROÛTE

Serves 6 to 8

This is yet another recipe that evokes that nostalgic, "Why don't people make this anymore?" feeling, like a beautiful picture from the old Larousse, a civil-war reenactment, or sleeping on a train. There is only one good reason to make this dish: because you can! Thankfully, people like Frank, Marco, and Emma (our kitchen mainstays and true Joe Beefers) see the value in making historically relevant dishes like this, and it stays with them forever and can live on. The most difficult part of this recipe is measuring the dough to cover the pâté. Although some pâtés are served hot, the salt content in this one means it only tastes good cold. We serve it with some mustard and a glass of Morgon.

DOUGH

4½ cups (550 g) all-purpose flour, plus more for dusting

1½ teaspoons salt

1 cup (225 g) cold unsalted butter, cut into ¼-inch/6-mm chunks

5 eggs

½ cup (125 ml) water

FILLING

About 1 pound (455 g) ground pork jowl (fresh guanciale)

2 pounds (900 g) ground pork

2 cloves garlic, chopped

1 tablespoon chopped fresh flat-leaf parsley

4 teaspoons salt

1 teaspoon pepper

1 teaspoon ground mace

2 tablespoons brandy

2 tablespoons all-purpose flour

2 eggs

½ cup (125 ml) whipping cream (35 percent butterfat)

1 egg yolk beaten with 1 teaspoon water for egg wash

7 sheets gelatin

2 cups (500 ml) chicken stock

¼ cup (60 ml) dry sherry

Salt and pepper

1. To make the dough, in a large bowl, mix together the flour and salt. Scatter the butter over the flour mixture, then squeeze it with your fingers, working it into the flour but still leaving some chunks. Add the eggs and work the dough gently with your hands until malleable. Slowly pour in half the water, mixing it in with your hands. When the water has been absorbed, work in the rest of the water. The dough should be firm and uneven looking.

2. Transfer the dough to a floured work surface. Using a rolling pin, flatten the dough into a rectangle. Wrap the rectangle in plastic wrap and place in the fridge for at least 1 hour while you work on your terrine filling.

3. To make the filling, in a large bowl, combine the ground meats, garlic, parsley, salt, pepper, mace, and brandy. In a small bowl, whisk together the flour, eggs, and cream until well blended. Add the cream mixture to the meat mixture and stir with a wooden spoon until you have one homogenous mix.

4. When the dough has rested for 1 hour, preheat the oven to 300°F (150°C). Then, on a floured work surface, roll out the dough into a rectangle about ¼ inch (6 mm) thick. This is the most technical part, because you want to roll enough dough to cover the terrine. We bake this dish in a 10 by 4 by 3¼-inch (25 by 10 by 8-cm) Le Creuset pot, but any enameled cast-iron pot of similar size will work well. Place the Creuset on the dough, denting the dough to imprint the size. Then cut out the dough so it is a little larger than the dented pattern, adding flaps on the two short ends (see drawing). Carefully lift up the dough and place it in the Creuset, pressing it down gently. Reserve the extra dough.

continued

La Pâte du Pâté en Croûte.

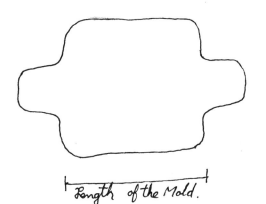

Length of the Mold.

* in order to fit a Le Creuset terrine mold.

+

Hole Made with an apple corer

5. Spoon the meat mixture into the dough-lined Creuset, spreading it evenly and smoothing the top. Fold the dough over the top of the meat mixture so it covers it completely. It doesn't have to look perfect where the sides meet. Using the extra dough, cut out a strip the length of the pot and lay it across the middle of the terrine to close the seam (as the dough will expand from the heat while baking).

6. Brush the dough with the egg wash. You can use any remaining dough to make decorative leaves, letters, or whatever you want and put them on top. Be sure to brush them with the wash, too.

7. In the middle of the dough, cut a quarter-size hole using an apple corer or a knife. Using the handle of a wooden spoon as a guide, make a small tube of aluminum foil. This is your chimney for the steam. The chimney is your first rule of *pâté en croûte*. Trust the chimney! Or, trust you will be cleaning the oven.

8. Place in the hot oven and bake for 35 to 40 minutes. The *pâté* is ready when an instant-read thermometer inserted through the chimney hole registers 158°F (70°C). Burnt crust or half-cooked meat is not appetizing, so a thermometer is key here.

9. In the meantime, bloom the gelatin sheets in a bowl of cool water to cover for 5 to 10 minutes, or until they soften and swell. Put a pot over medium-high heat and add the stock and sherry. Bring the stock mixture to a boil, season generously with salt and pepper, and remove from the heat. Gently squeeze the gelatin sheets, add to the stock mixture, and whisk until completely dissolved.

10. Remove the *pâté en croûte* from the oven and let cool for 45 minutes. Carefully pour the stock mixture into the foil chimney. Let the *pâté* cool completely before slicing and serving.

BLANQUETTE DE VEAU
aux CHICONS

Serves 4

This is the one stew you can get away with in the summer, yet crave in the winter. Veal chunks from the hind shank is the best meat for this; cheeks or shoulder is another option. All but the rear leg muscle will work. Of course, mashed potatoes or a marrow pilaf (rice baked with bone marrow instead of butter) is the perfect buddy. As a finishing touch, we like to pimp our *blanquette de veau* with truffles, cock's combs, foie gras, or small slices of lobster. It lends regality to an otherwise hearty and simple stew.

3 pounds (1.4 kg) boneless veal shank, cheeks, or shoulder, cubed

2 cups (500 ml) dry white wine

2 cups (500 ml) chicken stock

1 leek, white part only

1 carrot, peeled

1 small onion, stuck with 1 whole clove

1 celery stalk

1 sprig thyme

1 bay leaf

1 clove garlic

1 teaspoon salt

2 cups (500 ml) whipping cream (35 percent butterfat)

2 tablespoons Dijon mustard

2 heads Belgian endive, cored, halved lengthwise, and cubed

½ celery root, peeled and cut into 1-inch (2.5-cm) cubes

1 tablespoon chopped fresh tarragon

1. Preheat the oven to 375°F (190°C). In a Dutch oven or other heavy, lidded ovenproof pot, combine the veal, wine, stock, leek, carrot, onion, celery, thyme, bay leaf, garlic, and salt. Place over medium-high heat and bring to a boil, stirring occasionally. When you have a nice boil going, cover the pot and transfer it to the oven. Bake for 2 hours.

2. Remove the pot from the oven and then carefully proceed to remove and discard the vegetables and aromatics. (If you want to hold onto the carrots, you can always purée them along with potatoes to make a nice mash.) With a slotted spoon, remove the veal pieces and place them on a tray or plate close by.

3. Put the pot with the remaining liquid back on the stove top over medium heat. Stir in the cream and mustard and reduce, stirring occasionally, for 15 minutes, or until the sauce coats the back of a spoon.

4. Taste and adjust the seasoning, then return the meat to the pot and add the endives and celery root. Simmer for 8 to 10 minutes, or until the vegetables are tender. Add the tarragon during the last minute of cooking. Serve piping hot.

FILET DE CHEVAL À CHEVAL

Serves 4

Here in Canada, horse is the great divide between Anglophone and Francophone—more than politics, more than Celine Dion. Horse equals Napoleon versus Nelson, or Wolfe versus Montcalm on the Plains of Abraham. The French do two things that Anglophones find disgusting: eat frogs and eat horse. To Anglophones, horses are royalty. And it's understandable, as they're truly majestic. They're also really tasty.

We don't know anyone who raises horses for meat, yet the meat exists. So, if you don't want to eat horse that has been on growth hormones and clenbuterol, buy it from a trusted butcher. It has a high iron content and makes a delicious tenderloin or tartare.

2 tablespoons canola oil

4 slices bacon

2 tablespoons unsalted butter, plus more for frying

1 bay leaf or 1 sprig thyme (optional)

4 horse steaks, 8 to 10 ounces (225 to 280 g) each

1 cup (250 ml) Joe Beef Sauce Vin Rouge (page 250)

2 tablespoons Dijon mustard

4 eggs

4 slices brioche (optional)

1. Place a large sauté pan over high heat and add the oil. When the oil is hot, add the bacon and fry for about 5 minutes, or until nicely browned but not crisp (you are going to want to wrap it around the steak). Set aside.

2. Pour out the fat and wipe the pan clean. Add the 2 tablespoons butter to the same pan over medium heat. When the butter is bubbly, add the bay leaf. Now add the horse steaks to the pan and cook for 5 minutes on the first side. Turn and cook for 4 minutes on the second side. Transfer the steaks to a plate and let rest for 4 minutes, keeping them warm. Wipe the pan clean and set aside.

3. Meanwhile, in a small pot, warm the wine sauce over medium heat and whisk in the mustard. Remove from the heat and keep warm.

4. Add a little butter to the sauté pan and fry the eggs, then toast the brioche, if using. Wrap a slice of bacon around each steak, if you can, and then top the steak with an egg. Or, just place a bacon slice and an egg on top of each steak. If you have toasted brioche, slip a slice of toast under each steak. Pour a couple of spoonfuls of wine sauce over each portion, and you have the classic *filet de cheval à cheval*—"fillet of horse on horseback."

PIEDS-PAQUETS
with SAUCE CHARCUTIÈRE

Serves 4

If you're French or a Francophile, you know what these are supposed to be: sheep tripe and pig's trotters cooked together. We didn't know that, but we knew the name. We just made what we thought it ought to be and it turned out well, if completely unlike the original (we think). This is braised lamb and pig's trotter with greens and herbs, wrapped in caul fat. The sauce—a French classic with gherkins, mustard, and shallots—is also perfect with chops and liver.

2 pounds (about 1 kg) lamb neck or lamb shank

2 pig's trotters, each 6 inches (15 cm) long (just the trotter, not the whole leg)

¼ cup (60 ml) olive oil

1 cup (140 g) roughly diced, peeled carrot (about 1½-inch/4-cm chunks)

1 cup (140 g) roughly diced celery (about 1½-inch/4-cm chunks)

1 cup (115 g) roughly diced onion (about 1½-inch/4-cm chunks)

4 sprigs thyme

1 clove garlic

2 teaspoons salt

1 teaspoon pepper

2 cups (500 ml) dry white wine

Butter for greasing

SAUCE CHARCUTIÈRE

2 cups (500 ml) Beef Shank Stock (page 249)

3 tablespoons Dijon mustard

3 tablespoons unsalted butter

1 teaspoon red or white wine vinegar

16 small sour gherkins, sliced

2 tablespoons capers, drained and patted dry

1 French shallot, thinly diced

1 tablespoon chopped fresh tarragon

½ teaspoon cracked pepper

2 slices bacon, thick fall lardons (see Theory #3, page 166), crisped (optional)

PACKAGE

2 cups (400 g) chopped, blanched spinach (frozen is easiest)

2 tablespoons chopped fresh flat-leaf parsley

2 tablespoons chopped fresh basil

1 tablespoon chopped fresh sage

8 ounces (225 g) caul fat, thawed in the refrigerator if frozen and soaked in cold water until it can be gently stretched flat

2 tablespoons olive oil

Good Fries (page 154)

1. Preheat the oven to 350°F (180°C). Place the lamb, pig's trotters, and oil in a deep baking dish covered with buttered foil or a Dutch oven covered with its lid. Cover the meats with all the vegetables, the thyme, and the garlic. Sprinkle with the salt and pepper, and pour in the wine. Add water to barely cover the meat.

2. Cover with a sheet of buttered aluminum foil and place in the oven. Bake for 3½ to 4 hours, or until the trotters are easily pierced with a fork and the lamb is tender enough to shred. Check from time to time and add more water as needed to maintain the original level.

3. While the meats are cooking, make the sauce. Pour the stock into a small pot, bring to a simmer over high heat, and simmer until reduced by one-third. Stir in the mustard, butter, vinegar, gherkins, capers, shallot, tarragon, pepper, and lardons; reduce the heat to low, and cook for 5 minutes to blend the flavors. Taste and adjust the seasoning, adding more vinegar if you want a bit more bite. Remove from the heat and let cool before serving.

4. Remove the meats from the oven, uncover, and let cool. Remove the meats from the stock with a large slotted spoon, and transfer to a big plate or a tray. When the meats are cool enough to handle with your hands, start roughly shredding the lamb meat, discarding any bones. Place the lamb in a bowl. For the trotters, pull the meat off the bones with your hands, a knife, or a fork, discarding any bones and other unusable bits. The trotter meat is gelatinous, and it will be the glue you use to hold the packages together. Chop the trotter meat into small chunks and add to the lamb. Strain the cooking liquid through a fine-mesh sieve into a small bowl and set aside.

5. To make the packages, preheat the oven to 425°F (220°C). Add the spinach and all the herbs to the meats and mix well. Then add 1 cup (250 ml) of the strained cooking liquid and mix well with your hands. The mixture should feel malleable and moist. If it feels dry, add up to ½ cup (125 ml) more liquid. Taste and adjust the seasoning.

6. Form the meat mixture into 16 balls of equal size (about the size of a lemon). Lay the caul fat on a flat work surface, space the balls evenly on top, then cut the caul fat into squares large enough to encase the balls individually. Wrap each ball in caul fat, covering it completely.

7. Select a baking dish in which the balls will fit snugly, and oil it with the olive oil. Give each ball an elongated shape by squeezing it gently with your hands. Bake for 20 minutes, or until heated through and the tops are nicely browned.

8. Serve right away with the sauce and a pile of fries.

BROCHETTE DE LAPIN aux PRUNEAUX

Makes 6 skewers

We came up with this alternative to braised rabbit as a way to eat rabbit in the summer. If possible, ask the butcher to bone a rabbit for you. Be sure to distinguish between the legs and the loins (or saddle). In Canada, asking for the kidneys is no problem. In the United States, it is hit or miss.

Sometimes we like to serve the skewers with Gentleman Steak Sauce (page 251) for dipping, but they are good on their own, too. Another nice option is an easy pan jus, made by deglazing the pan with a shot of sherry, then adding ½ cup (125 ml) chicken stock and 2 tablespoons unsalted butter.

1 rabbit, divided into 2 legs, 2 loins, and 2 kidneys

4 slices bacon, cut into 3 pieces each

12 pitted prunes

1 red onion, cut into 12 pieces

2 tablespoons olive oil

1 teaspoon salt

2 large sprigs rosemary

1 tablespoon canola oil

1 tablespoon unsalted butter

1. Bone the legs and loins. Cut each leg and each loin into 6 equal pieces; leave the kidneys whole.

2. Have ready 6 bamboo skewers. Thread the following onto each skewer: 1 leg piece, 1 bacon piece, 1 prune, 1 loin piece, 1 onion piece. Repeat again.

3. Arrange the skewers on a platter. Drizzle the olive oil evenly over the skewers, then sprinkle with the salt.

Pluck the needles from the rosemary sprigs, and add a few pinches to each skewer.

4. Warm the canola oil and butter in a large frying pan over high heat. When the butter has melted and the fat is hot, add the skewers and cook, turning once, for 4 minutes on each side. Remove the pan from the heat and let the skewers rest for 3 minutes before serving.

PROFITEROLES DE CHÈVRE et CÉLERI, PURÉE DE TOMATES et PERSIL, R.I.P. Nicolas Jongleux

Serves 4

Nicolas Jongleux is a Montreal legend. Born and raised in Marsannay, in Burgundy, he grew up working in some of France's most influential kitchens, including, at age twenty-six, under Alain Chapel at the Michelin-three-star La Mère Charles in Mionnay. He came to Montreal under the guise of partnering in Le Cintra, where he worked for three years. From there he ran the seminal Les Caprices de Nicolas. David says: "He had more talent than anyone I've ever seen. I once watched him make sixty identical croissants by hand, no recipe, no scale, and he hadn't made croissants for more than five years. When he finished, there was not a drop of extra pastry, and each pastry was perfect."

He was also the kind of person who had such discipline all of his life, that he when he left France, he lived the experiences most of us had in our teens, in his thirties. He opened his last restaurant, Café Jongleux, in 1999, and committed suicide in the restaurant later that year. This recipe was a Nicolas classic.

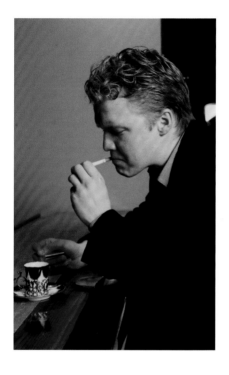

CHOUX PASTRY

1 cup (250 ml) water

½ cup (115 g) unsalted butter, cut into ½-inch (12-mm) cubes

¼ teaspoon salt

1 cup (130 g) all-purpose flour

4 eggs

CELERY ROOT AND GOAT CHEESE PURÉE

1 large celery root, peeled and diced

9 ounces (250 g) fresh goat cheese

Salt and pepper

Olive oil

PARSLEY PURÉE

1 cup (30 g) fresh flat-leaf parsley leaves

1 cup (30 g) fresh chervil leaves

¼ cup (60 ml) olive oil

1 tablespoon water

1 lemon, halved

Salt

TOMATO SAFFRON COULIS

2 tablespoons olive oil

1 clove garlic, minced

1 cup (170 g) peeled, seeded plum tomato pulp

Pinch of sugar

2 saffron threads

16 tiny sprigs chervil (optional)

Wedge of mimolette or Parmesan cheese (optional)

1. Preheat the oven to 400°F (200°C). Line a large rimmed baking sheet with parchment paper. In a heavy saucepan, combine the water, butter, and salt and bring to a full boil over high heat. Remove from the heat and add the flour all at once, stirring vigorously with a wooden spoon until the mixture forms a smooth ball that doesn't stick to the sides of the pan. Return the pan to medium-low heat and cook, stirring constantly, for 2 minutes. Remove from the heat and let cool for 5 minutes.

2. Using a stand mixer fitted with the paddle attachment, beat in the eggs one at a time, beating well after each addition, then continue beating until the dough is smooth and shiny.

3. With a spoon or a pastry bag fitted with a ¼-inch (6-mm) round tip, drop or pipe about 1 tablespoon of the dough onto the lined baking sheet for each profiterole, spacing them about 2 inches (5 cm) apart.You'll only use 16 pastries for this recipe, but the profiteroles can be baked and then stored in the freezer for up to 3 months.

4. Bake for 25 minutes, or until puffed, golden, and crisp. Turn off the oven and leave the choux on the pan in the oven until you are ready for them (be sure you take them out of the oven before step 8).

5. To make the celery root and goat cheese purée, in a saucepan, combine the celery root with water to cover, bring to a boil, and cook for about 15 minutes, or until tender. Drain and process in a food processor. The purée should look like runny mashed potatoes and should yield about 1 cup (250 ml). In a bowl, combine the celery root purée and goat cheese and mix until homogenous. Season with salt, pepper, and a little olive oil. Reserve at room temperature until needed.

6. To make the parsley purée, in the food processor, combine the parsley, chervil, half of the oil, and the water and process until smooth. With the motor running, slowly add the remaining oil. The purée should

have the thickness of yogurt. Season with lemon juice and salt.

7. To make the coulis, in a small pot, warm the oil over medium heat, add the garlic, and sauté until golden. Add the tomato pulp and sugar and simmer for 3 to 4 minutes, or until it thickens. Add the saffron at the last moment, then process in a blender until smooth. Keep warm until assembly.

8. Preheat the oven to 300°F (150°C). Using a small, serrated knife, cut the top one-fourth off each pastry. Keep the tops close by. With a small spoon or a clean piping bag fitted with a small, round tip, overstuff the base of each pastry until slightly full with the celery root and goat cheese purée. Replace the tops upside down.

9. Arrange the pastries on the same parchment-covered baking sheet. Place in the oven and bake for 4 to 5 minutes, or until the filling is hot.

10. While the pastries are baking, line up 4 shallow bowls (or a single platter if you're serving family style) and spoon 3 to 4 spoonfuls of the tomato coulis into each bowl (or cover the bottom of the platter with a thin layer).

11. When the pastries are ready, remove them from the oven and spoon a teaspoon-size dollop of the parsley purée in the upside-down cap of each one. Add a small chervil sprig to each dollop if you like. Place 4 pastries in each bowl, or put all of them on the platter. If you have the mimolette on hand, finely grate a little over each pastry before serving.

VEAL LIVER BRISKET

Serves 1

Some of our favorite customers—that is, Bobby Sontag—say that liver should always be served rare. This is (yet) another time where we disagree with him. Regarding Montreal smoked meat, we have one word: Schwartz's. Not unlike bagels, smoked meat preferences fuel wars and countless throwdowns. In fact, the best smoked meat is the one you prefer. If you can't get Montreal smoked beef brisket, you can substitute pastrami or even corned beef.

8 ounces (225 g) veal liver, cut into 4 thin slices

1 to 1½ teaspoons Montreal Steak Spice (page 250)

2 tablespoons neutral oil

4 slices Montreal smoked beef brisket, cut the same width and slightly thinner than the liver

1 large dill pickle

Prepared yellow mustard and ketchup for serving

1. Preheat the oven to 475°F (240°C). Season the liver slices liberally with the steak spice.

2. Select a nonstick frying pan or sauté pan large enough to hold all the liver slices in a single layer. Place over medium heat and add the oil. When the oil is hot, add the liver slices and sear, turning once, for 2 minutes on each side, or until done to your liking. Transfer the liver to a plate.

3. Add the smoked meat to the same pan over medium heat without any additional oil. Toss with tongs for about 1 minute, then remove from the heat.

4. Layer the meats "Napoleon style," alternating the liver and brisket. Cut the pickle lengthwise into medium slices, like you would for a burger, and place on top. Serve with the mustard and ketchup.

TURBOT au VERMOUTH DE CHAMBÉRY

Serves 2

We love Dover sole, or at least we used to. It's not as sound a menu choice these days, so instead we go for local turbot from the Gulf of Saint Lawrence. The classic turbot *au vin jaune* is exceptional, but said *vin jaune* can be really difficult to locate. A crisp, dry vermouth such as Vermouth de Chambéry will do.

1 French shallot, chopped

¼ cup (55 g) unsalted butter

1 sprig tarragon

Salt and pepper

½ cup (125 ml) dry white vermouth

1 cup (250 ml) whipping cream (35 percent butterfat)

½ cup (15 g) small, dried whole morels, hydrated in warm water to cover and drained

2 turbot fillets, about 8 ounces (225 g) each, preferably from whole fish, lifted by the fish monger

2 teaspoons chopped fresh chives

1. In a sauté pan, sweat the shallot in 2 tablespoons of the butter with the tarragon and a pinch each of salt and pepper for 3 or 4 minutes, or until soft and tender. Add the vermouth and simmer over medium heat until reduced by half. Add the cream and simmer for 3 to 4 minutes, until reduced by half, then add the morels and heat through for 2 minutes. Taste and add more salt and pepper as you like. The sauce should be the consistency of thin gravy and should taste delicious on its own. Remove from the heat, cover, and set aside.

2. Melt the remaining 2 tablespoons butter in a large frying pan or sauté pan over medium heat. When the butter stops foaming, add the fish and cook, turning once, for 3 to 4 minutes on each side, or until a golden brown crust forms on both sides.

3. Using a spatula, carefully lift up the fish and wipe the cooking fat from the pan. Replace the fish, spoon the sauce over, add the chives, and warm for 1 to 2 minutes. Cooked turbot falls apart so easily that we like to serve it directly from the pan at the table.

ÉPOISSES DE BOURGOGNE À L'ECHALOTE

Serves 4

If Parmesan is the king of cheese, Époisses is the cultural attaché. It's smelly in a way that makes you proud to like it. It's also red-wine compatible and awesome on a piece of steak. A washed-rind cheese, Époisses is made from milk from Burgundian cows and washed with the local marc de Bourgogne. It is crucial that you buy a good Époisses, and, in fact, only one or two brands make it to the United States and Canada. Sniff it before buying, and avoid one with a horse urine–window cleaner smell. Remember, too, warming up the cheese only amplifies the aroma. Sometimes Gilles Jourdenais at Fromagerie Atwater gets in tiny individual Époisses, which we try to use whenever possible.

This dish, which combines the cheese with shallots, used to be the classic Joe Beef drunk staff meal at 4 A.M. Eat it with toasted bread, a few rosettes of mâche, or on top of steak.

1½ cups (375 ml) dry red wine
4 large French shallots, finely chopped
1 sprig thyme
¼ teaspoon pepper
Pinch of sugar
2 tablespoons hazelnut oil
7 ounces (200 g) Époisses cheese
¼ cup (40 g) whole hazelnuts, toasted
4 slices pain levain, toasted

1. Preheat the oven to 425°F (220°C). In a small nonreactive saucepan, combine the wine, shallots, thyme, pepper, and sugar. Bring to a boil, then simmer over medium heat until the wine is reduced by half. Transfer to a bowl and let cool. Stir in the hazelnut oil.

2. Place the cheese in a small baking dish that you're proud to bring to the table, and cover it with the shallot mixture. Bake for 4 to 5 minutes, or until slightly melted. Serve with the hazelnuts and toast.

Note: When the Époisses comes out of the oven, you can flambé it with 1 tablespoon marc or a good brandy. And if you do, be careful. It is your responsibility and not ours if your date's rayon dress catches fire.

*I*t was May 3, 2010, and the plan was to meet at a nondescript bar in the basement of Place Bonaventure, Montreal's central station. When I arrived, Fred, Dave, and Jennifer (the photographer for this book) were on their second round of Campari and soda and their first plate of wings. Fred had a new recruit for his sermon of the train, and Dave and I exchanged knowing glances.

CHAPTER 3

TRAINS!

For the last six years, I had been so brainwashed on the merits of the great Canadian railroad that the previous summer I had taken the twenty-six-hour trip (advertised as twenty-one hours) on the Chaleur route from Montreal to the tip of mainland Canada, Gaspé, where I stayed for just two nights before heading home. "You want to be sure to take it on a Wednesday, as that's when they use the Budd [stainless-steel cars built in the 1950s by the Budd company, makers of the fabled California Zephyr], rather than the Renaissance [hand-me-downs from England purchased within the last ten years; 'uncomfortable, narrow, and ill-equipped,' according to Fred] equipment," Fred advised. So I did. I had a single roomette all done in chrome and Tiffany blue paint. I ate a foie gras parfait that Fred had packed and drank a bottle of Muscat that Dave said I would need. I fell asleep somewhere near Rivière-du-Loup and woke up on the gulf of the Saint Lawrence. It was strangely one of the most exotic trips I've ever taken. And here I was again about to set out on a seventeen-hour train trip to Moncton on the Ocean, the oldest continuously operated train route in North America.

At the bar, Fred was showing Jen his train manuals, while Dave and I witnessed people in suits engaging in after-office affairs before taking the suburban trains back home. "I like to read about trains while on the train," Fred was saying. You know how Trekkies probably lose their mind over the blueprint to the Starship Enterprise? That's how Fred is with the Renaissance car operating manual. He's just hoping there will be a mechanical breakdown and he'll be able to live out his dreams.

We finally boarded and unloaded in our side-by-side roomettes. Now, maybe we like a stronger gin and tonic than the average person, or maybe we like the fanfare of a nice bar setup. Or, maybe we're just drunks. Regardless, Fred brought his traveling-salesman bar kit, complete with bottles of vermouth, gin, Johnny Walker, and Fernet Branca. Knowing him well, I preempted any

catastrophies by grabbing bottles of soda and tonic, olives, lemons, limes, and cherries. We had cocktails and headed to the dining car.

The city was far behind us by the time we were onto Black Forest cake and our fifth bottle of Canadian wine. This was Dave's first time on a Canadian dining car, and knowing how much he hates to leave his family, I was surprised that he even agreed to come: "Hey, if Fred likes trains, I like trains, too."

Finally, we withdrew to our rooms, where in the agreeable company of one another we ate peanuts and listened to notorious train lover Neil Young's *Everyone Knows This Is Nowhere* on Dave's twenty-dollar speakers. We talked about how we would approach Fred's obsession in this book. The train lulled us sleepily and we listened patiently: "I want it to be a call to arms, a call to protect the railroad. . . ." **—ME**

The neighborhood of Point Saint Charles, or The Point, which lies directly beside Saint Henri, is one of the oldest working-class neighborhoods in the country. It is also where the Grand Trunk Railway Company incorporated in 1852, making it the oldest train hub in the country. This is where the harbor, the canal, and the railroads joined and where the row houses for the workers were crammed tight and piled high. It's these workers, along with the sailors and wharf rats, whom we imagine frequented the original Joe Beef somewhere between the 1870s and 1880s.

Up until the area was bull-dozed to make way for Expo 67, it remained a railroad haunt. A customer of ours who grew up in The Point drew us a map of the blocks around the rails. Twenty-seven bars were operating in about a four-block radius. They were set up so the men could jump off the train directly through the back door of a bar. There was the Moose Tavern, the Pall Mall, the 1 and 2, the Palomino, and the Olympic Tavern. He said you would walk into those places and they'd be buzzing with train radios and packed with men still in their work clothes, stinking of diesel fuel. The fact that we opened so close to this feels serendipitous and calming, and often reminds us of another era.

There was a time when the only way you could travel long distances

in this country was by train. And the only way that the railroads could compete with one another was by the service they provided on board. They boasted smoking parlors, piano bars, barber salons, and fashion shows. The Canadian National (CN) even had an onboard radio service, the CRBC, which was the model the Crown used to set up the Canadian Broadcasting Corporation in 1936. There were noble attendants, servers, cooks, and professional bartenders who had a fully stocked bar from which they made drinks in an array of real glasses. The premade bottled Césars and potato chips you get today were probably not an option. One of the main attractions of train travel was the dining car and the quality and array of food it offered. The kitchens were not always limited centralized setups made for ease and speed. Starting as early as 1872, the Delmonico dining car, which was

inaugurated in the U.S. Midwest, had a full kitchen, complete with stove tops for meats and sauces and ovens for fresh pastries. When we visited the Exporail Train Museum in Saint Constant (located a convenient twenty minutes away from Joe Beef), the archivist showed us the original cooking manuals that were given to the kitchen staff in 1912. Lake Winnipeg pickerel, crab Monte Cristo, ox tongue, Alberta sirloin with mash, Roquefort with crackers, stewed rhubarb—all dishes available en route.

Train passengers were the original locavores: It made sense that you picked up Alberta beef in the prairies and ate it outside of Calgary. It made sense that you were eating salmon as you departed Vancouver. More by necessity than choice, as the supplies for lengthy trans-Canadian trips were too heavy to carry, pickups for fruits, vegetables, and dairy

were scheduled across the country, and the cooks would in turn serve only the freshest provisions in the dining car. You would eat chowder and shellfish on Atlantic lines, "lumberjack" breakfasts through central Canada, and prime beef through the prairies.

One of the things I love most about train travel is the etiquette: You get on and get settled. You freshen up, put on a clean shirt or dress. Meet for drinks in the lounge for an hour. Get off during stops for cigarillos. Eat together and retire to another lounge for a nightcap. Go to the room, get ready for bed. Go to sleep in one province, wake up in another.

Call me nostalgic, but it's sad to think of what trains used to be, what they used to serve. Can you imagine a time when every aspect of train travel was Sunday's best? Now the food is equal to that of what you get

on airlines, and wi-fi is considered providing service. It's when I look through my old train books or visit Exporail that the pain is really felt.

Until 1974, Canada had two national train companies: Canadian National (CN) and Canadian Pacific Railway (CPR). In 1978, after decades of losing millions on passenger routes, CN and CPR merged and the passenger lines were taken over by the highly marketed sapphire blue and gold VIA Rail. Because this is not a chapter about economic feasibility, but rather nostalgia, we'll skip the politics and reasoning. The fact is, though the fanfare

is something only to be remembered, the routes still exist and there are fine dining cars with lounges and banquettes and room to have pre-packaged cheese and wine with your friends while you look out on some of the country's most beautiful scenery. Train travel takes longer and is only slightly less expensive than flying or driving, so the only raison d'être for the train is fun. If you're hungry, you can make the *foie de veau* in this book (page 95), or you can eat a can of tuna for sustenance. Likewise, if you want to go to the Gaspé, you can take the twenty-something-hour sleeper car, have wine, and meet

people, or you can drive the eight-hour autoroute. Like the beauty of people buying art not for trading, taking the train is for the hobby-ist in each of us. If efficiency is your only goal, then drop this book and eat a meal in a pill.

If I could take the train, some-how, each day, I would. When I am able to take the train, I often ride the metro train to the suburban train to the VIA train. And once I'm on, I never want to leave.

The following recipes are inspired by and meant for train travel. We wish we could eat these on the imaginary train ride of tomorrow. —**FM**

FRED'S TOP CANADIAN TRAIN ITINERARIES

1. THE HUDSON BAY

I flew to Winnipeg, took a nondescript cab to the train station, and then boarded the train at the end of the day. I was in the lounge section watching TV and thought I was alone, so I changed the curling channel after thirty minutes of boredom. Two older women with tight blue curls immediately chastised me for being so selfish. That's when I understood the Canadian love of curling.

By Law of Treaties, you can't be charged more than two dollars and fifty cents per freight box, so this train is a runner of sorts, with a lot of people sending provisions up north. Folks still depend on this train. *Coureurs des bois* (literally, "runners of the woods") are thought of almost as folklore now, but on this route, you actually see men with long beards who trap and skin animals for a living. It's the gateway to the north.

In Winnipeg, it was 60°F (15°C) and in Churchill -40°F (-40°C). It is practically the Arctic. I stayed in Churchill for three nights in March.

During my stay I went to the Gypsy Café, which is the "fancy" restaurant in town. The counter had the strangest setup. On one side was Gatorade, on the other, Dom Pérignon. There was a slide-in light box display of the menu, with items ranging from corn dogs and *poutine* to caribou and arctic char.

My big highlight was going out with Claude, the Arctic ranger. His business is skidoo expeditions, which I know nothing about. He took me out, just because he had to drop the flags for the upcoming qualifier to the Iditarod dog race. I thought I had dressed for winter, but Claude schooled me by lending me sealskin gloves, giant boots, gasoline-smelling pants, and a Hezbollah-looking face mask—and I was still cold. We toured for six hours through vast tundra. Because it's the Hudson Bay, you don't know if you're on ice on the bay or on the shore. He told me funny stories of French tourists crashing into one another, and showed me Arctic landmarks.

2. THE CANADIAN

In early spring, Allison was in Edmonton with her family, so I took the chance to ride the Canadian. I asked Paul Coffin to come, and, being the most relaxed guy, he said "sure." The Canadian is the longest and most proud route, running from Toronto to Vancouver over four days. We found the Budd train milk run to Toronto. We played tourist for the afternoon: picture at the landmark CN tower, peameal bacon at the St. Lawrence market, hung with Stephen Alexander at Cumbrae's meats. We left in the evening, around ten, and woke up the next day to real food from a real kitchen with real appliances. It's the only train in Canada that still has a full kitchen. It is an emblematic train with a true Canadian aura. If you haven't taken it, I highly suggest it. It is the only VIA route with a luxury option.

Yarmouth | Digby | Halifax
Via Dominion Atlantic Ry.

●8 Sat. Sam.	●6△ Sun. Dim.	●2△ Ex. Sun. Dim. exc.	Miles Milles	9 Atlantic Time/Heure Atlantique	●1 Ex. Sun. Dim. exc.	●7△ Fri. & Sun. Ven. & dim.	
				Dom. Atlantic Ry.			
05 05	16 20	12 05	0.0	Dp... Yarmouth Station.. Ar	17 05	00 10	
ƒ 05 44	ƒ 17 00	ƒ 12 45	28.8	.....Meteghan	ƒ 16 24	ƒ 23 29	..
ƒ 06 05	ƒ 17 23	ƒ 13 08	44.6	.....Weymouth	ƒ 16 01	ƒ 23 06	..
06 35	17 55	13 40	65.8	Ar...Digby Station ...Dp	15 30	22 35	
		13 55		Dp...Digby Wharf ....Dp	15 15		
ƒ 06 53	ƒ 18 13	ƒ 14 13	75.6	.....Deep Brook	ƒ 14 56	ƒ 22 16	..
ƒ 06 56	ƒ 18 16	ƒ 14 16	76.9	.....Cornwallis	ƒ 14 53	ƒ 22 13	..
07 10	18 30	14 30	86.0	...Annapolis Royal .. Ar	14 35	21 55	
ƒ 07 35	ƒ 18 55	ƒ 14 55	99.7	.....Bridgetown	ƒ 14 15	ƒ 21 35	..
ƒ 07 53	ƒ 19 13	ƒ 15 13	113.5	.....Middleton	ƒ 13 56	ƒ 21 16	..
08 03	19 23	15 23	120.8	.....Kingston	ƒ 14 15	ƒ 21 05	..
				(Greenwood)			
ƒ 08 20	ƒ 19 40	ƒ 15 40	132.0	.....Berwick	ƒ 13 29	ƒ 20 49	..
08 40	20 00	16 00	144 4	....Kentville ⓐ	13 20	20 30	..

Explanation of signs

ⓐ Meal Station.

● Air-conditioned R.D.C. (Rail Diesel Car) or news service. Checked baggage not : this equipment.

ƒ Stops on signal.

△ When statutory holidays are observed o... Trains 2, 3, 5, 6 and 7 will be annulled ... Trains 5, 6 and 7 will operate on Mond... operating on Mondays, Train 6 will leav... at 1735, arrive Halifax at 2320 and Trai... Halifax at 2330, arrive Kentville 0125 T...

Montréal | St. Jerome | Ste. Agathe | Mont Laurier

	Read down/De haut en bas					Read up/De bas en haut			
	167 Mon. Wed. & Fri. Lun. Mer. & Ven.	Miles Milles	13	Eastern Time/Heure de l'est	Altitude	164 Tue. & Thur. Mar. & Jeudi	172 Sun. only Dim. seul.	
86	18 15	0.0		Dp.....Gare Windsor Station...... Ar	109	12 35	21.00	
	♭ 18 20	2.0		....Westmount	152	12 27	20 52	
	♭ 18 25	4.7		....Montreal West	158	12 20	20 45	
	♭ 18 38	11.8		...Park Avenue (Jean Talon).....	191	12 07	20 32	
	♭ 18 43	15.5		....Bordeaux	76	ƒ 11 59	ƒ 20 24	
	♭ 18 54	22.9		....Ste-Rose	90	ƒ 11 49	ƒ 20 14	
	♭ 18 59	23.6		....Rosemere	91	ƒ 11 48	ƒ 20 13	

Equipment/Matériel

Montréal-Mont Laurier
Air-conditioned Rail Diesel Car.
Autorail climatisé.

Note A—No checked baggage handled.

Note A—Aucun bagage enregistré.

Explanation of signs

♥ Air-conditioned Rail Diesel Car.
Ⓜ Meal Station.
f Stops on signal.
▲ Convenient bus service via Canada Coach Lines between Galt and Kitchener.

Note D — Trains 337 and 338 — Carry checked baggage between Tor Galt, Woodstock, Windsor only, not to or from intermediate stat—

Explication des symboles

♥ Autorail climatisé.
Ⓜ Buffet à la gare.
f Arrêt sur signal.
▲ Service d'autobus Canada Coach Lines entre Galt et Kitchener.

Note D — Trains 337 et 338 — Service de bagage enregistré entre Tor Galt, Woodstock et Windsor seulement et non entre les gares i mediaires.

	Miles Milles	15 — Eastern Time/Heure de l'est	♥338 Daily Quot.	
		Royal York Hotel		
7 30	0.0	Dp...... Toronto Ⓜ ...... Ar	11 10	
7 40	4.5	...... West Toronto	11 00	
8 06	32.2	...... Milton	10 26	
8 35	57.2	...... Galt ▲	10 00	
8 12	87.8	...... Woodstock	09 29	
8 40	114.6	Ar...... London (C.P. Stn.) ...Dp	09 00	
8 50	114.6	Dp...... London (C.P. Stn.) .....Ar	07 50	
9 06	178.8	...... Chatham	07 32	
8 40	194.5	...... Tilbury	07 00	
	225.8	Ar...... Windsor ...... Dp		
		(Tecumseh Rd. and/et Crawford Ave.)		

Explanation of signs

Ⓜ Meal station.
b Flag stop to entrain passenger points north of Ste. Thérèse only.
f Stops on signal.

Explication des symboles

Ⓜ Buffet à la gare.
b Arrêt sur signal pour prendre voyageurs pour au-delà de Ste-Thérèse seulement.
f Arrêt sur signal.

Equipment/Matériel

Air-conditioned Rail Diesel Car. Autorail climatisé.

Montréal-Mont Laurier

	Milles	Eastern Time/Heure de l'est		Mar. & Jeudi	Dim. seul.
		Gare Windsor Station			
18 15	0.0	Dp..... Montréal, Que. Ⓜ ..... Ar	109	12 35	21 00
b 18 20	2.0	..... Westmount	152	12 27	20 52
b 18 25	4.7	..... Montreal West	158	12 20	20 45
b 18 38	11.8	..... Park Avenue (Jean Talon)	191	12 07	20 32
b 18 43	15.5	..... Bordeaux	76	f 11 59	f 20 24
b 18 54	22.9	..... Ste-Rose	90	f 11 49	f 20 14
b 18 56	23.6	..... Rosemere	91	f 11 48	f 20 13
b 18 59	25.6	Ar..... Ste-Thérèse ..... Dp	121	11 45	20 10
19 00	25.6	Dp..... Ste-Thérèse ..... Ar	121	11 45	20 10
19 05	29.8	..... Bouchard	232	f 11 37	f 20 02
19 08	32.8	..... St-Janvier	218	f 11 34	f 19 59
19 16	38.9	..... St-Jerome	308	11 27	19 52
f 19 30	47.5	..... Shawbridge	596	f 11 12	f 19 37
f 19 36	51.7	..... Piedmont (St-Sauveur) ..... (Mont-Gabriel)	547	f 11 04	f 19 29
19 42	54.7	..... Mont-Rolland (Ste-Adèle)	632	10 58	19 23
f 19 51	59.3	..... Ste-Marguerite	900	f 10 49	f 19 14
f 19 57	63.0	..... Val Morin	1018	f 10 42	f 19 07
f 20 01	65.2	..... Val David	1054	f 10 38	f 19 03
20 13	69.4	..... Ste-Agathe	1207	10 30	18 55
f 20 38	82.6	..... St-Faustin (Lac Carré)	1254	f 10 05	f 18 30
f 20 45	86.3	..... Morrison	889	f 09 58	f 18 23
f 20 53	90.6	..... St-Jovite	701	f 09 50	f 18 15
f 21 02	96.3	..... Mont-Tremblant	745	f 09 40	f 18 05
21 15	105.8	..... Labelle	749	09 27	17 52
f 21 35	119.0	..... Annonciation	816	f 09 07	f 17 32
f 21 42	122.5	..... Lacoste	850	f 09 01	f 17 26
f 21 54	129.3	..... Nominingue	835	f 08 51	f 17 16
f 22 11	140.2	..... Lac Saguay	1078	f 08 35	f 17 00
f 22 36	155.4	..... Barrette	793	f 08 11	f 16 36
22 50	163.8	Ar..... Mont-Laurier ..... Dp	733	08 00	16 25

3. THE ABITIBI

A few years back, our friend Adam Gollner wrote a nice piece in *Gourmet* magazine called "The Very Noble Train of the Huntsman," about our fishing trip to Club Kapitachuan and the eleven-hour route to northern Quebec. This route is in some way intimate to Joe Beef. It starts almost in our backyard and goes through The Point and Saint Henri backyards. Once you leave the island, you pass by Saint-Tite-des-Caps, where there is a huge country music festival: it's the Woodstock of RVs. Then at Hervey Junction the train splits in two, and the Saguenay makes its way to Jonquière and the Abitibi heads north to the outdoor country.

The route has trestles and tunnels, and after La Tuque, you're in the woods. A footnote that was (understandably) left out of the *Gourmet* story: We took a pile of local cheese up north, not knowing that back in Montreal there was a vast listeriosis scare. Men in black came to Joe Beef and demanded that Allison show them proof that the cheese was with us, and not at the restaurant. Meanwhile, we had started on our trip home and were (very quickly) made aware that we were at ground zero of the epicenter of an Ebola-like listeriosis outbreak. We felt odd and had the worst gas and stomach pain aboard the train. We then all crawled into bed for days. Part of me still thinks it was just the booze.

4. THE CHALEUR

What a train: This silver beauty inches its way along the Saint Lawrence River and the Chaleur Bay. You spot a lighthouse a few yards away. Three hours later, the Percé Rock. As you near cities you're moving slowly and so close to people's homes that you can see what they are watching on TV.

I love this train; I love the name, even if VIA Rail, in a move away from emotional nostalgia, generally abandoned names for destinations, that is, Montreal to the Gaspé. And what's a railroad claim to fame these days if it's not romance and nostalgia? I once got out of a mean parking ticket because I mentioned to the judge that I was on the Chaleur and it ran late because of the snow. And late it was, so late in fact that the run was cancelled halfway through. Right in Matapedia we backed up and I stayed at HoJo for two nights, and then took the bus to my destination. (Everything was wrong with that: I had a nice room onboard—my Christmas gift—I was largely hung over, and a 6:00 A.M. bus ride through rural New Brunswick is my equivalent of a *Twilight Zone* episode.)

Anyway, the train still runs, and the sights are still as gorgeous. I suggest you pack a French aristocrat picnic and a bar case, and choose a date when the acts of God aren't as prevalent.

y of Fundy Service | Service de la Baie De Fundy

"Princess of Acadia"

	Ex. Sun. Dim. exc.	10 — Atlantic Time/Heure de l'Atlantique	Ex. Sun. Dim. exc.
	10 50	Dp......... Saint John ....Ar	19 50
	13 35	Ar......... Digby ....Dp	17 05

l Service Available—Service de restaurant

IMPORTANT

For schedules and fares in effect after May 31, 1971, please consult local agent.

Pour horaires et tarifs en vigueur après le 31 mai, 1971, consulter l'agent local.

Havelock | Peterboro | Toronto

Read down/De haut en bas — Read up/De bas en haut

	♥381 Note A	♥383 Note A Sun. only Dim. seul.	♥381 Note A Sat. only Sam. seul.	♥381 Note A Ex. Sat. and Sun. Sam. et dim. exc.	14 Eastern Time/Heure de l'est	♥380 Note A Ex. Sun. Dim. exc.	♥382 Note A Sun. only Dim. seul.	♥380
	17 45	17 45	07 10	06 10	Dp. Havelock Ar	20 00	23 59	
	17 55	17 55	f 07 20	f 06 20	Norwood	f 19 50	f 23 37	
	f 18 07	f 18 07	f 07 32	f 06 32	Indian River	f 19 40	f 23 35	
	18 20	18 20	07 45	06 45	Peterboro	19 20	23 20	
	f 18 33	f 18 33	f 07 56	f 06 58	Cavan	f 19 06	f 23 09	
	f 18 42	f 18 42	f 08 07	f 07 07	Drexel	f 18 55	f 23 00	
	f 18 48	f 18 48	f 08 13	f 07 13	Manvers	f 18 48	f 22 54	
	f 18 54	f 18 54	f 08 19	f 07 19	Pontypool	f 18 42	f 22 48	
	f 19 06	f 19 06	f 08 31	f 07 31	Burketon	f 18 31	f 22 36	

edericton   TRAINS!

schedule | Horaires des autobus

Baltimore & Ohio Dining Car Service

THE GREAT LAKES LIMITED DINNER

To expedite service, kindly write your order on check, as our waiters are not permitted to accept verbal orders. Please pay waiter on presentation of your check.

Soup du Jour   Melon Balls in Grape Juice   Jellied Bouillon

Golden Omelet with Fried Tomatoes - 1.50
Grilled Lake Trout, Lemon Butter - 1.65
Tender Fried Chicken, Southern Style - 1.85
Casserole of Sweetbreads and Fresh Peas, Bearnaise - 1.90
Roast Leg of Lamb, Currant Jelly - 1.85
Broiled Selected Sirloin Steak - 3.00

Potatoes, Hashed Brown   Corn and Green Pepper Saute

Salad — Chopped Combination, French Dressing

Ice Cream   Sliced Peaches, Cream   Pie
Cheese and Crackers

Coffee   Sanka   Tea   Postum   Milk

All **B&O** Trains
to and from
DETROIT use
**MICHIGAN
CENTRAL
STATION**

HOT WEATHER SUGGESTION - 1.50

Cold Jellied Consomme
Stuffed Tomato, Crab Salad
Olives, Potato Chips

Rolls and Butter   Beverage

H. O. McAbee
Manager, Dining Car
and Commissary Department
Baltimore, Maryland
847

"THE IMPERIAL" MID-DAY
A LA CARTE

RELISHES
SLICED CUCUMBERS 45   YOUNG ONIONS 15
CANAPE OF CAVIAR 70   RADISHES 25   MIXED PICKLES 15
TOMATO JUICE 20   CHOW CHOW 15

Grapefruit Cocktail 35

SOUP 30

FISH
BROILED LAKE SUPERIOR TROUT, MAITRE D'HOTEL 70
FRIED LAKE SUPERIOR WHITEFISH, TARTAR SAUCE 70

ENTREES, ROASTS, ETC.
FRESH MUSHROOM OMELET 60
INDIVIDUAL CHICKEN PIE 85
GRILLED LAMB CHOP WITH NEW PEAS 65

CHOPS, STEAKS, ETC. FROM THE GRILL
BROILED OR FRIED CHICKEN (HALF) 1.25
"RED BRAND" SMALL STEAK 1.00
SIRLOIN STEAK 1.50   COUNTRY SAUSAGES 60
CHOPS (ONE) 45 (TWO) 85   BACON AND EGGS 65
BACON (3 STRIPS) 35 (6 STRIPS) 65   BROILED OR FRIED HAM (FULL CUT) 65
WITH 1 EGG 55 WITH 2 EGGS 65
(Bacon served with other Order 15, or Individual Mushrooms 25)

INDIVIDUAL POT OF BAKED BEANS, (HOT OR COLD) 35

EGGS, OMELETS, ETC.
BOILED (ONE) 20 (TWO) 35   FRIED (ONE) 20 (TWO) 35
POACHED ON TOAST (ONE) 20 (TWO) 40
PLAIN 45.   TOMATO OR CHEESE 50.   JELLY, SAVORY, SPANISH OR HAM 60

VEGETABLES
BAKED POTATOES 25   BOILED OR MASHED POTATOES 20
POTATOES 30
FRENCH FRIED OR HASHED BROWNED POTATOES 25
NEW BEETS 20   NEW GREEN PEAS 20
BEETS 20   FRESH ASPARAGUS DRAWN BUTTER 50

COLD DISHES
CHICKEN 85
BEEF 75   HAM 75   LAMB 75   TOMATO SURPRISE 40
SARDINES 60   CANADIAN SARDINES. FANCY PACK 35
(With Potato Salad 15 cents Extra)

SALADS
(WITH FRENCH OR MAYONNAISE DRESSING)
COMBINATION 45   LETTUCE AND TOMATO 45   HEAD LETTUCE
WALDORF 50   BEET AND EGG
ASPARAGUS 50
(THOUSAND ISLAND DRESSING 10)

It is with pleasure and pride that we call attention to the desire
and willingness of all our employees to give their utmost in service. . .
special attention and they as well as ourselves would appreciate
any items as well as your commendations.

. . . menu card in envelope, ready
. . . to dining car steward.

Link of Empire. When the *first transcontinental train from Montreal rolled over the new steel path to the Pacific, fifty years ago, it carried the destinies of a nation—of an Empire! For the newly-completed Canadian Pacific Railway not only formed the visible link of the newly confederated Provinces, it opened the way to unbroken world-communications within the Empire—a fact of profound significance in Imperial policy. If a united Empire has stood as the bulwark of civilization in the succeeding years, a vital contribution to that unity was made by the men of faith and courage who planned and built the Canadian Pacific Railway fifty years ago.

The original equipment of the first transcontinental train is being reconditioned and its arrival at Port Moody is being re-enacted on July 3, in celebration of its own and Vancouver's Golden Jubilee.

JUL 18 1936

Painting by MARIUS HUBERT-ROBERT

THE CHATEAU FRONTENAC

Salute to our Farmers and Dietitians

CANADIAN PACIFIC DINING CARS OFFER NEW SALAD BOWL MENUS ■ FOR 1936 ■

Breakfast
FRUITS
Orange   Orange Juice
Banana with Cream
. . . Stewed Rhubarb
Apple Juice

.65
Fruit or Cereal
Poached or Scrambled Eggs
or Bacon
Muffins or Biscuits
Coffee   Milk

.85
Fruit and Cereal
Scrambled or Fried Eggs
Pan Cakes, Currant Jelly
Bacon with Egg
Marmalade or Jam
Muffins or Biscuits
Coffee   Milk

$1.00
Fruit and Cereal
Broiled or Creamed Fish
Chop with Bacon
Bacon or Fried Potatoes
Marmalade or Jam
Muffins or Biscuits
Coffee   Milk

Luncheon
Price opposite each item includes the full course Luncheon
Canadian Pea Soup
Consomme (Hot or Cold)
Fried, Grilled or Baked Fish, 75
Chicken Salad, Mayonnaise, 75
Spanish Omelet, 90
Roast Loin of Lamb, Red Currant Jelly, 1.00
Calf's Sweetbreads, Milanaise, 1.00
Boiled, Mashed or Fried Potatoes
Creamed Spinach   Carrots Vichy
Chocolate Custard Pudding
Banana Cream Pie
Bread   Rolls
Tea   Coffee   Milk
(Iced Tea or Coffee)

Dinner
Price opposite each item . . . full course Dinner
Sliced Egg, Ravigote or . . .
Puree Jackson   Consomme (. . .
Fried or Broiled Fish, . . .
Asparagus Omelet, Supreme Sa. . .
Steak and Mushroom Pie, . . .
Roast Chicken with Bacon, Bread S. . .
"Red Brand" Sirloin Steak, Can. . .
Pacific Style, 1.50
Boiled, Mashed or Au Gratin Pota. . .
Creamed Cauliflower   Green . . .
Waldorf Salad, Mayonnaise . . .
Fruit Custard Pudding   Strawberry Ta. . .
Ice Cream   Canadian Cheese and Crack. . .
Bread or Rolls
Tea   Coffee
(Iced Tea or Coffee)   Milk

CANADIAN PACIFIC DINING CAR SERVICE

CANADIAN PACIFIC - CANADIAN NATIONAL
POOLED TRAIN SERVICE

Luncheon Suggestions

Price opposite each item includes the full course Luncheon

Canadian Pea Soup   Consomme (Hot or Cold)

Fried or Grilled Fish, 75

Combination Salad, 75

Irish Stew, Dublin Style, 90

Calf's Sweetbreads, Bordelaise, 1.00

Assorted Cold Cuts, Potato Salad, 1.00

Boiled or Mashed Potatoes

Cauliflower, Polonaise   or   Boiled Onions

Chocolate Custard Pudding   Berry . . .

Bread   Rolls

Tea   Coffee

(Iced Tea or Coffee)

LE GRAND SETUP DE CAVIAR

Serves 4

As we write this, it seems much more acceptable to spend $18 for an entire appetizer than it does to spend $180 an ounce for real caviar. What makes this setup grand is the ceremonial feel it has, like something you could get on the Orient Express. Feel free to use any kind of fish eggs: whitefish, salmon, trout, or even smoked or preserved fish. It's also crucial that what you save on the real caviar, you spend on Champagne and on an overpriced silver serving dish from eBay.

Eat it in your bed or on the bus.

BLINI

⅓ cup (40 g) all-purpose flour, sifted
⅔ cup (85 g) buckwheat flour
¼ teaspoon salt
1 tablespoon baking powder
1 egg
1 cup (250 ml) water
2 tablespoons neutral oil, plus more for cooking
1 teaspoon sugar
Melted unsalted butter for serving

1 small container mújol (Spanish mullet caviar) or Canadian or American sturgeon caviar (1 ounce/30 g per person)
4 hard-boiled eggs, peeled and whites and yolks separated and chopped (or pushed through a coarse-mesh sieve)
¼ cup (10 g) chopped fresh chives
2 lemons, halved
½ cup (125 ml) crème fraîche (see Smorgasbord insert)
2 tablespoons grated fresh horseradish

1. To make the blini, in a bowl, sift together the all-purpose flour, buckwheat flour, salt, and baking powder. In another bowl, whisk together the egg, water, oil, and sugar until well mixed. Whisk together the dry ingredients and wet ingredients briefly. It is better to have tiny clumps than rubbery dough.

2. Place a nonstick frying pan over medium heat and add 1 teaspoon of oil. When the pan is hot, drop in the batter by spoonfuls, forming silver dollar–size blini. When the tops begin to set, flip the blini carefully. Continue to cook until firm. They should take 2 to 3 minutes total to fry. Transfer to a warm tray and cover with a kitchen towel to keep warm. Repeat with the remaining batter. You should have about 24 blini. Just before serving, brush with melted butter.

3. To serve, place the caviar, eggs, chives, lemons, crème fraiche, and horseradish in serving dishes alongside the warm blini. Build as you see fit.

TINY SAUSAGE LINKS

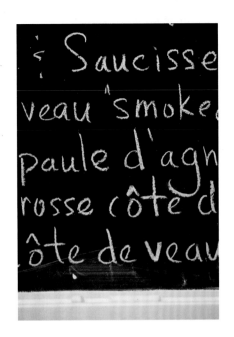

Makes about thirty 3-inch (7.5-cm) links,
enough for a large family breakfast

You can make sausage links or you can make patties, which are a lazy man's links. If you opt for links, you will need a sausage stuffer. You may also have to special order the casings from your butcher. It is a good idea to double the recipe, too, because it is easier to work with a larger amount. These are good breakfast sausages, but they also shine with kraut, lentils, or duck. Enjoy with a nice glass of Hungarian wine, or with a nice Hungarian man, i.e., artist Peter Hoffer.

1 pound (455 g) ground pork

1 pound (455 g) ground veal, turkey, or duck

½ cup (40 g) rolled oats

¼ cup (60 ml) ice water

¼ cup (75 g) maple syrup

1 tablespoon Sriracha sauce

2 teaspoons salt

2 tablespoons powdered sage

1 tablespoon pepper

1 teaspoon garlic powder

½ teaspoon ground ginger

Canola oil for frying

2 bundles ¾ to 1-inch (2 to 2.5-cm) lamb casings, if making links

1. In a large bowl, combine the pork, veal, oats, ice water, maple syrup, Sriracha sauce, salt, sage, pepper, garlic powder, and ginger. Mix thoroughly with your hands. In a frying pan, heat a little canola oil over medium heat. Fry a small test patty and correct the seasoning if needed.

2. Now, if you want to make patties rather than links, form the meat mixture into flattened golf balls. Return the frying pan to medium heat, add a little more oil, and then the patties. Fry, turning once, for about 3 minutes on each side, or until just cooked through. Serve hot.

3. If you are feeling ambitious, load the meat mixture into the sausage stuffer. Slide the casing onto the stuffing tube and begin to stuff. The casing should be full and tight, but not full enough to burst when you begin to pinch the links. Stuffing sausage takes Yoda-like patience at the beginning. That's why most folks say screw it and make patties instead. But making your own links is a skill, and with practice, you'll be stuffing casings like a pro. To form the links, press your forefinger and thumb together to make a slight indent in the casing about every 3 inches (7.5 cm) or every second sausage, then twist each indent about 3 turns.

4. Finally, fry the sausages in a frying pan with a little oil, turning to brown all sides, for 4 to 5 minutes, or until just cooked through. Serve hot.

CANARD et SAUCISSE

Serves 2

This dish is not surprising in taste (it's duck, sausage, and potato—what can go wrong?), nor very feminine (in other words, it's not pretty). We like the look a lot, because the fingerlings, duck pieces, and links are all the same size and shape. This is the best way to enjoy duck in the middle of the winter.

¼ cup (60 ml) canola oil

Salt

1 boneless duck breast, a little less than 1 pound (about 420 g)

10 fingerling potatoes, parboiled and peeled

10 Tiny Sausage Links (page 93)

1 sprig thyme

1 French shallot, thinly sliced

1 tablespoon ketchup

¼ cup (60 ml) Beef Shank Stock (page 249)

1 tablespoon unsalted butter

1. In a frying pan, heat 2 tablespoons of the oil over medium heat. Salt the duck breast on both sides and place, skin side down, in the pan. Sear for 4 minutes, then turn and continue cooking for 3 minutes on the other side; it should be medium-rare. Set the duck aside in a warm spot.

2. Pour the fat out of the pan. Return the pan to medium-high heat and add the remaining 2 tablespoons oil. Then add the potatoes, links, and thyme and cook, turning the potatoes and links every now and again, for 8 minutes. You want those potatoes to soak up all that fat the links release. Now add the shallot and ketchup and mix well. Finally add the stock and butter to the mix. Stir for another 2 minutes, just enough to warm everything up evenly.

3. Cut the duck into slices similar in size to the links. Divide the duck, spuds, and links between 2 plates, and pour the sauce from the pan on top.

DINING CAR CALF LIVER

Serves 2

This recipe is taken from an old Canadian National Railway menu. It became an instant Joe Beef classic, which goes to show: people love train food.

1 long slice calf liver, about 10 ounces (280 g) and 1½ inches (4 cm) thick

6 tablespoons (55 g) unsalted butter

½ cup (85 g) diced cooked ham

1 shallot, finely chopped

½ cup (40 g) finely chopped white mushrooms

1 tablespoon Cognac

Salt and pepper

½ clove garlic, minced

1 tablespoon finely chopped fresh flat-leaf parsley

½ cup (55 g) toasted bread cubes (from 1 slice stale white bread)

½ cup (55 g) grated Parmesan cheese

1 tablespoon Dijon mustard

¼ cup (10 g) chopped fresh chives

½ cup (125 ml) Beef Shank Stock (page 249)

1. Preheat the oven to 400°F (200°C). With a long sharp knife, carefully slice open the piece of liver like a wallet.

2. To make the stuffing, grab a sauté pan and melt 2 tablespoons butter over medium heat. It seems like a lot of butter because it is. After 2 minutes, add the ham and the shallot. Sweat it for a minute or two and then add the mushrooms, Cognac, and ¼ teaspoon salt to draw the water from the mushrooms. Stir in the garlic, parsley, and a pinch of pepper and cook for 3 minutes. Lastly, add the bread and mix everything together. Remove from the heat and let cool.

3. Spoon the stuffing carefully into the veal wallet. Unlike a real wallet, you want this one only three-quarters full. Squeeze the top to make sure that the bottom is full. Now sew the top shut with bamboo skewers. It doesn't have to be perfect; just shut it so the stuffing doesn't fall out.

4. In a small cocotte or other small flameproof casserole, melt 2 tablespoons butter with a pinch each of salt and pepper over medium heat. When the butter is foaming, fit the liver in the pan and place in the oven for 12 minutes.

5. Time to make the herb crust: Melt the remaining 2 tablespoons butter, let cool, then mix with the Parmesan, mustard, and chives.

6. After 12 minutes, take the liver out but don't turn off the oven. With a spoon, smear the buttery crust on top of the liver. Add the stock to the pan, return the pan to the oven, and bake for another 5 minutes, or until a thermometer inserted into the thickest part reads 135°F (58°C).

7. Take out the skewers, let the liver rest for a minute, then slice and serve.

PORK FISH STICKS

Serves 6

The idea here is to get great pulled pork but in the shape of High Liner Captain's fish sticks. If you don't have a proper fryer, you can still do this recipe—just don't attempt it drunk and/or naked. You can use a thick-bottomed pot and a deep-fat thermometer, and of course, have a fire extinguisher nearby. Try these sticks with any of the suggested dips for Cornflake Eel Nuggets (page 134), or serve on mashed potatoes with onion jus.

Pulled pork from Scallops with
    Pulled Pork (page 30)

6 sheets gelatin

1½ cups (375 ml) BBQ Sauce (page 176)

3 tablespoons chopped French shallots

Salt and pepper

BREADING

2 cups (255 g) all-purpose flour

2 tablespoons Old Bay seasoning
    (optional)

4 eggs

1 cup (250 ml) milk

Salt and pepper

4 cups (170 g) *panko* (Japanese bread
    crumbs), crushed in the bag(s)
    between your hands to powder a bit

Canola oil for deep-frying

1. At Joe Beef, we smoke the pork butt for 10 hours for this recipe. If you have a smoking device (see page 146), we suggest you use it. But if not, no problem; just roast it in the oven as directed. When the pork is ready, shred it and set it aside; do not add the BBQ Sauce yet.

2. Bloom the gelatin sheets in a bowl of cool water to cover for 5 to 10 minutes, or until they soften and swell. Meanwhile, heat the BBQ Sauce in a large saucepan over medium heat until warmed through. Remove the saucepan from the heat. Gently squeeze the gelatin sheets, add to the sauce, and whisk until completely dissolved. Add the shredded pork to the sauce and mix well. Stir in the shallots, taste, and correct the seasoning with salt and pepper.

3. Line a rimmed baking sheet with plastic wrap. Transfer the meat mixture to the baking sheet and press well and evenly. Cover with plastic wrap and refrigerate for at least 2 hours or up to 4 days.

4. To ready the breading, set up three bowls. In a shallow bowl, mix together the flour and the Old Bay seasoning. In a second bowl, whisk together the eggs, milk, and a pinch each of salt and pepper. Put the *panko* in a third bowl.

5. Unmold the chilled meat mixture on a cutting board by turning the baking sheet upside down and using your fingers to gently remove the meat (it's okay if it breaks up a little as you can re-form it with your hands). Cut the meat into fish stick–sized sticks. Now, set up the bowl assembly line. *Carefully* toss the sticks in the flour, then in the egg mixture, and then, with a clean hand, in the *panko*. If you feel unsure of the resistance of your breaded crust, you can repeat the egg and *panko* steps, hence doubling the crust. Lay the pork sticks on a clean baking sheet and refrigerate uncovered in a single layer for about 15 minutes to dry out a bit.

6. Meanwhile, pour the oil to a depth of 3 inches (7.5 cm) into your deep fryer and heat to 350°F (180°C). Working in batches of 5 or 6 sticks, fry for 3 to 4 minutes, until golden and crisp. (Remember to let your fryer return to its initial temperature between batches; respect that little orange light!) Remove the sticks from the oil, pat dry with paper towels, and let cool for 3 or 4 minutes. Season to taste with salt and pepper and serve.

BOX OF PULLMAN LOAF

Serves 1

George Pullman was a fervent industrialist and a train man. He created the sleeping car, the hotel car, and eventually the dining car. Some say the Pullman sandwich loaf was designed after his cars. Others say it was designed to fit into the cube-shaped train shelves. Either way, this is an easy dish we would love to eat for breakfast—on the train, of course. This recipe makes one serving; use up the rest of the Pullman loaf making more boxes.

1 unsliced loaf day-old Pullman (sandwich) bread (works best if the bread is cold)

2 tablespoons unsalted butter

1 smoked mackerel fillet or a few slices smoked salmon

3 eggs

2 tablespoons whipping cream (35 percent butterfat)

Salt and pepper

1 tablespoon crème fraîche or sour cream

1 teaspoon chopped fresh chives

Few shavings fresh horseradish

Caviar for garnish (optional)

1. Basically, what you are doing here is building a big box of buttered bread, a little home for your eggs. Start by removing a slice about 2 inches (5 cm) thick from the loaf. Cut off the crusts from the slice, then remove its core by cutting a square hole in the middle. Keep in mind that the hole has to be big enough to contain three scrambled eggs and the delicious fish.

2. Preheat the oven on a low setting. Melt 1 tablespoon of the butter in a nonstick frying pan—or better, use a breakfast griddle—over low heat and slowly color the box on all sides. Put the box on a plate along with the fish and place the plate in the oven to heat the fish and keep the box warm.

3. In a small bowl, whisk together the eggs, cream, and a little salt and pepper. Scramble the eggs over low heat in the remaining butter in the same pan (or a new pan if you used a griddle for the bread). When they are almost set, nonchalantly add the warm pieces of fish. Heat the ensemble through.

4. Place the ensemble in the box. Garnish with the crème fraîche, chives, and horseradish. We also find a teaspoon of caviar to be a nice touch.

PEAMEAL BACON

Makes about 4 pounds (1.8 kg)

Even though peameal has nothing to do with the bacon we know and love, many still refer to it as "Canadian bacon." They call it that in Canada, the place on both sides of Quebec—joking, joking. . . . Part of the history of Montreal is an overdramatized opposition to Toronto. Maybe it's hockey, maybe it's the separatist thing, or maybe it's just a friendly rivalry. Regardless, we love Toronto. It's where our favorite butcher, Stephen Alexander, has his shops (Cumbrae's), and it's the national capital of oyster bars (Rodney's, Oyster Boy, Starfish). It's also home to Kids in the Hall, John Candy, the Black Hoof, and, of course, the Saint Lawrence Market, where you can get a peameal bacon bun with maple mustard.

Peameal is not made with peas anymore. Like most aspects of life, ranging from food to plastic, peameal is being taken over by corn. We make our peameal with dried yellow peas crushed in the processor. The purpose of peas or cornmeal is to wick and dry, thus preventing spoilage. You will let the meat brine for a minimum of four full days, ninety-six hours, in the fridge. It is necessary to have a brine injector; they sell them nowadays for under ten bucks in big stores.

3 quarts (3 liters) cold water

1 cup (300 g) maple syrup

⅔ cup (150 g) kosher salt

2 tablespoons Prague powder #1 cure (optional)

10 peppercorns

1 tablespoon mustard seeds

1 bay leaf

4½ pounds (2 kg) boneless lean pork loin

1½ cups (215 g) coarse cornmeal or 1½ cups (340 g) dried yellow peas, roughly milled in a food processor

1. In a plastic (preferably) container large enough to hold both the brine and the meat, mix together the water, maple syrup, salt, cure, and spices.

2. Scoop out a scant 1 cup (200 ml) brine, and use it to load the brine injector. Then, inject the loin every ¾ to 1 inch (2 to 2.5 cm), inserting the needle about ¾ inch (2 cm) deep. Try to distribute the brine evenly over the loin. Place the loin in the container with the remaining brine, and keep the meat submerged with the help of a plate or an object of a similar build. Cover and refrigerate for 4 full days.

3. Remove the loin from the brine and pat it dry. Then roll it in the meal of your choosing. Give it a day's rest, uncovered, in the fridge, so the meal and meat form as one.

4. You have two options on cooking it: you can slice it and griddle it for a minute on each side (for thin slices that is), or you can bake it at 375°F (190°C) for about an hour, or until it has a core temperature of 142°F (61°C), then slice it. I like it the first way, especially when it gets a bit burnt on the edges and I have added a dash of maple syrup that caramelizes a bit toward the end.

CHICKEN JALFREZI

Serves 4

This recipe is an homage. While aboard the Ocean, en route to Prince Edward Island, we had three choices for dinner: haddock Dugléré, chicken *jalfrezi*, or fish chowder and sandwich. Meredith went for the chicken, everyone else had haddock. Fred looked at Meredith's, knew it was better, and talked the entire trip about ordering it on our return. As we made our way back to Quebec, all he wanted was a warm and true *jalfrezi*.

So we're back on the train, in our favorite booth, two bottles of wine down when the attendant comes to our table. Fred orders. "Sorry, sir, all we have left are ham sandwiches and Pringles." Devastation in the form of a one-hour rant about the decline of the railroad ensues.

The *jalfrezi* had such an impact that we wanted to get it into this chapter. So we asked ex–Joe Beefer and curry pro Kaunteya Nundy to come up with a classic *jalfrezi*. Not surprisingly, he came up with a recipe that put the VIA Rail version to shame. This is for Fred. And this is what Kaunteya had to say about the dish: "I asked my family what *jalfrezi* means, and I was told by my Bengali grandmother [Calcutta region] that *jal* means 'hot' and *frezi* means 'fry.' This is a very Anglo-Indian dish that was invented by the British. My mom, Shobhna Nundy, and I created this recipe. We made it three times to make sure that it was just right and would not blow away the 'white folks' from a spicy [heat] level."

SPICE MIX

2 teaspoons coriander seeds

2 teaspoons cumin seeds

½ cinnamon stick

2 bay leaves

2 dried red chiles

Seeds from 4 green cardamom pods

6 whole cloves

½ teaspoon fennel seeds

½ teaspoon ground turmeric

JALFREZI

5 tablespoons (75 ml) vegetable oil

2 pounds (900 g) boneless, skinless chicken thighs, halved

Salt and pepper

3 onions, finely chopped

4 cloves garlic, finely minced

½-inch (12-mm) piece fresh ginger, peeled and finely minced or grated

2 green chiles, finely chopped

4 to 5 tablespoons (60 to 75 ml) red wine vinegar

6 canned plum tomatoes, lightly pressed with a fork

2 tablespoons ketchup

1 large green bell pepper, seeded and cut into 1-inch (2.5-cm) squares

1 large red bell pepper, diced into 1-inch (2.5-cm) squares

1 teaspoon ghee (clarified butter)

2 tablespoons plain yogurt

Coarsely chopped fresh coriander for garnish

BASMATI RICE

2 cups (400 g) basmati rice

4 cups (1 liter) water

2 bay leaves

2 whole cloves

2 green cardamom pods

Pinch of saffron threads

Pinch of salt

3 to 4 teaspoons butter, melted

Lightly toasted slivered almonds for garnish

Note: There are two ways to make Basmati rice. The quick and dirty way, aka boil and drain, or the traditional way. This is the traditional way.

1. To prepare the spice mix, in a small sauté pan, combine the coriander, cumin, cinnamon, bay leaves, dried chiles, and cardamom and roast over medium heat for about 4 minutes, or until a very fragrant cumin aroma is released. Let cool. Transfer to a spice grinder, add the cloves and fennel seeds, and grind to a fine powder. Pour into a small bowl, add the turmeric and mix well. Set aside.

2. To make the *jalfrezi*, preheat a large, thick-bottomed stew pot over high heat and add the vegetable oil. At the same time, season the chicken thighs with salt and pepper. When the oil just begins to smoke, using tongs, place the thigh pieces into the pot and sear until golden brown on all sides. This should take 4 to 6 minutes. Remove the thighs with a slotted spoon to a large plate and set aside.

3. Add the onions, garlic, ginger, and green chiles to the pot and sauté, scraping the bottom of the pot as you stir. After about 7 minutes, reduce the heat to medium and season with

salt and pepper. This will cause the onions to release some of their liquid, which will make it easier to dislodge the browned chicken bits from the bottom of the pot as you stir. When the onions are lightly caramelized, deglaze the pot with the vinegar and continue to scrape the bottom of the pot.

4. Return the chicken to the pot along with any juices that accumulated on the plate while it rested. Add the spice mix and stir together all the ingredients so the spices adhere to the chicken pieces. Now add the tomatoes, ketchup, and the bell peppers and mix well. Add just enough water to cover the top of the chicken, raise the heat to high, and stir constantly. When the mixture is about to boil, cover the pot, reduce the heat to medium-low, and simmer for 15 to 20 minutes, or until the chicken is cooked through.

5. Uncover and raise the heat to medium-high to evaporate the excess water and to thicken. When the dish starts to thicken slightly and a light sheen of oil is visible on the surface, add the ghee. Move the chicken pieces to the sides of the pot, creating a well in the center. Mix the yogurt into the liquid in the well, then remove from the heat. The ghee and yogurt will enrich the sauce.

6. While the *jalfrezi* is cooking, prepare the rice. Preheat the oven to 375°F (190°C). Rinse the rice until most of the starch is removed. We like to do this by rubbing the grains between our palms under cool running water. Drain the rice well, then place it in a heavy ovenproof pot with a tight-fitting lid. Add the water, bay leaves, cloves, cardamom pods, saffron, and salt.

7. Place the pot on the stove top over high heat and bring to a boil, stirring occasionally. When the rice is boiling, cover the pot tightly with aluminum foil and then the lid and place in the oven for 20 minutes. Remove the rice from the oven and let it sit, still covered, for another 10 minutes.

8. To serve, transfer the *jalfrezi* to a warmed serving dish and garnish with the fresh coriander. Remove the lid and foil from the rice pot. The rice should be "standing," very aromatic, and slightly orange from the saffron. Fluff the rice with a fork and drizzle the melted butter on top for an even richer, nuttier flavor. Garnish with the slivered almonds for a traditional finish. Serve the *jalfrezi* with the rice.

Route of the Diesel Electric Streamliners

BEER CHEESE

Serves 4

This recipe is from a trip that Fred took with Allison and her parents to the Czech Republic: "I was thirty, traveling in the back of an Opel minivan loaded with adults. The bottles of beer were always too small and the stops never frequent enough. This was back when I was ignoring a little gluten issue and drinking vast quantities of Czechvar/Budvar. Basically, this trip was like the Griswolds in Prague.

"While visiting an old brewery's beer garden, I noticed a 'little things to eat with beer' section of the menu. It was full of pickled herring, *utopenec* (pickled sausage), and cheese. We ordered them all, and when the cheese arrived, it was like a gathering of all of the cheese leftovers blended with beer. It was unsightly and completely delicious."

You will need four (4-ounce) cheese molds with holes or four Styrofoam coffee cups with holes poked in the bottoms and sides, plus four paper coffee filters to make the cheese.

4½ ounces (130 g) quark cheese
4½ ounces (130 g) cream cheese
3½ ounces (100 g) blue cheese
½ cup (125 ml) pilsner beer
1 teaspoon salt
½ clove garlic, finely minced
Hefty pinch of paprika

ACCOMPANIMENTS
Rye bread slices panfried in butter and rubbed with a garlic clove
Pickled cherry or banana peppers
Sour Crudités (page 177)

1. Leave the cheeses at room temperature for about 1 hour.

2. In a small pot, warm the beer over medium heat and then remove from the heat.

3. In a food processor, combine the cheeses, beer, salt, garlic, and paprika and process until smooth and homogenous, stopping to scrape down the sides of the bowl as needed.

4. If you are using Styrofoam cups (see note above), use a hot nail or small pointed knife blade to poke holes in each cup, spacing them every square inch (2.5 cm). You should have about 30 holes. Dampen the coffee filters, and line each perforated Styrofoam cup or drainage cup with a filter.

5. Divide the cheese mixture into 4 equal portions, and put a portion in each lined cup. Put the cups on a rimmed plate, cover with plastic wrap, and refrigerate overnight.

6. Unmold the cheeses and place each portion on a plate. Serve with the rye bread, pickled peppers, and crudités.

LENTILS LIKE BAKED BEANS

Serves 4

This great side dish has a bit of a Quebecois-lumberjack-in-Bollywood taste. It is red lentils cooked like dahl, seasoned like baked beans. It is a pork chop's best friend, or will mate with a hefty breakfast.

4 slices bacon, finely diced

1 onion, finely chopped

½ teaspoon minced garlic

2 cups (400 g) red lentils, picked over and rinsed

4 cups (1 liter) water

¼ cup (60 ml) ketchup

2 tablespoons maple syrup, plus more as needed

2 tablespoons neutral oil

1 tablespoon cider vinegar, plus more as needed

2 tablespoons Colman's dry mustard

1 teaspoon pepper, plus more as needed

1 bay leaf

Salt

1. Preheat the oven to 350°F (180°C). In an ovenproof pot with a lid, fry the bacon over medium-high heat until crisp. Add the onion and cook, stirring, for about 4 minutes, or until softened. Then add the garlic and cook for 1 minute longer.

2. Add the lentils, water, ketchup, maple syrup, oil, vinegar, mustard, pepper, and bay leaf. Stir well and season with salt. Bring to a boil. Cover, place in the oven, and bake for 45 minutes, or until the lentils are tender.

3. Taste and correct the seasoning with salt, pepper, maple syrup, and vinegar. Serve hot now or later.

NEW ENGLAND CLAM CHOWDER

Serves 4 to 6

It's tough to find real chowder in this city, so we promised we would always have delicious homemade chowder by the cup or bowl at McKiernan. Ours is made with fresh Carr's PEI clams.

½ cup (115 g) unsalted butter

6 celery stalks, chopped

3 large onions, chopped

9 ounces (250 g) bacon, cut into ¼-inch squares

2 large spuds, preferably Yukon Gold, peeled and diced

Fistful of all-purpose flour

4 cups (1 liter) 2-percent milk

Salt and pepper

15 large cherrystone clams, preferably from PEI; 20 little-necks; or 4 pounds (1.8 kg) savoury (aka varnish) or manila clams, well scrubbed and free of sand

One 12-ounce (375-ml) can beer

Pringles, fresh chives, and chopped celery heart (if not too bitter) for garnish

1. In a large stockpot, melt the butter over medium heat. Add the celery, onions, and bacon and cook for 6 to 7 minutes, or until the onion is translucent and the bacon is cooked and glossy but not yet crisp.

2. Add the spuds and flour to the pot and stir steadily until all of the bacon fat and butter drink up the flour. (A flat spatula and flat-bottomed pot make a difference to the job, since once the flour is in the pot, it sticks in about 4 minutes if you're not paying attention.) Add the milk and drop the heat to low. Season with salt and pepper and leave the chowder to cook, uncovered.

3. Meanwhile, in another large stockpot, combine the clams and the beer over high heat. Use only half of the beer; drink the rest. Too much beer will make the chowder curdle. Cover and cook for about 5 minutes, or until the clams open. Remove from the heat, uncover, and pick out and discard any clams that failed to open. When cool enough to handle, remove the clams from their shells, capturing any juice in the pan. Discard the shells and set the meats aside. Strain the juice through the finest-mesh sieve available and set aside.

4. Slice the clam meats. Check to see if the potatoes are cooked, and if they are, add the clam meats and strained juice.

5. The chowder is ready to eat, but it is better when it is one day old. Cover and refrigerate and reheat the next day, adding more milk if it is too thick. Serve with Pringles on the side and topped with chives and celery heart. Repeat recipe twice a week for 2 years.

W henever I'm close to a body of water, part of me believes I should have been a sailor, a fisherman, or an aquaculturist. The sea calls certain people, and in my subconscious, I feel as though I might have been a stevedore in a past life. When I am by the sea, I feel truly happy. A friend of ours who once worked as a private chef in an exclusive fly-fishing resort in the Queen Charlotte Islands (British Columbia) told me that it was not uncommon to see executives break down and start weeping about their wasted lives while hip deep in a northern river during the spring salmon run.

CHAPTER 4

 # THE SEAWAY SNACK BAR

We are geographically wellborn in Montreal, sitting on the shores of the seafood superhighway that is the Saint Lawrence Seaway. From the Gaspé Peninsula to Kamouraska, Montreal to Portland, Maine, the seaway has a tremendous influence on what we eat. And just as the crabs, oysters, eels, and lobsters inspire the Joe Beef menu, the visual elements of these parts inspire the Joe Beef soul. We like the craft of the waterfront: the wharves, piers, wooden boats, skiffs, cedar-shake homes, canoes, buoys, weathered signs, traps, and brick-paved alleys. We thrive on the smell of humidity and the taste of salt air. I wish we could bottle them and breathe them in our restaurants.

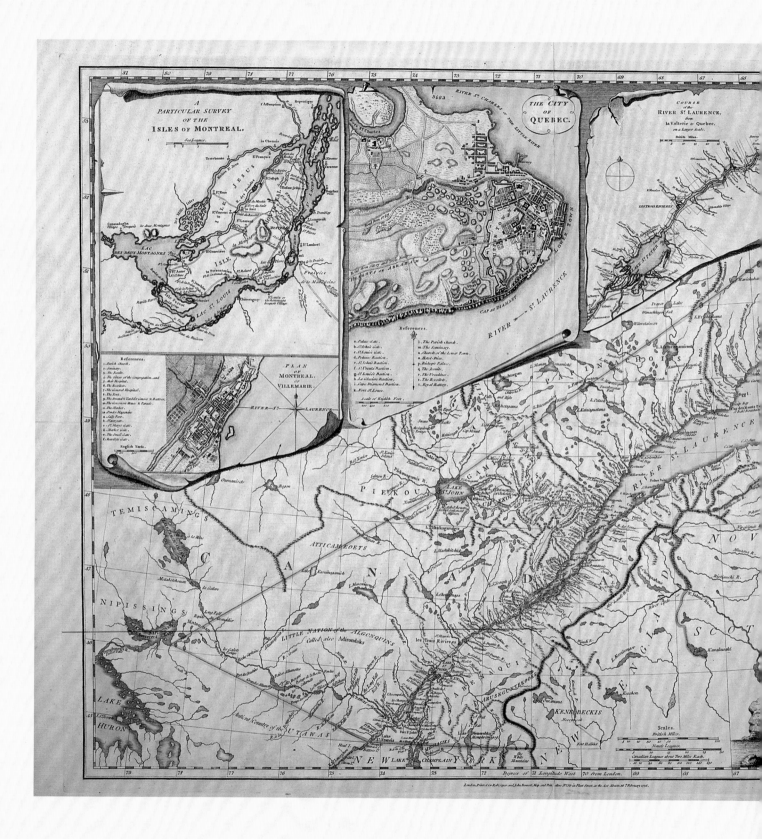

Our families have deep roots in the Bas Du Fleuve (lower Saint Lawrence) area, as do most native Quebecers, as it was here that Samuel Champlain dug his claim to Nouvelle-France, moving west from Tadoussac to Montreal. In *Champlain's Dream* (Random House, 2008), David Hackett Fischer describes the great explorer's awe at what he discovers: "Champlain mapped the area with much attention to the river, its islands, and the terrain. On the north bank of the river he literally put Cartier's name [for Montreal] 'Montréal' on the map—its first published appearance. Champlain and his men were surprised by the fertility of the land. Everywhere they found wildlife in unimaginable numbers. They came upon an island covered with 'so many herons that the air was completely filled with them.' Above Montreal were the rapids, a roaring cataract of white water. . . . The roar is so loud that one would have said it was thunder, as the air rang with the sound. It was a place of beauty and danger."

I have a cottage in Kamouraska, which lies about halfway between Montreal and the Gaspé, and have spent many summer vacations at the village of Notre-Dame-du-Portage, the beginning of a famous portage route that settlers once used to avoid paddling around the Gaspé Peninsula. Heading east, one of the first major stops on the portage is the old paper-mill town of Cabano, where it's possible to put your boat back in

the water. It's also where Fred's dad is from!

The portage routes are among the many gems of old roads in Quebec. If you want to take the ultimate seafood road trip, plan a long weekend driving Route 132, known as the Navigator's Highway or the Route of the Sea. It begins on the border of New York, comes up through Montreal, passes south of Quebec City, and then through Kamouraska, Rivière-du-Loup, Matane, Gaspé, and Percé. It takes you alongside the Saint Lawrence River, Gaspé Bay, and Chaleur Bay. Water is at every (curvy) turn and it's completely intoxicating. Plus, it's a great route for *casse-croûtes*.

The bounty of the Gulf of the Saint Lawrence accounts for a lot of what we sell at Joe Beef: black sturgeon, herring, cod, turbot, sea trout, whelk, Matane shrimp, snow crab, eel, smelt, small boat by-catch halibut, and other line-catch sturgeon. We also use a few farmed products, namely rainbow and white trout and Gaspé and Saguenay char. We get razor clams from La Mer, the main seafood purveyor-broker to Montreal. We've always had a special relationship with its owner, John Melatakos, who has supported us from day one. John, in turn, buys them from the mysterious fisherman John Doyle, who works on the Northern Shore, between Havre Saint Pierre and Natashquan. Another of our important purveyors is Bernard Lauzier of Kamouraska, from whom we get

gorgeous smoked eel. It's because of him that we sell around thirty pounds (about fourteen kilograms) of smoked eel per week—a great feat for any place not in Berlin or Hamburg.

The Saint Lawrence River (along with, maybe, maple syrup) is the *sang du pays* (blood of the country). It marked the reference points for the fur trade and was the obvious entry to Nouvelle-France and the new frontier. When you read of Cartier's and Champlain's explorations down the river—the countless belugas in the seaway, the firs and the oaks sidelining the rapids, the eels and trout in the archipelagos—you realize (if you have been recently) that it has remained relatively unchanged. We try to keep as much of a connection as possible with this region by keeping close relationships with purveyors, trying out new goods, and visiting as much as we can.

PRINCE EDWARD ISLAND

For those of you who don't know, the Maritimes, an area in eastern Canada made up of the four provinces of New Brunswick, Newfoundland, Nova Scotia, and Prince Edward Island, or PEI for short, is the veritable seafood buffet for Montreal. Prince Edward Island is the biggest supplier, and Quebec and Ontario the biggest purchasers. PEI is where the ocean meets the Saint Lawrence River, and the water, reportedly, is about one-third less salty than the ocean on the coast of, say, Maine. Dunes that lie miles beyond the island shelter the water, control the tidal flow, and create small, idyllic, and opportune saltwater beds. These are perfect shellfish breeding grounds: the colder the water, the longer the lobsters keep their shells on, which means more meat under

the shell. The fresher the water, the fatter the oysters.

We love seafood at Joe Beef, and sometimes it's the only thing we want to sell. But for years we were slaves to the local fish market—not that it's bad; really, it's great—and the market is what every restaurant in Montreal uses. That is, until we met John Bil, a gypsy vagrant king and a three-time Canadian oyster-shucking champion. Originally from Toronto, John has lived intermittently in Prince Edward Island for about fifteen years, working in every aspect of the shellfish industry. He has great stories, which he shared with customers while shucking at Joe Beef, and has more sweet (shellfish) contacts than you can dream of. This is a guy who drives (fast) in a minivan whose license plate reads "oysters." Did you know that you can wrap a trout and a bit of butter and lemon in foil and cook it on an engine block? For John, that's a weekly occurrence. We've seen him driving while eating stew that he made in the truck. He's the kind of guy who crashes at friends' houses for months on end, buys clothes and things while he's there, yet manages to leave with exactly what he arrived with. He has stuff stowed around the country.

Before John came to Joe Beef, we were sourcing acceptable shellfish. Now, thanks to his contacts, we're getting the best: the small and large quahogs, steamer clams, lobsters, (unreal) scallops, mussels, and oysters. Acting as a broker of sorts to Joe Beef and others, John owns and runs a restaurant called Ship to Shore with his partner, the mussel magnate, Stephen Stewart. Ship to Shore is a trailer on the side of the ocean, located in "Planet Darnley" (Darnley, PEI, population "60 to 100, excluding campground"); their front yard is basically an oyster lease full of perfect oysters (which we serve at Joe Beef as John Bil Private Reserves). His place is an excellent seafood restaurant/fish shop that is in the swear-to-god middle of nowhere, closed for eight months of the year and crazy for the four it is open, and has a suggestion box that leads directly to the garbage.

We had always wanted to visit John and meet some of the purveyors we have been dealing with over the years. Also, we wanted to see if he actually had a home with running water and electricity. So last spring we took the seventeen-hour train ride to Moncton, New Brunswick, and then drove another three-plus hours to Darnley to visit the man himself.

THE TALE OF WADE, BEAVER, AND THE *KNOTTY HOOKER*

Our trip was three full days. On the first morning, we arrived at the Stanley Bridge Wharf to go mussel fishing. Two boats were docked: the freshly hosed down and ready-to-go *Pure Mussel 2* and the pastoral *Knotty Hooker*. The first was full of a ragtag crew of young guys: Captain Shane, Wade, Beaver, and the boys were getting ready to go out for their second of what would be four trips that day. We jumped aboard and set out onto the crystal clear waters of New London Bay. After a full twenty-four hours of travel, it felt like we had finally arrived in the Maritimes.

The first thing we noticed is how clean the water is—we could easily see 20 feet (6 meters) down. There are 20 different farmers in New London Bay (approximately 130 in all of PEI), all using the long-line system. Long lines are attached to buoys for as far as you can see, and they work like this: The lines are attached to anchors and are sunk to the bottom of the sea. On each line, twenty-foot socks, or "seed collectors," are attached, suspended in the water, alternating with buoys, so you have sock, buoy, sock, buoy, sock, buoy for miles. The mussels harvest on the socks. The production cycle runs two years, which means the line is pulled up two years after it was dropped.

To us, this all seemed like an intricate system of who owns what and where. But these guys had been working on the boats since their teens, so they knew where their maze of lines began. We would stop in what seemed to us to be a

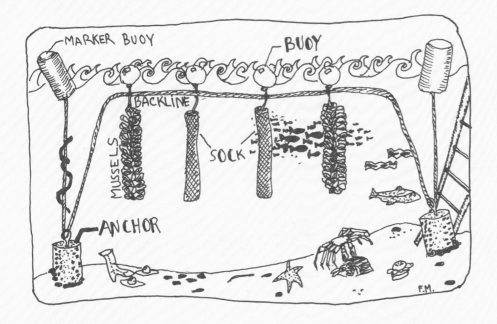

Labels on illustration: MARKER BUOY · BUOY · BACKLINE · MUSSELS · SOCK · ANCHOR · F.M.

completely random spot, and Shane would put the boat into neutral while one of the boys hooked a line and the rest of the crew started pulling up endless feet of muddy mussel-packed socks. Shane would cut the sock at the end and one of the crew would hoist it over his shoulder like a bag of potatoes and dump it into one of many blue, dumpster-size, plant-bound bins. Along with the ropes came little sea treasures like crab, fish skeletons, and the occasional piece of plastic (we asked if they had ever pulled up Sponge Bob Square Pants, but they completely ignored us). It's truly a filthy job for such an amazingly sustainable, clean product. If we learned anything from the trip, it's that mussels are a truly green food and should be eaten as much as possible. It also got our mussel juices flowing in terms of what we like to put on the menu and what we like to eat at home.

The boys on the boat were all great guys: funny, kind, and hard-working. As we headed back to the wharf, first mate Wade told us he would make great cover material and struck a few poses for Jennifer, the photographer. We got into the jeep and set out for Kensington for lunch, with Meredith pining in silence, imagining a simple life by the sea with the fisherman Wade. A connection was made that day, and Wade and the crew of *Pure Mussel 2* were in her thoughts for the rest of the week.

TOURING CONFEDERATION COVE

Kensington seems to be one of those towns where people don't lock their cars, kids wander around the streets at night unchaperoned, and pickled pork neck bone outsells hot dogs. Starved after our hours at sea and

craving filter coffee (well, espresso, but we didn't want to risk getting lynched for asking), Fred took us to an old diner he had previously visited that was now located in the middle of the PEI Lions Club. Faded provincial flags hung around a dining room full of large, circular tables. Half restaurant, half town hall, there were beautiful photographs of the queen and her mother, along with landscape photographs of potatoes. Our lunch was cheeseburgers, liver and onions, fried clams, chicken wings, iceberg lettuce with ranch dressing, onion rings, and 7UP. We were the only people under age sixty, and our sizable meal for four cost us a very reasonable forty-seven dollars (without the senior discount).

After lunch, we headed west to Borden-Carleton, which sits directly under the Confederation Bridge that connects mainland New Brunswick to the island and where just adjacent sits the Confederation Cove Mussel Company. The company produces more than 10 million pounds (4.5 million kilograms) of mussels per year: 6 million (2.7 million kilograms) are exported to the United States, 3 million (1.4 million kilograms) stay in Canada, and the rest are frozen and distributed worldwide. When Stephen Stewart started harvesting mussels in 1986, he worked 2,000 acres of ocean and everyone thought he was nuts. Today, he has 10,000 acres, a few boats, and the plant. His partnership in Ship to Shore allows for good access to willing buyers like Joe Beef through John. Stephen is a scientist, engineer, and a Forbes-level entrepreneur and restaurateur all in one. He's a true Maritimes renaissance man and is always willing to chat, whether it be about any detail of the mussel-production process, the antiaging merits of starfish, Molson Canadian, or poker.

Stephen gave us a tour of the plant, which is essentially a flowing saltwater assembly line and is positively pristine compared to a slaughterhouse. The plant has two main sections, one for cleaning the fresh mussels and the other for processing the frozen mussels. The process of transferring the mussels out of their blue bins and into netted bags takes in clean saltwater and puts back clean saltwater, with no by-products. The plant actually smelled good. The cold, oxygenated rooms can hold up to 300,000 pounds (13,600 kilograms) of mussels at a time if necessary, but usually little product is left at the end of the day. All of the machinery was designed by Stephen and is patented and used around

the world. From what we witnessed, if there is such a thing as a completely sustainable product, it has to be mussels, or at least Confederation Cove blue mussels.

After the tour, we jumped in the back of Stephen's truck and he took us next door to By the Water, a gigantic lobster pound. Here we met the owner, Kevin MacDonald, who walked us through six holding tanks that together can hold up to 350,000 pounds (160,000 kilograms) of lobster. We watched men in rubber suits wading in water up to their chests between tens of thousands of lobsters, sorting and removing the sold bunch from the rest.

This facility, like the mussel plant, is completely pristine, pumping over 1,000 gallons (4,000 liters) of fresh seawater per minute between the ocean and the plant. The tanks held some of the biggest lobsters we have ever seen. According to *Guinness World Records*, the largest recorded lobster in the world was caught in Nova Scotia and weighed 44.4 pounds (20.1 kilograms). When eating big (older)

lobsters, a little respect should be observed. We bought a 7-pounder (3.2 kilograms) to make our breakfast lobster and (uncharacteristically) dreaded killing and cooking it. It sat in a cold tub in the backyard of our little bungalow on the ocean until two hours before our departure. We think we did well by it.

The next day, we went back to Stanley Bridge Wharf to Carr's Shellfish. Carr's is a prime supplier for us, and we've been selling their shellfish by the crate since our opening. Owner Phyllis Carr is like shellfish royalty, a duchess of oysters. She can be found managing her lobster pound or working across the bridge at the oyster bar. She introduced us to Phillip Boute, an employee and true islander who was chosen to teach us how to tong (harvest) oysters.

First, Phillip showed us how to find the great spots and how to feel for a good catch. The process is kind of like holding two huge rakes and blindly grabbing at disintegrated pebbles. As we all took turns learning, Phillip told us how he tongs in

his dreams. Some people put on suits and go to an office to support their kids. Phillip puts on his fisherman slicks and sits alone in a boat tonging for oysters for six hours to support his four kids. Some people may call this banal, he (and we!) calls it Zen.

When we got back to land, we met up with Phyllis again, who walked us through the Carr's own Stanley Bridge Marine Aquarium and Manor of Birds. The aquarium was closed as it was being renovated but we walked through the manor of birds. This experience definitely wins the "strangest moment of the trip" award. Home to North America's largest collection of mounted birds—the more than seven hundred specimens are the work of taxidermist *extraordinaire* William Labrie (originally from Kamouraska)—the manor was eerie, bizarre, and beautiful, the kind of place you'd expect to see the ghost of Vincent Price.

That night we made *mouclade* (page 125), drank PEI's homegrown and herbaceously delicious Myriad Strait Gin, and promptly fell asleep. (Apparently, there is a huge moonshine tradition in PEI, not unlike the old days of distilling in the Appalachians. We only heard about PEI's backwater moonshine, of course; seeing as moonshine is illegal, we would never touch the stuff.)

THE WILD, WILD (UP) WEST

On our final day, we headed to an area the locals call Up West. On our way, we drove past the Stanley Bridge Wharf, saw that a lobster boat had just come in, and went to investigate. It was here that we met a lobster fisherman named Dales Dorion, who owns the stunning *Miss Bay View*. I'm a big boy at six feet three, but in my eyes, Dales seems bigger than life. A lobster fisherman working with two friends on an impeccably clean boat, he commands more respect than anyone I've ever met. He has the piercing blue eyes

SHATTUCK & JONES
INCORPORATED

FISH OF ALL KINDS

128 FANEUIL HALL MARKET

BOSTON March 25, 1916

Mr. A. Grenier,
        94 Rue St. Jean,
                Quebec, Canada

Dear Sir:

        At the request of Isaac Locke
Co. of this city we are inclosing a copy
of our weekly quotation list showing
the different varieties of fish now in
market and approximate prices.

        We have had many years experience
in supplying the better class of trade,
Clubs, Hotels etc. with all kinds of
sea food in their season and feel confident
that our goods and service will meet with
your approval.

        We have placed your name on our mailing
list in order that you may receive our
quotations regularly and trust you may find
some items of interest thereon.

        Hoping to hear from you with an order
which will have our best attention, we are

        Very truly yours,

        SHATTUCK & JONES, INC.

        Per. Allen E. Newton

of an alpha male Alaskan malamute and, at age sixty-four, could make quick work of a seasoned street fighter. At the same time, he gives off a favorite grandpa, Santa Claus–like warmth. I don't believe I could have said anything to him that he would have found remotely interesting, so I said nothing. Everyone was shocked, as they had never seen me be so silent.

Up West was rumored to be a wild frontier populated by fishermen and PEI natives who have never left the island, so we expected to see a raw and rugged landscape governed by lawless men. Well, that's not exactly what we experienced. The closest to it was when we stopped at an old, eerie wharf populated with rows of colorful shacks in which we assumed fishermen slept. The wharf gave off a rundown-fisherman's-post, bone-chilling-cold-in-May kind of feeling. The office displayed the requisite naked-women calendar, and each man we saw had a few missing teeth and homemade tattoos.

We tried to ask a few questions, but felt like complete urbanites, so we quickly left.

We continued up the peninsula, wary of meeting a sort of *Heart of Darkness* fate. Thankfully, there was no bloated Brando, only Randy Cooke's friendly face. Randy has a plant in Howard's Cove, and his oysters are the famous Cooke's Cove Malpeques. The plant sits right on the water looking out toward the gulf, with dunes and Randy's oyster leases lying somewhere in between. It's the kind of place that makes you shiver as you stare out at the water. We sampled the Cook's Cove goods, and took a few crates home for dinner.

Prince Edward Island is a rugged and unforgiving place, with few people and even fewer chives and espressos. The people are the salt of the earth, which we mean in the best possible way. For instance, the locals refuse to call the cassoulet on the Ship to Shore menu cassoulet, "because it's just pork 'n' beans." And when we asked an oyster fisherman his ultimate dream, he said, "I would like to spend the afternoon drinking one beer, playing guitar in the boat, and tonging." The raw resources from the ocean provide a livelihood to most people who live on the island, judging from the oyster boats that lay up against most homes (it's possible to take your catch of clams or oysters to any plant and supplement your income). PEI is a small part of the Maritimes, but a big part of Joe Beef.

MORE ON OYSTERS

Although the Malpeque oyster is, in our minds, the perfect oyster, at any given time you'll find Cook's Cove, John Bil Private Reserves, Carr's, and Colville Bay's oysters listed on the Joe Beef blackboard. We also love the Beausoleils brought to us by Amédé Savoie, Maurice Daigle, and Léon Lanteigne from Neguac, New Brunswick; Galways from the Kelly family in Ireland; and, of course, Glidden Points from Maine and various Puget Sound oysters from Taylor Shellfish Farms.

During the winter months, temperatures on the East Coast can easily drop to –22°F (–30°C) for weeks on end. Since few people have the chainsaws and deep-sea diving equipment it takes to harvest under ice, we can't order much from this area during this period. So every winter, we order a variety of shellfish from the Out Landish Shellfish Guild, a dozen folks who farm and transport seafood on the gorgeous

Cortes, Quadra, and Read islands, which are part of the Discovery Islands and Desolation Sound in British Columbia. We've been buying from the guild for several years and consider Victor and Kathy McLaggan, two of the founders, to be good friends. We haven't met the other founders, but we assume that one day over beers, they will follow suit. From late December to mid-April, we purchase clams (manila, littleneck, savoury), Gallo and Edulis mussels, gorgeous home-canned smoked swimmer scallops, smoked oysters, and various mixed-size tray oysters and beach angels.

The sea on the West Coast, where Out Landish is located, is warmer than the sea on the East Coast, and the oysters grow fast and are plumper. They're delicious and meaty, great fried or baked. You can show them off in our Chinatown recipe (see page 123). Raw and on the half shell, they are definitely a handful and not for beginners. It took me

a while to tackle a dozen gem-size marina's top drawers with a pint of beer. After eating Malpeques all year long, I'm always happy to sit down with a dozen Out Landish oysters. They are welcome arrivals in the doldrums of the winter.

I adore British Columbia's seafood and fish and it's an amazing place; I worked at the Sooke Harbour House on Vancouver Island fifteen years ago and loved it. But British Columbia is far from Montreal, and we don't like to use product that's been on a plane. That said, Out Landish Shellfish Guild has been part of Joe Beef since we opened, and we'd like to keep it that way as long as they will bear us. (I hope this mention brings them more customers. Those guys rock, and they'll always be part of the Joe Beef perfect winter dirty dozen.)

The recipes that follow are inspired by the bounty of the Saint Lawrence: our seafood snack bar.
—DM

HOT OYSTERS ON THE RADIO

Serves 4

When we started Joe Beef, the town was suffering from a weird vibe, a kind of up-the-ante feeling with regard to food: people went out to eat like college kids drink beer. If someone was doing testicles, you could count on someone else to pair them with pizza. Feet were kept on chickens, and heads and eyeballs were served as sides. There was no end in sight, much less vegetables.

To put a damper on the frenzied quest for more, we thought that maybe the next ingredient should be inedible: not gold shavings, but what about an old radio? Doesn't "oysters on the radio" sound good? When we ran out of radios, we used bags of sugar, erotic novels, or old album covers.

The oysters themselves are simple: plump specimens topped with crisp bacon, chives, potatoes, eggs, cream, and some bread crumbs. Serve yours on any inedible ingredient of choice.

12 big, meaty oysters

Coarse salt for partially filling pan

4 slices bacon, finely diced

¼ cup (120 g) peeled and finely diced small potatoes

1 clove garlic, finely chopped

2 egg yolks

⅓ cup (80 ml) whipping cream (35 percent butterfat)

1 tablespoon chopped fresh chives

¼ cup (30 g) finely grated aged Cheddar cheese

Salt and pepper

¼ cup (30 g) dried bread crumbs

¼ cup (55 g) unsalted butter, cut into 12 equal pieces

1. Shuck the oysters, pouring the liquor into a cup and keeping the oysters on their bottom shells. Set the oysters and liquor aside. A good trick for cooking the oysters is to fill a big cast-iron frying pan about half full with coarse salt, put it in the oven, and preheat the oven to 450°F (230°C), then heat the pan for an extra 15 minutes. This will help to accelerate the cooking process.

2. Place the potatoes and salted water to cover in a small pot over medium-high heat. Boil for 2 to 3 minutes, or until slightly softened. Drain the potatoes, let cool, and pat dry. Meanwhile, in another frying pan, crisp the bacon over medium-high heat until light brown. Add the potatoes to the pan and cook, stirring occasionally, for about 4 minutes, or until tender. Add the garlic and cook for another minute. Remove from the heat.

3. In a bowl, rapidly whisk together the egg yolks, the cream, and whatever oyster liquor you were able to gather. Add the chives, Cheddar, a pinch each of salt and pepper, and the bacon-potato mixture and whisk to mix. Divide evenly among the oysters, spooning it on top. Dust the tops with the bread crumbs, then finish with a piece of butter.

4. Pull the cast-iron pan out of the oven and carefully nest the oysters in the hot salt. Return the pan to the oven and cook for 4 to 7 minutes, or until the tops start to turn golden. Serve immediately.

OYSTERS #37

Serves 4

We cannot *not* dedicate this recipe to the New Dynasty restaurant in Montreal's Chinatown. Every Joe Beef cook has woken up at least once with an odd burn in his or her gut from the MSG and a soy sauce stain on his or her mouth after eating there. At New Dynasty, the tables are covered and the lights are really bright, not unlike Dexter's murder rooms! The kitchen serves until 5:00 A.M., and the boss is patient with drunks who are loud and drunks who fall asleep at the table (that is, Peter Meehan).

Here you can find every sea crawler you dare to eat: eel, jellyfish (served with cold chicken), huge live crabs, winkles, hacked-up crispy lobster, razor clams, and more. Inevitably, we start a meal at New Dynasty with the big Vancouver oysters, steamed with black bean sauce, one or two each, and a hefty pour of cold beer from a teapot.

For this recipe, we use Gigas oysters from our friend Victor McLaggan of Cortes Island, British Columbia. They are as big as my feet and a bitch to open, but they have huge meats that can be over-cooked without much sorrow. This is a case, unlike real life, where it's easy to feel inept with a big one. If possible, ask your fish guy to open the oysters. If you can't get these big oysters where you live, use smaller shucked oysters and bake them in ramekins. You'll probably have sauce left over, so store it in the fridge and use it on chicken, duck, or anything else that sounds good.

⅔ cup (160 ml) water

⅔ cup (160 ml) soy sauce

1 tablespoon sugar

2 tablespoons peeled and minced fresh ginger

2 tablespoons minced garlic

2 tablespoons chopped green onion

2 tablespoons salted black beans, soaked for 1 hour in water and drained

1 tablespoon toasted sesame oil

1 little dried chile or a few dried chile flakes

4 big oysters

1. In a small pot, combine the water, soy sauce, and sugar and bring to a boil. Add the ginger, garlic, green onion, black beans, sesame oil, and chile; stir well, and remove from the heat. Transfer to a plastic container, let cool, cover, and refrigerate for at least 2 hours or, ideally, overnight to let the flavors mingle.

2. Shuck the oysters, pouring the liquor into a cup and saving it for another use and keeping the oysters on their bottom shells. Pour water to a depth of about ½ inch (12 mm) into the bottom of a large, flat pan with a lid. Or, even better, if you own a bamboo steamer large enough to hold all the oysters, set it up over water. Bring the water to a boil.

3. Gently place the oysters in the pan, using crumpled aluminum foil to help stabilize them. You want the oysters cup up and no leaks. Spoon a good tablespoon of the condiment onto each oyster and put the lid on the pan. Cook for about 5 minutes, or until you see that the oysters have shrunk a little. If there is a loss of condiment, replenish. Eat the oysters piping hot with plastic chopsticks.

MOUCLADE

Serves 4

We do not have a story for this recipe. Sorry.

1 carrot, peeled and finely diced

1 celery stalk, finely diced

1 small onion, finely diced

1 small PEI or Yukon Gold potato, finely diced

3 tablespoons unsalted butter

2 pounds (900 g) PEI mussels, washed and picked through

½ cup (125 ml) dry white wine

¾ cup (180 ml) whipping cream (35 percent butterfat)

1 egg yolk

1 tablespoon chopped fresh tarragon

1. In a sauté pan over medium heat, sweat the carrot, celery, onion, and potato in 2 tablespoons of the butter for 3 to 4 minutes, or until the onion is translucent. Set aside.

2. In a pot with a lid, combine the mussels and wine, cover, place over high heat, and steam for 4 or 5 minutes, or until the mussels open. Discard any mussels that failed to open. Then, take the mussels one by one and remove the top shell, allowing the mussel liquor to fall back into the pan. Set the mussels in their bottom shells, meat side up, in a shallow bowl.

3. Simmer the mussel juice over medium heat until reduced by half. Add the remaining 1 tablespoon butter and the cream, bring to a boil, and remove from the heat.

4. Buzz the sauce with a hand blender and add the egg yolk and tarragon. Add the sweated vegetables and return the pan to low heat. Do not allow the sauce to boil or the egg will curdle.

5. When the sauce is nice and warm, pour it on top of the mussels and serve immediately.

SQUID STUFFED
with LOBSTER

Serves 4

1 small live lobster, about 1¼ pounds (570 g)

⅓ cup (40 g) alphabet pasta

3 tablespoons tomato sauce

2 tablespoons Hellmann's or Best Foods mayonnaise

Few dashes of Tabasco sauce

Dash of Pernod or ouzo

2 tablespoons chopped fresh flat-leaf parsley

Salt and pepper

Olive oil for sautéing and dressing

1½ cups (375 ml) water

2 tablespoons unsalted butter

4 squid, head and body 6 to 7 inches (15 to 18 cm) long (if smaller, use 8 squid), cleaned (see sidebar)

3 tablespoons escargot butter (see Whelks with Escargot Butter, page 131)

2 tablespoons dried bread crumbs

4 handfuls cress or arugula

Fred worked at Toqué! in the early 1990s, and one of his many tasks was cleaning squid. Every so often, the Anglophone sous chef would order from the Quebecois fishmonger at La Mer, and one day "15 pounds" of squid was heard as "50 pounds." That week Fred cleaned 150 pounds of squid. He couldn't smell squid for about ten years without feeling sick, but he's back on the squid train now. The only way he can bear it, though, is filled with lobster and cooked in lobster juice.

1. Bring a large pot of salted water to a boil, add the lobster, and cook for 5 minutes. Pull the lobster out of the pot, discard the water, and chill the lobster.

2. Shell the lobster, keeping as much meat as possible. Dice the meat into ¼-inch (6-mm) cubes, and keep the shells. Set both aside.

3. Bring a small pot of water to a boil, add the pasta, and boil for about 4 minutes, or until shy of al dente. Drain and transfer to a decent-size bowl.

4. Add the lobster meat, tomato sauce, mayo, Tabasco, Pernod, and parsley to the pasta and stir to mix. Season with salt and pepper and set aside.

5. Crush the lobster shells into 1-inch pieces. In a sauté pan, sauté the shells in a film of olive oil over medium-high heat until the lobster water is gone from the shells. Add the water and unsalted butter and simmer over medium heat for about 20 minutes. Don't let it become dry, but almost dry. You should have about ½ cup (125 ml) liquid. Strain the liquid and set aside.

6. Preheat the oven to 425°F (220°C). Stuff the pasta mixture into the squid tubes, and seal the open end of each tube with a couple of nonmentholated toothpicks. Just stick them right across the opening, pinching the tentacles into the opening. Lay the stuffed beauties side by side in a baking dish or baking pan. It should be a snug fit so the pan is less likely to dry out. Pour the strained lobster juice over them, then top with a few pats of escargot butter and the bread crumbs.

7. Bake for about 15 minutes, or until bubbly. Remove the toothpicks and serve with a handful of olive oil–dressed cress (greens) on each plate.

HOW TO CLEAN SQUID: A BRIEF EXPLANATION

1. Wear gloves; many people have contact allergies to squid. Clean the squid in the sink under cold running water.

2. Rip off the head. It's the part from which the legs hang down.

3. Pinch away the beak. It's on the center, nestled among the legs.

4. Slide out the blades. There are two of them, plasticlike, along the inside of the tube.

5. Peel off the dark skin.

6. Rinse the squid well, inside and out, to eliminate all traces of mucus and sand.

SMELT MAYONNAISE

Serves 4

David's childhood memories inspired this recipe: "When I was a kid, my father and his in-laws would go fishing off the Rivière-du-Loup Wharf. They would come back with buckets full of smelt that they caught using bamboo fishing sticks. We would get out the Robin Hood flour and start frying them up. They're delicious and what's better, they're small so you know that they're not feasting on anything dubious at the bottom of the sea." We serve smelt piled high on a plate with mayo on the side.

2 cups (310 g) corn or all-purpose flour
Salt and pepper
½ cup (125 ml) evaporated 2-percent milk
1 egg yolk
20 or so smelt (4 or 5 per person)
Fresh parsley for serving
Peanut oil for deep-frying
Mayonnaise (page 175) for serving
Lemon wedges for serving

1. In a shallow bowl, mix the flour with a pinch each of salt and pepper. In another bowl, whisk together the milk and egg yolk until blended. Soak the smelt, 4 or 5 at a time, in the milk mixture for a couple of minutes and then coat them with the flour mixture. Set aside on a plate. Wash the parsley and thoroughly pat it dry.

2. Pour the oil to a depth of 3 inches/ 7.5 cm (or according to the manufacturer's instructions) into your deep fryer or a deep sauté pan and heat to 350°F (180°C). Add the parsley and fry until crisp, 1 to 1½ minutes. Drain on paper towels. Working in batches, fry the smelt for 4 to 5 minutes, or until golden. Drain briefly on paper towels, patting the smelt dry.

3. Serve the smelt with the deep-fried parsley, mayonnaise, and lemon wedges.

WHELKS with ESCARGOT BUTTER

Serves 4

Whelks are giant marine snails. In towns along the Saint Lawrence (like Kamouraska), you can find them in gallon jars, marinated in brine or white vinegar. At Joe Beef, we buy whelks fresh from La Mer, Montreal's big seafood broker, and serve them with escargot butter.

In Burgundy, chefs are judged by their snail butter. Literally. You can work under three different Michelin-starred chefs and they'll all tell you that there is only one way to make escargot butter—and each way will be completely different. This classic recipe is the escargot butter that drowned Montreal after Expo 67 (see page 52). If you're not a whelk fan, you can enjoy the butter slipped under the skin of a chicken before it is roasted, on a steak, over mashed potatoes, or just spread on toast.

ESCARGOT BUTTER

1 pound (455 g) salted butter, at room temperature

3 cloves garlic, finely chopped (or more if desired)

About ½ cup (15 g) chopped fresh flat-leaf parsley

3 tablespoons bread crumbs

¼ cup (50 g) almond powder

¼ cup (60 ml) pastis

1 teaspoon salt

½ teaspoon pepper

4 drops of Tabasco sauce

16 whelks, handpicked and individually smelled to make sure they are fresh (discard any that don't smell like food)

12 cups (3 liters) water

½ cup (115 g) salt

1. Prepare the escargot butter first. In a food processor, combine the butter, garlic, parsley, bread crumbs, almond powder, pastis, salt, pepper, and Tabasco and process until creamy. Scoop into a bowl, cover, and store in the fridge.

2. Soak the whelks in cold water to cover for 2 hours, changing the water 2 or 3 times.

3. Drain the whelks. In a small stockpot, bring the water and salt to a boil over high heat. Add the whelks, lower the heat to medium, and simmer for 15 minutes. While the whelks are cooking, remove the escargot butter from the fridge to soften, and preheat the oven to 450°F (230°C).

4. When the whelks are ready, drain and let cool for 5 to 10 minutes, then rinse the shells. Using a fondue fork, remove the meats from the shells. Reserve the shells. Clean the meats by removing any muddy or sandy appendages, and then rinse the meats.

5. Make 4 or 5 neat little slices, ¼ inch (6 mm) deep across each meat, and carefully put the meats back into their shells. Dab a spackle of escargot butter on the opening of each whelk, effectively closing it shut. Place the whelks in a small gratin dish (from which you should eat them).

6. Bake for 10 to 14 minutes, or until the butter is crackling and bubbling. Serve piping hot.

STEAMERS

Serves 4

We wouldn't call ourselves purists (like John Bil), but we tend to agree that steamed clams served with anything other than their own broth and butter is an abomination. We also think PEI might just have the prettiest white sand–dug clams we have ever seen.

2 pounds (900 g) soft-shell clams, any New England or Maritime clam will do

6 tablespoons (85 g) unsalted butter

1. Fill a 1-gallon (4-liter) stockpot with 1 inch (2.5 cm) of water and set over high heat to boil.

2. While the water is reaching a boil, wash the clams with a brush vigor-ously under cold water, inspecting them for sand.

3. When the water is boiling, pour in the clams and cook for 5 minutes. Meanwhile, put the butter in a little pan and melt it over low heat.

4. Check on the clams. You'll know they're ready when all the shells have opened. Pour them into a colander set over a bowl to catch any clam liquor. Discard any clams that didn't open.

5. Serve the clams, the butter, and the clam liquor in three separate bowls. As you eat, peel away the tough skin from the clams' append-ages, rinse them in the hot liquor, and dunk in the butter.

SMORGASBORD

Serves 4 to 6

We never went hungry as kids. And we have no inherent fear of the next Great Depression or anxiety about canned food. Still, we always want more. Wanting and eating four of the Swedish shrimp-egg things you can buy in the restaurant at IKEA is a good example of that.

Another good example is how we would have piled more stuff on this modest toast if we could have fit it: a can of sardines from Bretagne, maybe, or quails stuffed with crab hiding in the corner. Our first reaction on seeing this photo was, "Shit, we forgot clams." There are thirty items here, and if we do another book, we will put in sixty, we promise (just so we don't run out of food).

Disclaimer: In no way do we aspire or pretend to serve authentic Scandinavian food. This is just our view projected onto a classic. The closest we have been to Scandinavia is Fred Heimlich-maneuvering a Dane who choked on the biggest oyster ever eaten raw. And it was a weird experience because it was like they kissed; they were shy around each other for the rest of the evening.

In the list that follows, an asterisk means a recipe is included. If there's no *, it means the item is straightforward and you can figure it out. We suggest serving the items on rye bread or a baguette sliced lengthwise and buttered. You then eat your open-faced sandwich with a fork and knife. Or, you can do as we do: add condiments and eat it like a military strategist, portioning, placing, moving, and rationing.

Regarding yields: the smorgasbord is more of a concept than a straightforward recipe. The smorgasbord shown here serves 4 to 6, and includes every single thing listed. You don't have to follow our lead (though we would be pleased). Typically we put 4 or 5 proteins and 4 or 5 condiments on the average smorgasbord. Following this rule, each of the small recipes serves four.

1. Grated fresh horseradish
2. Dijon mustard
3. Black Pepper Crème Fraîche*
4. Cucumber Salad*
5. Dill Butter*
6. Smoked Mackerel*
7. Whitefish eggs
8. Mújol (grey mullet) eggs (cheap caviar)
9. Dill flowers
10. Caper berries
11. Maple Smoked Kamouraska Eel*
12. Pickled Eggs with Celery and Horseradish*
13. Char Tartare*
14. Aquavit Onions*
15. Cured Char with Gin*
16. Canned Scandinavian sprats
17. Fresh Gaspé snow crab
18. Beets
19. French breakfast radishes with unsalted butter
20. Dutch-style matjes herring
21. Smoked Rainbow Trout*
22. Nova Scotian "Salmon" Gundy*
23. One big Carr's oyster
24. Potato Salad with Cider Vinegar and Shallot*
25. Smoked West Coast Oysters* (scrub the shell if you are placing it directly on the bread)
26. Cold poached lobster
27. Smoked Sturgeon*
28. Smoked Scallops*
29. Scandinavian salmon spread in a tube
30. Onion from "salmon" gundy

MAPLE SMOKED KAMOURASKA EEL

8 ounces (225 g) smoked eel (from the
 Saint Lawrence, if possible), filleted
 and skinned
2 tablespoons maple syrup
Salt and pepper

1. Preheat the broiler. Cut the eel into
4 equal pieces, place on a rimmed
baking sheet, and baste with some of
the maple syrup.

2. Broil the eel for 1 to 2 minutes, or
until it bubbles. Remove, baste with
the remaining maple syrup, and
then broil again for a minute or two.
Remove from the broiler, season with
salt and pepper (they should stick to
the syrup), and serve warm.

PICKLED EGGS WITH CELERY AND HORSERADISH

Here is a recipe for a brine that is
sufficient to pickle up to 10 normal-
size eggs. If you are using quail eggs,
you can obviously pickle a lot more.
The day we took this picture we had
quail eggs, but truly, our favorite
eggs are the smallest hen eggs
available: the peewees. We even love
the name, and their size is perfect
because you can gobble up two or
three. Remember to leave your eggs
at room temperature for an hour
before cooking them.

10 chicken or quail eggs
1 cup (250 ml) water
1 cup (250 ml) distilled white vinegar
1½ tablespoons sugar
1 tablespoon mustard seeds
1 sprig tarragon
1 celery stalk, cut into matchsticks
2 slices fresh horseradish, each ¼ inch
 (6 mm) thick

1. Place the eggs in a pot in cold water
to cover, bring to a boil, and boil for
3 minutes for quail eggs or 7 minutes
for chicken eggs. Chill in an ice bath,
then peel and refrigerate.

2. To make the brine, in a saucepan,
combine the water, vinegar, and
sugar and bring to a boil. Put your
eggs in a Mason jar, and put the
mustard seeds, tarragon, celery, and
horseradish on top. Pour in the boiling mix and seal the jar. Store in the
fridge.

3. The eggs are ready to eat after
1 week. They will keep in the refrigerator for up to 1 month.

BLACK PEPPER CRÈME FRAÎCHE

We can't stress enough the importance of cleanliness when doing a recipe of this sort. That means a good washing of the jar and other equipment and yourself.

2 cups (500 ml) whipping cream (35 percent butterfat)
¼ cup (60 ml) buttermilk
Pinch of black pepper

1. Combine the cream and buttermilk in a measuring pitcher and stir until you get a thick yogurt consistency. Transfer to a jar, cover with cheesecloth or muslin, and secure with a rubber band. Leave at room temperature for 12 hours.

2. The crème fraîche is now ready to use. If you want to drain off some liquid so it is thicker, spoon it into a sieve lined with a coffee filter placed over a bowl, and put the setup in the fridge for a few hours. Add the pepper to the cream just before serving.

CUCUMBER SALAD

4 Lebanese cucumbers, or 1 English cucumber
1 teaspoon kosher salt
¼ cup (60 ml) white vinegar
¼ cup (60 ml) water
Pepper
1 tablespoon sugar
1 tablespoon mustard seeds

1. Thinly slice the cucumbers and place in a colander. Lightly rub the salt into the slices while tossing them. Place the colander over a bowl and let drain for about 15 minutes. Place the cucumber slices in a bowl and set aside.

2. In a small saucepan, bring the vinegar, water, pepper to taste, sugar, and mustard seeds to a boil. Remove from the heat, pour the mixture over the cucumber slices, and refrigerate for 1 hour. Add more pepper to taste before serving.

DILL BUTTER

1 cup (225 g) unsalted butter, at room temperature
⅓ cup (10 g) finely chopped fresh dill
2 tablespoons Dijon mustard
Salt and pepper

1. In a bowl, work together the butter, dill, and mustard until smooth. Season with salt and pepper to taste. Scoop onto a sheet of plastic wrap and, using the wrap, shape into a cylinder the diameter of a silver dollar. Wrap in the plastic wrap and refrigerate for about 3 hours, or until firm.

2. You may use the butter now, leave it in the fridge longer, or freeze it to use later. (It is good on poached fish or poultry.)

SMOKED MACKEREL OR RAINBOW TROUT

You will need a smoker that can be controlled or a grill and a chip box for this recipe and a supply of maple wood or maple wood chips.

4 cups (1 liter) water
1 rounded cup (240 g) salt
¼ cup (60 ml) soy sauce
⅓ cup (100 g) Grade B (dark) maple syrup
4 whole mackerel or rainbow trout, 10 to 16 ounces (280 to 455 g) each, gutted

1. In a thick-bottomed pot, combine the water, salt, soy sauce, and maple syrup and bring almost to a boil over medium-high heat, stirring to dissolve the salt. Take it off the stove and chill it in the fridge.

2. Lay the fish in a plastic container with a tight-fitting lid, cover with the cold brine, and cover with the lid. Refrigerate for 6 hours.

3. When you are ready to smoke, start your smoker. It should be barely warm when you start, and it should take about 30 minutes to reach 85°F (30°C)—inside the smoker that is. It is now that the fish take on that distinctive crust that makes them look smoked. After 1½ hours, the smoker should be at 150°F (65°C). At the 2-hour mark, it should reach 200°F (95°C). At this point, the internal temperature of the fish should read (on a good-quality, well-calibrated electronic thermometer) about 140°F (60°C). Make sure there is always a good cloud of smoke. (I suggest taking readings at 20-minute intervals to make sure you don't overshoot that 140°F mark.)

4. You can store the smoked fish in the fridge for up to a week, or you can freeze it for up to a month.

2. Remove the fish from the bag, rinse well under cool water, and pat dry. Cover with the remaining dill, slip the fish into a new bag, and refrigerate again for at least 8 or up to 10 hours so the cure can even out.

3. Remove the fish from the bag, slice thinly, and serve.

NOVA SCOTIAN "SALMON" GUNDY

This tangy herring pickle somehow made its way from northern Europe to Nova Scotia, where you can find it in every grocery store. It's like roll mops but less sweet. Here the classic preparation is done not with salted herring but with fresh salmon, which we salt the living daylights out of, then desalt and pickle in jars. It screams saltines and mustard.

The Nova Scotians will tell you that the name *Gundy* is Nova Scotian, but the Brits, the French, and the Jamaicans all claim it for their own, too.

1 large piece skinned wild salmon fillet, about 12 ounces (340 g), pinboned
¾ cup (210 g) pickling salt
1 small onion, sliced
1 cup (250 ml) distilled white vinegar
¼ cup (50 g) sugar
1 tablespoon classic pickling spice, in a cloth bag

1. Cut the salmon into 1-inch (2.5-cm) cubes and place in a bowl. Add the salt, toss to mix, cover, and refrigerate overnight.

2. Rinse the salmon cubes under cool water to remove the salt, place in a clean bowl, add cold water to cover, and soak in the refrigerator for 2 hours.

3. In a large, widemouthed Mason jar or wire-bale canning jar, place a layer of fish, then a layer of onion slices. Repeat.

4. In a covered saucepan, combine the vinegar, sugar, and pickling spice and bring to a boil. Remove from the heat and let infuse for 10 minutes. Discard the bag of spices and pour the boiling mix over the fish and onion. Seal the jar, let cool, and refrigerate.

5. Give the salmon and onion a day or two to pickle. They will keep in the refrigerator for up to a month.

POTATO SALAD WITH CIDER VINEGAR AND SHALLOT

8 ounces (225 g) small potatoes, skin on
1 tablespoon cider vinegar
¼ cup (60 ml) whipping cream (35 percent butterfat)
2 tablespoons Dijon mustard
1 French shallot, finely chopped
Leaves from 2 sprigs tarragon, finely chopped
Salt and pepper

1. Boil the potatoes as you would normally, drain them, and immediately pour the vinegar over them. Let them cool off for 5 to 10 minutes.

2. Whip the cream gently just to thicken it. Fold in the mustard, shallot, and tarragon. Season with salt and pepper.

3. When the potatoes have cooled, toss them gently with the cream. Add more salt and pepper to taste.

SMOKED WEST COAST OYSTERS

For each large oyster, make a cure of 1 tablespoon each soy sauce and canola oil and 1 teaspoon brown sugar. Be sure to use huge West Coast oysters (Gigas). We shuck them, brush on the cure, and then smoke them on their bottom shell in heavy smoke until they register a core temperature of 140°F (60°C).

SMOKED STURGEON AND SCALLOPS

The Smoked Mackerel brine is adequate for processing other fish as well, but the curing time may differ. The dense, thick flesh of sturgeon, for example, may take up to 24 hours at the same temperature. We soak scallops in the brine for 30 minutes, and then smoke them for about an hour, or until they register a core temperature of 140°F (60°C).

CHAR TARTARE

8 ounces (225 g) skinned artic
    char fillet (steel head trout would
    also do)

½ lemon

1 tablespoon chopped fresh chives

1 French shallot, finely diced

Salt and pepper

1 tablespoon grape seed oil

Fresh horseradish for serving

1. Rinse the fish and pat dry. With
your sharpest knife, remove the brown
flesh on the skinned side, not too
much, just a little. Cut the fish into
¼-inch (6-mm) cubes, transferring
the pieces to a cool bowl as you go.

2. Add about 1 teaspoon lemon juice,
the chives, shallot, and a generous
pinch each of salt and pepper and
stir. Taste and rectify if need be,
then mix in the oil.

3. Serve within 15 minutes. Shave
horseradish to order.

AQUAVIT ONIONS

One 8-ounce (224-g) jar sour cocktail
    onions

¼ cup (60 ml) aquavit

1. Open the jar of onions, remove
¼ cup (60 ml) of the liquid, and
replace it with the aquavit. (You can
also use vodka in place of aquavit
and then add 20 caraway seeds and
10 coriander seeds.)

2. Leave for 3 or 4 days (at least).
Open and serve.

CURED CHAR WITH GIN

1 pound (455 g) skin-on arctic char
    fillet, pinboned (or you can use
    sockeye salmon)

⅓ cup (65 g) packed brown sugar

⅓ cup (65 g) granulated sugar

⅓ cup (75 g) salt

1 tablespoon peppercorns

3 tablespoons gin

½ cup (20 g) chopped fresh dill

1. If you have 1 fillet, cut it into
2 equal pieces. If you have 2 fillets,
they should be of equal size. In a
small bowl, mix together the sugars,
salt, peppercorns, and gin to form a
paste. Divide the paste evenly among
the 4 sides of the fish pieces. Using
half of the dill, cover the flesh side of
both pieces, and then join the sides
together. Slip the sandwiched pieces
into a lock-top plastic bag, press out
the air, and seal closed. Place the
bag between 2 plates, place the setup
in the fridge, and leave for 8 hours.

RAZOR CLAMS VIDEO LOTTERY TERMINAL, aka Clams Casino

Serves 4

According to argumentalist extraordinaire John Bil, these are actually called "stuffies."

Everyone seems to agree that this is a great way to eat razor clams, as it's not uncommon for us to sell one hundred pounds (forty-five kilograms) per week at Joe Beef. We get our clams from the elusive fisherman John Doyle, who lives on the northern coast of the Saint Lawrence. To our knowledge, no commercial fisheries in Canada sell razor clams. If you want to prepare clams this way, but can't find razor, quahog will do.

24 razor clams, alive and wiggly

¼ cup (55 g) unsalted butter, at room temperature

4 slices bacon, diced and fried until crisp

2 tablespoons dried bread crumbs

2 tablespoons mayonnaise

2 tablespoons chopped fresh flat-leaf parsley

1 clove garlic, finely chopped

Dash of Tabasco sauce

Dash of pastis

Salt and pepper

¼ cup (30 g) grated Parmesan cheese

1. The shells of razor clams cut like real knives, so working with these shellfish calls for caution. They are also thin and brittle, so you have to handle them delicately. Rinse the clams carefully and then steam them in the biggest pot you have in about 1 inch (2.5 cm) of water. Count about 4 minutes from the moment you have steam.

2. Carefully remove the clams from the cooking liquid (also called the liquor), strain the liquid into a bowl, and set aside. Cautiously separate the shell of each clam in two by running a paring knife between the two parts, and remove the clam meat. When all of the meats are free of their shells, find the 16 to 20 nicest shells and give them a good rinse.

3. Remove the part that looks like a crater at one end of each clam; cut just an inch (2.5 cm) of that. Then remove the black bulging sac located in the middle. Rinse them again briefly. Once you have clean clams and clear liquor, combine them, cover, and refrigerate until you are ready to proceed with the rest of the recipe. You can leave them overnight.

4. Preheat the broiler. Chop the clam meats roughly—let's say, 25 pieces total. Place in a bowl, add the butter, bacon, bread crumbs, mayo, parsley, garlic, Tabasco, and pastis, and mix well. Add a couple spoonfuls of the liquor as necessary to obtain a texture like peanut butter (freeze any leftover liquor to add to chowder), season with salt and pepper, and mix again. Distribute the mixture evenly among the reserved shells, then top evenly with the cheese.

5. Arrange on a rimmed baking sheet and broil for 4 to 7 minutes, or until bubbly and golden. There is a fine line between perfect and overcooked, so keep a watchful eye. Serve immediately.

CORNFLAKE EEL NUGGETS

Serves 4

All of the eels of the world begin and return to the Sargasso Sea: can you imagine a more disgusting place to swim? It sounds like the scariest place on earth. In the course of their journey, some of those eels swim down the Saint Lawrence River, near the shores of Kamouraska, Quebec. And some of those eels get caught in weir traps by guys like Bernard Lauzier. Bernard smokes and brines eels and sturgeon, both of which we use at all three restaurants for many dishes, including this one right here. Eel is so meaty and delicious; Fred refers to it as the "undersea tenderloin."

8 ounces (225 g) smoked eel, cleaned and skinned (or you can use smoked sturgeon or hot-smoked salmon)

8 ounces (225 g) potatoes, peeled, boiled until tender, drained, and mashed with a fork

2 egg yolks, lightly beaten

2 tablespoons chopped fresh chives

1 tablespoon prepared mustard

1 tablespoon finely diced shallot

Salt and pepper

CRUST

1 cup (130 g) all-purpose flour seasoned with 1 teaspoon each salt and pepper

2 eggs

1 cup (250 ml) milk

2 cups (170 g) crushed cornflakes

Canola oil for deep-frying

ACCOMPANIMENTS

BBQ Sauce (page 176)

Honey Mustard (recipe follows)

Classic Tartar Sauce (recipe follows)

Piri Piri Honey (recipe follows)

Babylon Plum Jam (page 160)

Lemon wedges

1. Preheat the oven to 400°F (200°C). Place the eel on a baking sheet and warm in the oven for 5 minutes. Bring it out and inspect it for pin-bones and extract any you find while it is still warm. Place the eel in a bowl and, using a fork, shred it.

2. Add the potatoes, egg yolks, chives, mustard, and shallot to the eel and mix well. Season with salt and pepper to taste. If the texture appears too soft to form a consistent nugget, mix in a tablespoon or two of crushed cornflakes (from the crust ingredients) to help bind the ingredients. Refrigerate for about 20 minutes or so, or until chilled.

3. Using your hands, shape the eel mixture into rectangular nuggets about 1 by 1½ inches (2.5 by 4 cm).

4. To make the crust, set up your 3-bowl assembly line: put the seasoned flour in a shallow bowl, whisk together the eggs and milk in a second shallow bowl, and put the crushed cornflakes in a third bowl. Carefully yet generously coat each nugget in the flour, then dunk it in the egg bath, and finally give it a good roll in the crumbs. Reshape to make sure you have that negligently perfect nugget form. Now, put all the nuggets through the triple coating again. Refrigerate for about 10 minutes to help the crust "set."

5. Pour the oil to a depth of 3 inches (7.5 cm) into your deep fryer (or according to the manufacturer's instructions) and heat to 350°F (180°C). (Or, use a thick-bottomed, high-sided pot and a deep-fat thermometer.) Working in batches, fry the nuggets for 4 to 5 minutes, or until they get that classic nugget color. Drain briefly on paper towels, pat them dry, and serve with one or all of the sauces.

continued

CORNFLAKE EEL NUGGETS, continued

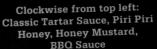

Clockwise from top left: Classic Tartar Sauce, Piri Piri Honey, Honey Mustard, BBQ Sauce

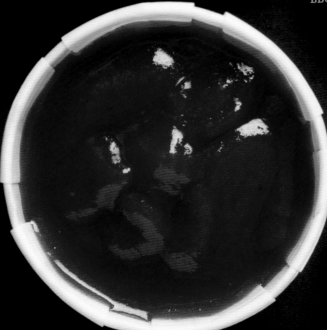

HONEY MUSTARD

Mix together ¼ cup (60 ml) strong Dijon mustard, ¼ cup (85 g) honey, and 1 tablespoon each mustard seeds and chopped fresh dill.

CLASSIC TARTAR SAUCE

Mix together ½ cup (125 ml) mayonnaise; 1 tablespoon each finely chopped capers, gherkins, tarragon, and shallot; a pinch of sugar; a dash or two of Tabasco sauce; and 1 tablespoon pickle brine.

PIRI PIRI HONEY

Warm ¼ cup (85 g) honey for about 30 seconds, then mix in 1 or 2 piri piri (African bird) or other small crushed dried chiles.

BAKED COMMON CRAB

Serves 4

Of all the crab we receive at the restaurant, West Coast Dungeness and the common crab from the Saint Lawrence (tourteau, brown crab, or Jonah) are our favorites. Many of the same guys who fish for lobster in these areas also fish for crab. But oddly enough, these crabs don't make it to Montreal. Instead, they're highjacked somewhere along the way for the Asian market. The crab is typically picked clean and frozen in blocks, shipped to China (for example), sawed, and only then sent back in one-pound (455-gram) packs. Although we make a point of using PEI or Quebec crab, Maine seems to understand the game a bit better. At Portland's Browne Trading Company, you can buy fresh, handpicked Jonah crab, meat and claws: our dream.

Whatever crab you buy (or catch!), make very sure to check the meat closely for bits of shell and cartilage that might have been left.

SAUCE

½ cup (125 ml) whipping cream (35 percent butterfat)

¼ cup (60 ml) light soy sauce

¼ cup (60 ml) mayonnaise

1 tablespoon ketchup

2 egg yolks

1 teaspoon Asian fish sauce

1 teaspoon peeled and grated fresh ginger

1 teaspoon grated garlic

1 pound (455 g) crabmeat, drained and picked over for shell bits and cartilage (if you're buying frozen crabmeat, a standard 14-ounce/400-g block is fine)

4 Brussels sprouts, trimmed and finely shaved

¼ cup (10 g) minced fresh chives or green onion tops

1 Thai bird chile, finely chopped

2 tablespoons *panko* (Japanese bread crumbs)

1. Preheat the oven to 400°F (200°C).

2. To make the sauce, in a bowl, whisk together the cream, soy sauce, mayonnaise, ketchup, egg yolks, fish sauce, ginger, and garlic.

3. Add the crab, Brussels sprouts, chives, and chile to the sauce and mix well. Divide the mixture evenly among 4 ramekins. Dust the top of each dish with one-fourth of the *panko*.

4. Bake for 10 to 12 minutes, or until brown and bubbly. Serve piping hot.

MACKEREL BENEDICT

Serves 1

When we wrote "mackerel" on the blackboard menu, it didn't sell, so we renamed it silver tail and a star was born. Now when we serve silver tail with bacon and sage, or in a breakfast Benedict, it flies out of the kitchen. We sell so much that our supplier thinks we might be feeding farmed killer whales in the backyard. Our guys at McKiernan Luncheonette do a great job of smoking 50 pounds (23 kilograms) every week, which culminates with the Saturday brunch mackerel Benedict, with eggs, hollandaise, maple syrup, and an English muffin.

This isn't much of a recipe. It's more of an idea. If you don't like or can't get smoked mackerel, substitute with smoked trout, no problem. You can use store-bought English muffins, or make the recipe for blini on page 91, only shaping them a bit bigger. Use 3 or 4 tablespoons of hollandaise (page 177) per serving, and drizzle a bit of maple syrup on the fish and then warm it a little under the broiler for 3 to 4 minutes. Also spread a bit of honey mustard (page 136)

on the muffin for an "undercover taste agent." As you can see from the picture, we use a whole mackerel for each serving (see Smorgasbord insert for how to smoke a whole 10- to 16-ounce/280- to 455-g mackerel for this recipe). It is indeed pretty, but it is the pits to use because of the bones. We prefer pinboned fillets, one per person, served with a pair of poached eggs. And eggs love chopped fresh chives.

*G*rowing up in the suburbs of Montreal, I was an awkward, little country boy. My backyard was my homestead (made to look a lot bigger by the extending woods of the psychiatric hospital just behind), and it is where I spent the majority of my first twenty years (the backyard, not the hospital). I have a picture of me on the day of the high-school prom, not in a suit posing with some cute classmate, but in my backyard garden holding a big head of lettuce I had grown.

CHAPTER 5

THE SMOKER

I learned about gardening in the same way I've learned about most things in my life: part from just doing and part from the Reader's Digest *L'Art de Vivre au Temps Jadis* (*The Art of Living in the Old Days*), a book I pulled from my parents' shelves. My grandparents had these kinds of books, too: *How to Settle in the Woods, How to Build a Homestead, How to Make Brambleberry Jelly, How to Generate Your Own Electricity*. Boxes in the basement held copies of *Mother Earth News* magazine or books on Vermont folk medicine, all of them filled with ideas and projects.

When I was twelve, the next-door neighbors had a pile of bricks near the foundation of their home just waiting to be stolen. I grabbed some bricks, dragged them to my house, and then stuck them together with clay and began to build what became my first makeshift smoker. I didn't get to use it for long because, much to my surprise, I got a Little Chief smoker for my birthday the next year. Pastrami, almonds, bacon, and beef jerky were my menu mainstays, and my neighbor and best friend, Matthew

"La Matematica non è un'opinione." (Mathematics is not an opinion.)

—Wally Ricciardelli

Roberts, was always there to sample the goods (and the bads, like smoked eggs and banana gum made from pine sap and bananas). Thus, my smoking journey was launched.

A quick disclaimer before I go on: I understand that building smokers has been cool for so long that it's no longer cool, and we are by no means the first to embark on a how-to of smoking techniques. We're no Apostles of Bacon, and we know that the world needs another praise of pork like it needs another celebrity TV dance show. That being said, preserving and salting meats have always been a big part of the Quebecois culture, starting with the *coureurs des bois* tradition, and they are a big part of Joe Beef culture, too.

Fast forward to 2009: Liverpool House and McKiernan Luncheonette had been built and the shared back garden was starting to thrive. Dave and I had always talked about

having a smoker (which is why we held onto the chimney when we first moved into the Joe Beef space) and the time just seemed right. We had seen a little smoker at Monas (the Montreal equivalent of JB Prince kitchenware in New York) that cost two thousand dollars. Allison said to wait. Because she's usually right and because I had no choice, I waited. But in the spring of 2009, with paycheck in hand and nothing else to spend the money on, I secretly bought a MIG welding machine for a thousand dollars so we could build a smoker on our own.

It was to be neither a southern BBQ pit smoker, nor a northern cold smoker suitable for making a batch of fish *boucanné*. I wanted it to have a cabinet, which is unusual these days, so I didn't have any plans to follow. I just used my imagination. In my head, I could picture a smoker that might have been used at the Montreal smoked-meat shops, like Lester's or Schwartz's, at the turn of the twentieth century. After I shared my plans with Dave and Allison, we all agreed that the Joe Beef smoker should look something like this (see page 148).

My dad always draws models of planes or machines on letter-size graph paper, a practice that I inherited. (A lot of things at Joe Beef have

started as sketches on those pads. It's a good way to orient yourself with space and volume.) So I drew the plan for the smoker. When I put my ideas down on paper, I could see and understand how the smoke would progress, how the smoker would draw, where the damper should go, and so on. The process of drawing the plan forced me to read, to dig up more information. When I have an idea, or when I have a build going on, I feel like a crackhead looking for a rock. I'm completely obsessed and I'll do anything to finish the project, including sabotaging the restaurant by hijacking the kitchen staff to help me. This totally screws the staff's prep time and generally pisses off everyone, especially my partners.

An area was set aside in the backyard for construction. This was when the garden only took up about half the space it does today. In one of the daily pilgrimages to the hardware store, I bought a metal chop saw, a black welding helmet, metal brushes, a plethora of metal grinders, and a welder's hammer. Quincaillerie Notre-Dame, aka Rona hardware, is one block east of the restaurants on the same street and thank god for that. It's the oldest hardware store in Montreal, and walking inside is like stepping back in time (excluding the Slap Chops on

sale near the cash register). Because Rona services an industrial neighborhood, it still sells pipe wrenches for the guys who install gas pipes and tools for railroad workers. Speaking with any of Rona's staff, whether about plumbing or welding, is a completely humbling experience. If you need one screw, they will sell you one screw. It's that kind of place.

It took ten days to build the smoker. Max, an old Joe Beefer, and

François Coté (another staff member) worked on the smoker every day before service. We would still be welding when the first customers of the night arrived, creating disgusting fumes of smoke and the smell of flux and ruining their *apéros* on the terrace. Our favorite welder (and Italian), Wally Ricciardelli was on speed dial and instrumental in giving advice on all things metal. The days passed in a

blur of measurements, hard work, and Dilallo burgers (neither Dave nor I have ever lost any of our many pounds while working on a new project, although we always believe we will). Once the smoker was welded, the guys at Rona dropped by with thirty bags of concrete, which all of us mixed by hand. We dug the hole, made the foundation, tied the rods, and poured the concrete. The next day it took six of us

to lift the smoker to its position and bolt it into place. The smoker sits on the back wall of Joe Beef; on the other side is the dish pit.

There are complex rules about smoke dynamics that I didn't know then (or now, really) but had a feeling about, so I was happy when it all started to work: the firebox burning, the baffle directing heat, and the chimney smoking. It's been easy to use and maintain since the beginning. As a river finds its bed in soil, the smoke goes where it wants to, and our cooks have mastered its little imperfections. We realized that airflow in a smoker is finicky: you want smoke, but not too much; you want heat, but in good proportion. I wanted to combine the smoker with a gas burner, but the gas burner was way too hot, so that idea was out. The perfect temperature is 225°F (110°C), and we're able to maintain that temperature until November (at which point we start making nova-cured fish, cold-smoked hams, and the like). The smoker isn't chrome or mechanized, but we think it's handsome, if only because it looks like it's always been there.

A year later, at any given time, the smoker could contain three dozen racks of ribs, two pig heads, a dozen pork butts, twelve rabbit summer sausages, and lots of duck, chicken, and rabbit legs. It is used five days a week throughout a good part of the year, making prep time more interesting for the kitchen, and creating new "classics" on the menu for the customers. The smoked duck legs (page 151) are a good example. When you add the element of smoke, the dish becomes completely different.

One evening, Habs player Roman Hamrlik sat by himself at the Liverpool bar with a Czechvar and the duck legs. The next week, a bunch of other Czech and Slovak players came to try the same thing. We can't really say it is a Liverpool House classic, but it is definitely an expectation that we'll serve Czechvar and duck legs during hockey season now. The smoker also gave rise to the Joe Beef ribs, which are now a phenomenon because the recipe was aired on the popular Quebec television program, *À la di Stasio*. Because of Josée di Stasio, we sell an average of forty racks of ribs per night between Joe Beef and Liverpool House, and we get the chance to meet people from all corners of Quebec who are willing to drive three hours for dinner (because Josée said to).

The following recipes were inspired by the Joe Beef smoker.
—FM

BUILDING YOUR OWN SMOKER

I HAVE ALWAYS HAD A FASCINATION with utilitarian objects, whether it be a globe on wheels with a liquor cabinet inside, Felco #2 pruning shears, the perfect *verre à vin d'Alsace*, or a nice smoker. And apart from the eBay bills, this fascination feels healthy. When my head is populated by projects, the work feels less like a job and more like inspired fun. François, Emma, Manu, Marco, and all of the Joe Beef staff seem to feel the same way; they show up to work wanting to make summer sausage, wanting to sew cloth casings, or just wanting to talk about getting back to the roots of making good baloney.

Because we built the smoker on our own, we understand it more fully. We also understand that most people who want to start smoking won't have the space (or the desire) to build a freestanding smoker like ours. As a result, we're providing two options for smoking at home: (1) building your own smoker (similar to ours) or (2) building a wood-chip device for an outdoor grill (see The Hot Délicieux Sandwich on page 151). We have included the original plan for our smoker here, and have based our instructions accordingly. We understand that this plan will probably be useless for you. But we can't fake an original, so you should see the information below as more of a "plan fantastic," like a time-travel machine or the floor plan to Grizzly Adams's cabin.

A WORD ON SAFE WELDING

I am in no way a professional welder. I took welding in agricultural college and practiced here and there for a few years. One thing I know, though, is how to work safely. To start, cover your eyes with safety glasses when you cut, assemble, or handle steel tubes. Weld with your full-face helmet on. I had cataract surgery at age twenty-eight, probably from being courageous. Cover your head and wear inflammable long sleeves and pant legs, even when grinding: the shower of sparks can and will ignite anything. Wear your cuffs outside of your work boots. No lighter in your pockets; that's just stupid. Wear welding gloves (not ones that are old and transparent). If it rains or the ground is wet, wait it out. Use an approved extension cord. Warn people nearby when you're about to weld by screaming "WELDING!"

A (VERY MINIMUM) LIST OF TOOLS

- MIG, flux core, or stick welder (220 volts operation is a must)
- 12-inch (30-cm) abrasive chop saw
- 4½-inch (11-cm) abrasive grinder with grinding wheel and wire-brush wheel
- Soapstone marking chalk
- Welder hammer
- Large welder vise grip
- 2 magnetic squares
- Arc-welding helmet
- 1 piece heavy steel scrap, to use as a weight
- Cutting pliers (in case the wire sticks)
- Proper and sufficient flux core wire
- Powerful electric drill with ½-inch (12-mm) metal bit
- Measuring tape
- Acetylene torch kit or MAPP TurboTorch

LIST OF CUTS

All the tubing used is square steel with walls ⅛ inch (3 mm) thick (see diagram).

For the main body frame:
- four 1½ × 1½ × 60 inches (4 × 4 × 152 cm)
- four 1 × 1 × 69 inches (2.5 × 2.5 × 175 cm)
- four 1 × 1 × 46 inches (2.5 × 2.5 × 117 cm)
- four 1 × 1 × 21 inches (2.5 × 2.5 × 53 cm)
- four 1 × 1 × 22 inches (2.5 × 2.5 × 56 cm)
- two ¼ × 2½ × 26 inches (6 mm × 6 cm × 66 cm) [strap for the base]
- fourteen angle 1 × 1 × 23 inches (2.5 × 2.5 × 58 cm) [for the racks]

For the doors:
- four 1 × 1 × 48 inches (2.5 × 2.5 × 122 cm)
- four 1 × 1 × 36 inches (2.5 × 2.5 × 91.5 cm)

For the firebox:
- four 1 × 1 × 17 inches (2.5 × 2.5 × 43 cm)
- two 1 × 1 × 24 inches (2.5 × 2.5 × 61 cm)
- two 1 × 1 × 22 inches (2.5 × 2.5 × 56 cm)

For the exterior, using sheet metal ⅛ inch (3 mm) thick:
- one 72 × 48 inches (183 × 122 cm)
- two 72 × 24 inches (183 × 61 cm)
- one 48 × 24 inches (122 × 61 cm)
- two 36 × 48 inches (91.5 × 122 cm)
- one 24 × 30 inches (61 × 76 cm)

For the firebox doors and top, using sheet metal ¼ inch (6 mm) thick:
- one 24-inch (61-cm) square
- one 6 × 21 inches (15 × 53 cm)
- one 24 × 18 inches (61 × 46 cm)

The door handles and hinges pin are ½-inch (12-mm) steel rod, bent with a torch. Cut and then position with ½-inch (12-mm) ID washers welded in place. The tube for the hinges is ⅝-inch (1.5 cm) interior diameter for ⅛-inch (3-mm) wall thickness.

1. Draw the plan, calculating the cutting lengths. It's a lot of fun to look for other smoker references in books like *The Practical Handyman's Encyclopedia* and old welding guides, but I'm sure you can also just use the dreary World Wide Web.

2. Establish a comprehensive list of materials.

3. Order and purchase the materials from your local steel supplier.

4. Measure the steel twice and mark (accurately) once before cutting with a band or chop saw.

5. Prepare your welder MIG, flux core, or stick in a safe and dry area.

6. Mock fit all of your tubes.

7. Tack weld (read: temporarily set before final weld) the front and back panel, check the square by taking two opposite cross measures; they have to be even. If all is even, finish the welds.

8. Assemble the front to the back with the connecting tubes. If it warps, straighten with a small jack or a ratchet strap.

9. Assemble and weld the door frames and the firebox.

10. Cover the frame with pre-measured and cut steel sheets. Number them to avoid mistakes. Airproof the smoker by tack welding the exterior and interior.

11. Measure, cut, and bend the rods with a torch for the handles and the hinges.

12. Same for the grate for the firebox.

13. Paint the exterior with commercial stove paint.

14. Install the damper and the thermometer.

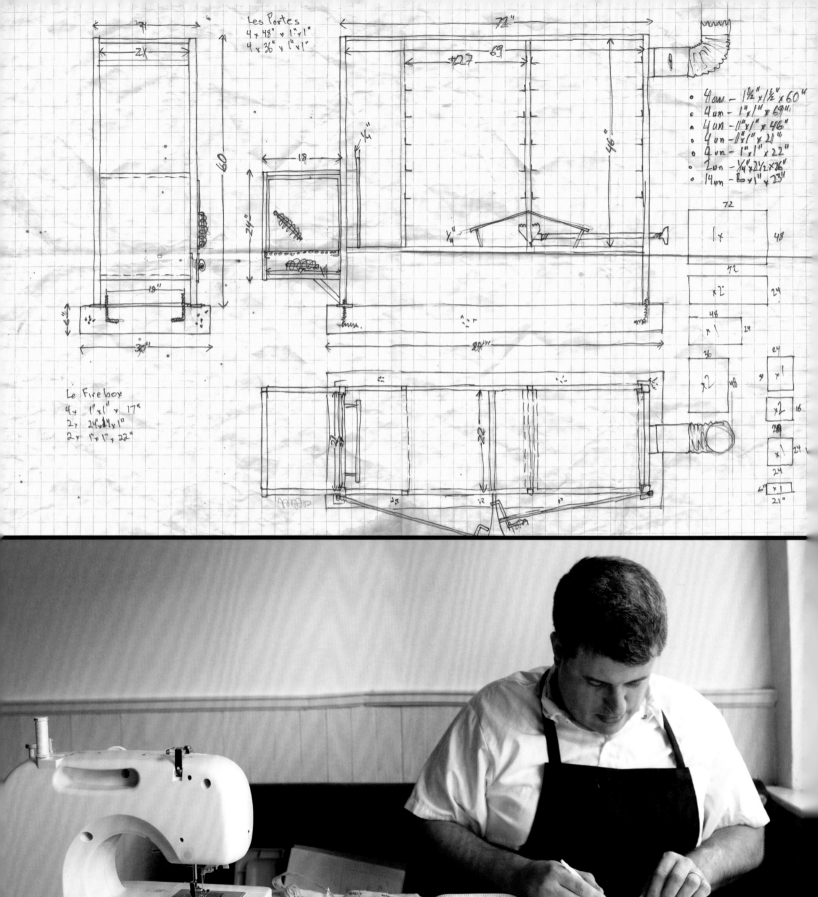

THE HOT DÉLICIEUX SANDWICH

Makes 4 hefty sandwiches

Even though places like St. Hubert Rotisserie have been serving the "hot chicken sandwich" since the 1930s, no factual proof exists that it originated in Quebec. Our only proof is that we haven't seen it outside the province, whereas inside, it's a weekly staple. It's basically hot, shredded chicken, served with *galvaude* (peas and gravy, usually a *poutine* variation) and two pieces of white bread.

In this recipe, you have four meat options: pork, duck, rabbit, or chicken. They're all hot and they're all delicious. For pork, use the pulled pork recipe in Scallops with Pulled Pork (page 30). For the other meats, there are three steps: (1) cure it, (2) smoke it, and (3) confit it. If you don't have a smoker can, you will need to dig up an empty 1-quart (1-liter) tin can for step 2. If you live in the States, D'Artagnan (www.dartagnan.com) will deliver the duck fat you need in step 4 to your door. If not, use bacon fat.

The gravy is the perfect clone of the local *poulet* barbecue sauce. It's not a hot sauce, but it's also not that thickish gravy that tastes like spinach and baking soda. It's zingier, a cross between BBQ sauce and gravy. It is classic on these sandwiches, but it's also good, minus the bread, on duck, pork, *poutine*, or yes, chicken.

SMOKED MEATS

¼ cup (55 g) kosher salt

¼ cup (50 g) packed brown sugar

1 clove garlic, chopped

1 tablespoon peppercorns

6 whole duck, rabbit, or chicken legs

About 1 quart (1 liter) all-natural wood chips

About 2 tablespoons olive oil

9 cups (about 2 kg) rendered duck fat

DELICIOUS GRAVY

1 small onion, finely chopped

1 teaspoon minced garlic

¼ cup (60 ml) roast chicken, duck, or pork drippings

¼ cup (30 g) all-purpose flour

¼ teaspoon cayenne pepper

2 teaspoons Colman's dry mustard

1 teaspoon celery salt

½ teaspoon allspice

½ teaspoon pepper

2 tablespoons HP Sauce or Gentleman Steak Sauce (page 251)

1¼ cups (300 ml) tomato juice (we use Heinz)

2 cups (500 ml) chicken stock

Salt

8 slices white bread

1 cup (140 g) frozen or very fresh shelled peas

Good Fries (page 154), crinkle cut

continued

1. To cure the meat, in a small bowl, mix together the salt, sugar, garlic, and peppercorns. Rub the mixture into the legs thoroughly. Place the cured legs in 1 or more lock-top plastic bags and refrigerate for 4 hours. When the time is up, remove them from the bag(s), rinse off the cure, and pat dry with paper towels.

2. To smoke the meat, start the BBQ on low-medium setting. To prepare the smoker can (or a 1-quart/1-liter tin can), fill it to the top with the wood chips. Cover the entire can with aluminum foil and poke 3 or 4 holes in the top. By now the BBQ should be hot and smoking. Place the can on the fire on the opposite side of where you will put the meat.

3. In a large enough bowl, coat the legs with the oil. Put the legs on the BBQ, close the lid, and smoke for 45 minutes. There should be a good amount of smoke billowing out near the end. Now remember, you're not cooking the meat here. You are smoking it for flavor.

4. To confit the meat, preheat the oven to 300°F (150°C). Pour the duck fat into a large (big enough for 6 legs) baking dish and let it melt. When the fat is melted and liquid, nestle the 6 smoked legs in it, side by side. If you're using duck or rabbit legs, cook in the oven for 3½ hours; for

chicken, cook for 2½ hours. You know you're on the right track when after 45 minutes the bubbles in the fat start rising to the top like a glass of 7UP long after it's been poured.

5. Meanwhile, make the gravy. In a saucepan, sweat the onion and garlic in the drippings over medium heat for 4 to 5 minutes, or until slightly colored. Add the flour and stir well with a wooden spoon. Add the cayenne, mustard, celery salt, allspice, and pepper and stir for another minute or two, then add the HP sauce. Stir again for a minute and then add the tomato juice and the stock.

Whisk about 10 turns, reduce the heat to low, and simmer for 20 minutes. Strain the gravy; you should have about 2 cups (500 ml). Season with salt. Just before serving, reheat until piping hot.

6. When the time is up on the confit, remove the pan from the oven and let cool for 30 minutes. Take the legs out of the fat. Now you have confit legs. If you want to stop here and not make the sandwich, we don't blame you. You can enjoy the legs on their own. (Confit legs are the best leftovers: an absolute treat and they taste better in the days after.) If you are going ahead with the sandwiches, while the legs are still warm, pull the meat off the bones and then pull the meat apart using either your fingers or 2 forks.

7. Get out 4 plates, and put 1 bread slice on each plate. Divide the meat evenly among the bread slices. Pour half of the hot gravy over the meat and bread. Top the sandwiches with the remaining bread slices. Add the peas (thawed, if using frozen) to the remaining gravy and put on the heat for 2 to 3 minutes, enough to warm a little. Pour the gravy and peas over the top of the sandwiches. Serve with the fries.

SMOKED BABY BACK RIBS

Makes 4 racks; serves 4 to 6

Our use of ribs extends beyond a plate of ribs. We use them in gnocchi and in potato soup, and we will cut them into three, remove the bones, and make a McKiernan ribs sandwich. As lard was a staple at the turn of the century, so are ribs at Joe Beef. We provide two ways of cooking: roasting and smoking. Serve with Good Fries (page 154).

2 tablespoons smoked paprika

2 tablespoons garlic powder

2 tablespoons Colman's dry mustard

2 tablespoons pepper

½ teaspoon ground bay leaf

4 racks baby back ribs, about 1½ pounds (680 g) each

One (12-ounce/375-ml) bottle beer, if roasting the racks

BBQ Sauce (page 176)

About 1 quart (1 liter) all-natural wood chips

1. Preheat the oven to 325°F (165°C). In a small bowl, mix together the paprika, garlic powder, mustard, pepper, and bay. Place the rib racks in a roasting pan and coat them generously with the spice mix, then shake off the excess. Pour the beer between the ribs. Cover with aluminum foil.

2. Roast for 2½ hours. During the last 30 minutes, remove the foil and coat the racks with the BBQ sauce so the surface is well glazed.

3. To smoke the ribs, the first thing to do is to find out if your BBQ can maintain the target temperature. Get an oven thermometer and test it; if it holds a temperature between 210° and 230°F (100° and 110°C) for a good

20 minutes, you're fine. Also, because the racks require a 4-hour smoke time, it's clever to check for a good supply of gas. The ingredients are the same for smoking as for roasting except for the beer. In other words, you mix the spices together and coat the racks with the mixture. Next, fill the smoker can (or any 1-quart/ 1-liter tin can) to the top with the wood chips. Cover the entire can with aluminum foil and poke 3 or 4 holes in the top.

4. Nowadays, most BBQs have 3 burners: light only the left one, turning it to low-medium; your ribs will cook on the right. You may want to put an aluminum cake pan filled with water under the grill rack, to prevent flare-ups and to provide moisture. Place the ribs on the right side, place the can on the opposite side, and close the lid. Check now and again to make sure the temperature does not go above 240°F (115°C), adjusting the flame as needed. After 2 hours, check the ribs. Are they too soft or too hard on the edges? Listen to the force and adjust. They should be ready in 4 hours. When I smoke ribs, I like to keep the BBQ sauce on the side and dip the ribs.

GOOD FRIES

Serves 4

The best fries are done with potatoes that have never seen the cold. It has something to do with starch converting to sugar at certain temperatures. If you're interested in the specifics, check out Harold McGee's *On Food and Cooking: The Science and Lore of the Kitchen*. At the restaurant, we use a russet potato from the Île d'Orléans in the Saint Lawrence River (which Cartier originally named the Isle of Bacchus because of the native vines that covered the landscape), but you can use anything similar.

This recipe really is made to work with a deep fryer. If you don't have a small one at home, a 5-quart (5-liter) thick-bottomed, high-sided pot and a deep-frying thermometer will work. We use half canola oil and half beef fat, which always makes better fries the second day. If you can get your hands on rendered beef leaf fat (the fat from around the kidneys), definitely use that. If this is all too much, you can use peanut oil. We don't, as we can't piss off both the vegetarians and the allergics.

A few years back we started tossing our fries in escargot butter (its name comes from its use, not its contents; it's basically garlic butter) and now we can't stop. We also like to add a little grated pecorino as we toss.

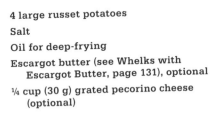

4 large russet potatoes

Salt

Oil for deep-frying

Escargot butter (see Whelks with Escargot Butter, page 131), optional

¼ cup (30 g) grated pecorino cheese (optional)

1. Peel the potatoes and cut into ⅜-inch (1-cm) sticks—the size of a Crayola crayon. Place the sticks in a deep bowl, sprinkle in 1 tablespoon salt, and mix in with your hands. Pour in just enough hot tap water to cover. Let sit for 1 hour.

2. Drain the potatoes, rinse well in cold water, and dry well with a salad spinner or a kitchen towel.

3. Pour the oil to a depth of 3 inches (7.5 cm) into your deep fryer and heat to 260°F (125°C). Working in batches, fry the potatoes for 4 to 6 minutes, or until almost tender. Drain in the basket and place on a baking sheet.

4. Now heat the oil in the fryer to 360°F (185°C) in preparation for a quick double fry. Again working in batches, fry the potatoes briefly to crisp them up but not color the outside. They should still be a nice blond color. Scoop them out of the oil, allow the oil to heat up again to the 360°F, and then fry them one last time until crisp. Do the taste test to see if they are ready, then pat them dry with paper towels.

5. Serve immediately sprinkled with salt or tossed in the butter with or without the cheese.

LIVERPOOL HOUSE RABBIT SAUSAGE

*Makes 6 sausages, each about 8 inches (20 cm) long
and 3 inches (7.5 cm) in diameter*

When Fred travels, the first place he always goes is to a grocery store. Forget the idyllic markets and the virile butchers; he has this immense fascination with supermarkets. Nothing compares to landing in Paris at 9:00 A.M. and heading to the loaded yogurt aisle of a Monoprix. He feels the same when he's visiting western Canada, checking out the sausage sections. Far from artisanal anything, we're sure, but the array is crazy: midget baloney, cotton-sack summer sausage, skinless Mennonite, headcheese, jerky of all kinds, and on and on.

It's a fun challenge to take an old commercial sausage and just make it honest again: good meats and real smoke. This one we made with Emma, who was chef de cuisine at Liverpool House at the time. We suggest the use of muslin bags for this sausage in particular. You might find them online, or, as a proper Joe Beefer, you can sew them yourself (see Note). The penetration of smoke is much better and you don't need a stuffer. You just do it by hand.

3 pounds (1.4 kg) boneless rabbit, cut into 1-inch (2.5-cm) cubes

1 pound (455 g) boneless lean pork loin, cut into 1-inch (2.5-cm) cubes

2 pounds (900 g) fat pork cheek or fatback, cut into cubes

3 tablespoons kosher salt

1½ cups (375 ml) water

½ cup (110 g) powdered milk

¼ cup (30 g) Colman's dry mustard

2 tablespoons sugar

2 tablespoons ground black pepper

1 teaspoon Prague powder #1

6 (2⅜ by 24-inch/6 by 61-cm) sausage casings (we buy them from sausagemaker.com)

Butcher string for tying the casings

POACHING INGREDIENTS

2 onions, each studded with three cloves

4 bay leaves

Preserved Stone Fruits (page 161) for serving

1. In a large bowl, combine the rabbit, pork loin, pork cheek, salt, water, powdered milk, dry mustard, sugar, pepper, and Prague powder and mix well. Cover and refrigerate for at least 2 hours or up to overnight.

2. Fit your meat grinder with a plate with medium-size holes (³/₈ inch/ 10 mm). Slowly pass the meat mixture through the grinder. Using your hands, stuff 1 pound (455 g) of meat into each casing by inserting small balls of the meat mixture and squeezing the casing to compact the mixture. (If your casings are too long, just trim them to size.) Tie 'em up with butcher string. Place the sausages on a tray, cover with a cloth, and let sit at room temperature for 1 hour.

3. To smoke the sausages, preheat the smoker to a chamber temperature of 200°F (93°C). (To smoke your sausages on a barbecue, follow the smoking instructions for the Hot Délicieux Sandwich, page 151.) Hang the sausages in the smoker (we hang them from a grill using small stainless-steel hooks) and smoke them until they reach a core temperature of 152°F (67°C). That's about 3 hours at 185°F/85°C (the chamber temperature will drop a bit once the sausages are inside). We figure if you have a smoker, a meat thermometer is probably not such a big deal for you. Be sure to spray the sausages with water every 30 minutes. When the sausages are finished smoking, let them cool for a day.

4. Alternatively, poach the sausages in simmering water with the onions and bay leaves for 30 to 40 minutes, or until they reach a core temperature of 152°F (67°C).

5. Serve the sausages with a pocket-knife, crackers, and the stone fruit preserve, preferably while on a fishing trip. The sausages will keep for a week (if poached) to 10 days (if smoked) wrapped in aluminum foil in the refrigerator.

Note: *To make your own casings, cut unbleached muslin cloth into 14 by 6½-inch (35 by 16.5-cm) rectangles. Fold in half lengthwise and sew along the long and one short side to make a 14 by 3¼-inch (35 by 8-cm) bag. Wash the casings before use.*

PORCHETTA ALLA JOE BEEF

Serves 6 to 8

Porchetta is something you want to eat lukewarm: work on it in the morning, cook it in the afternoon, take it out, and eat it an hour or so later. We're aware that a traditional *porchetta* is a whole stuffed pig; this is our version and has little affiliation with the Italian classic. Because you wrap the pork belly around the shoulder, you need a pretty skinny piece of Boston butt. We buy a 5-pound (2.3-kg) shoulder, slice it lengthwise, and use half (freeze the other half for another time). This recipe may look labor-intensive, but it won't be, especially if you get your butcher to do all of the trimming for you.

4-pound (1.8-kg) piece pork belly, skin removed and reserved

2.5-pound (1.1-kg) cylinder Boston butt (pork shoulder)

8 sprigs rosemary

2 cloves garlic

½ jalapeño chile

2 tablespoons fennel seeds

¼ cup (60 ml) white vermouth

2 tablespoons salt

1 tablespoon pepper

¼ cup (60 ml) olive oil

Canola oil for coating

2 large carrots, halved crosswise

Potato Dinner Rolls (recipe follows)

Babylon Plum Jam (recipe follows)

1. You want to be sure that the belly width and the butt length are the same, and that they don't look like a cartoon hot dog (big wiener, small bun). So if they are not identical, do some trimming. Now, preheat the oven to 350°F (180°C).

2. For the seasoning paste, in a food processor, combine the rosemary, garlic, chile, fennel seeds, vermouth, salt, pepper, and olive oil and process until a paste forms. Or, use a mortar and pestle.

3. Rub the paste on the butt and the belly, inside and out. Wrap the butt in the belly, fat side out. Then stack the wrapped pork butt on the belly skin; in a perfect world, it would be the same size. Roll tightly and tie securely with kitchen twine. Coat the outside with canola oil.

4. Line up the carrots, to make a support, on the bottom of a roasting pan. Place the tied pork on top. Roast for 2 hours. Lower the temperature to 275°F (135°C) and continue to roast for 5 hours more. You are slow roasting pig fat here, so it's much better to slightly overcook than to undercook. The smell, just as much as the look, should clue you in to its doneness.

5. Remove from the oven and let rest for 30 minutes. Snip the twine, slice, and serve with the rolls and jam.

POTATO DINNER ROLLS

Makes 12 rolls

You know those cheap dinner rolls you eat at your grandma's house on Sunday nights? The supersoft, semiattached kind you buy in plastic bags? These are those dinner rolls. The base of the recipe is mashed potato, so it's important to start this recipe as soon as you've just finished making mashed potatoes. These are perfect to serve with a pulled pork sandwich or on *porchetta*.

2¼ teaspoons (1 package) active dry yeast

1 tablespoon sugar

6 tablespoons (90 ml) lukewarm water

1 egg

⅔ cup (160 ml) milk, at room temperature

½ cup (100 g) warm mashed potatoes

3½ cups (510 g) all-purpose flour, plus more for rolling

1 tablespoon salt

⅓ cup (75 ml) rendered bacon fat, melted and cooled to room temperature

continued

1. In a small bowl, combine the yeast and sugar with the water and let sit for 15 minutes, until frothy.

2. Using a stand mixer fitted with the dough hook, knead together the egg, milk, mashed potatoes, and the yeast mixture on low speed. Add the flour and salt and knead for 4 minutes. Add the bacon fat by the spoonful and mix until the dough is homogenous. You want to have a smooth dough consistency. It should taste like raw mashed-potato bread dough—in other words, not very good.

3. Transfer the dough to an oiled bowl and set it in a warm place. Let the dough rise for an hour, or until doubled in size. Transfer the dough to a lightly floured work surface, punch it down, and knead it for a minute. Divide the dough into 12 equal pieces (2½ to 2¾ ounces/ 70 to 75 g each; remember to use your scale!). Roll each piece between the palm of your hand and the floured work surface, pressing down gently. Line a rimmed baking sheet with parchment paper and oil the sides. Place the dough balls, seam-side down, on the baking sheet ¼ inch (6 mm) apart, so when they rise they attach to one another. Let rise for 45 minutes in a warm place, or until doubled in size. Meanwhile, preheat the oven to 375°F (190°C).

4. Bake the rolls for 20 to 25 minutes, or until very lightly browned. They should not turn golden brown, but instead look like the cheap grocery-store doughy rolls that your grandma serves. Remove from the oven and let cool on a rack for 15 minutes before tearing apart and serving.

BABYLON PLUM JAM

Makes about 1½ pints (680 ml)

The spice and heat in this jam make it more at ease with meats and cheese than toast. As for the Babylon term, it's simply in relation to the avid devotion that the world's kitchen has for reggae music!

1½ pounds (680 g) plums (about 10), pitted and chopped
2¼ cups (455 g) sugar
¼ cup (60 ml) distilled white vinegar
1 small fresh or dried red chile
2 tablespoons ground ginger
½ cup (105 g) mustard seeds

1. In a heavy saucepan, combine the plums, sugar, and vinegar and let stand for 1 hour.

2. Place the pan over low heat and cook, stirring occasionally, for 1 hour, or until the mixture thickens.

3. Add the chile, ginger, and mustard seeds and continue to cook, stirring, for about 15 minutes, or until you have the right jammy consistency. It should be thick, not soupy. If you're using big plums, you may have to keep it on the heat for a bit longer to cook away the extra water. Remove and discard the chile. If you don't want chunky jam, buzz it with a hand blender.

4. Let cool for 10 minutes before serving or jarring. The jam will keep for up to a month stored in a tightly sealed container in the refrigerator.

PRESERVED STONE FRUITS

Makes about 2 pints (1 liter)

This is Fred's mom, Suzanne's, recipe. It is an old Belgian Walloon standard—a quick and tasty pickle that is good with pork roast and sausages. You can also mix the "brine" with nut oil as a dressing for beets. And use it to give a welcome buzz to a bland wine sauce: just a drop or two.

This pickling solution works well with almost any stone fruit. The amount of liquid you need will vary according to the stone fruit(s) you use. Here, the amount has been geared to 1 pound (455 g) cherries and/or Italian plums. You may need to adjust it if you use other stone fruits. Because we are deathly afraid of preserves gone wrong (from watching an old episode of *Quincy, M.E.*, where the culprit was botulism), we suggest using superclean plastic containers and always refrigerating the preserves.

1 pound (455 g) large dark cherries or Italian plums or half cherries and half plums

1 cinnamon stick

1 bay leaf

2 cups (500 ml) white wine vinegar

1 cup (250 ml) water

1 cup (200 g) packed Demerara or brown sugar

1. Rinse the fruits and wipe dry. Burn the tip of a safety pin briefly to sterilize, then prick each plum about 8 times and each cherry about 4 times.

2. Divide the fruits into your containers of choice and pack tight; divide the cinnamon stick and the bay leaf evenly among the containers.

3. In a saucepan, combine the vinegar, water, and sugar and bring to a boil, stirring to dissolve the sugar. Remove from the heat and pour over the fruits. Let the fruits temper for about 2 minutes, then cover and promptly place in the fridge.

4. Give the fruits at least a week to pickle properly before serving. They will keep for up to 2 months.

SMOKED CHEDDAR with DOUGHNUTS

Makes 20 to 24 doughnuts, depending on size

Pier Luc Dallaire has worked for us for five years (and counting) as a cook, busboy, bartender, oyster shucker, and now, a real French waiter! His dad, Bertrand, was a kindred soul gardener, and his mom, Huguette, made these killer doughnuts. They rise with baking powder, not yeast. And you will often find them at weekend country flea markets. The Isle-aux-Grues cheese (page 276) is a great Quebec product that we couldn't resist smoking. Together they sing.

2¾ cups (350 g) all-purpose flour, plus more for dusting

1 tablespoon baking powder

½ teaspoon salt

¼ teaspoon freshly grated nutmeg

¼ teaspoon ground cinnamon

¼ cup (55 g) unsalted butter, at room temperature

½ cup (100 g) sugar

2 eggs

¼ cup (60 ml) whipping cream (35 percent butterfat)

¼ cup (60 ml) milk

1 teaspoon vanilla extract

Canola oil for deep-frying

1 cup (300 g) maple syrup

8 thin slices Smoked Cheddar (recipe follows)

1. In a bowl, stir together the flour, baking powder, salt, nutmeg, and cinnamon. Set aside.

2. In a second bowl, cream the butter with the sugar until smooth. Add the eggs, one at a time, beating after each addition until combined. Slowly add the cream and milk, mixing until combined, and then mix in the vanilla. Lastly, add the flour mixture and stir until a stiff dough forms.

3. On a floured countertop, roll out the dough about ½ inch (12 mm) thick. With a doughnut cutter, cut out the doughnuts. We prefer a smaller doughnut, but it is up to you.

4. Pour the oil to a depth of 3 inches (7.5 cm) into your deep fryer (or according to the manufacturer's instructions) and heat to 350°F (180°C). (Or, use a thick-bottomed, high-sided pot and a deep-fat thermometer.) Working in batches, add the doughnuts and fry for 3 to 4 minutes, or until they are a nice light brown. Drain on paper towels.

5. In a small saucepan, bring the maple syrup to a boil over high heat, then lower the heat and simmer for 5 minutes. With your trusty tongs, dip and coat the doughnuts with the syrup. Serve 4 to 6 doughnuts per person with a couple of slices of the Smoked Cheddar each.

continued

SMOKED CHEDDAR

2-pound (900-g) block Cheddar cheese

1 tablespoon Canadian whisky

2 tablespoons maple syrup

1. Combine the cheese, whisky, and syrup in a large freezer bag. Seal the bag and place it in the freezer for 4 hours.

2. Start your smoker and heat it to 85° to 105°F (30° to 40°C); you want to keep the smoke "cold," that is, at a slow smolder, using mostly wood chips.

3. Insert a remote thermometer into the cheese and place it in the smoker. Smoke the cheese until it reaches an internal temperature of 39°F (4°C). The smoked cheese will keep in the fridge for up to 1 month, wrapped tightly in plastic.

TALL TALES, TASTE, AND A FEW THEORIES

Je n'ai jamais un service qui ne finit pas.
(I've never seen a service not end.)

—Nicolas Jongleux, to a *stagiaire* during a particularly hellish night

WHEN YOU'VE BEEN in the restaurant business for more than fifteen years, you begin to develop ideas about the way things work. And after years of these ideas being legitimized, they become theories: how you know when a cook is going to last, why you can't trust people with thin lips, why catering always seems like a nice idea but never is, and so on.

A FEW THEORIES

The following section is a collection of these random theories. It is the equivalent of a thought experiment, like the Éclair Velveeta (page 170) or the Joe Beef Double Down (page 173), one-off items on our menu. The customers who order these dishes are immediately endearing to us, forever noted in the "good" book.

Theory #1
Square plates: Like a man wearing a tuxedo top with shorts, square plates do not work with Joe Beef food. They look heavy in a waiter's hands and are awkward to fit on the table. The food looks unappetizing; it's like eating a culinary version of a Malevich

painting. Even in Paris, you'll go to the oldest of brasseries (so old they've been designated as World Heritage sites), where the toilets are so antiquated they can't be outfitted for the handicapped, and you'll see raw tuna whiz by on a square plate. French food doesn't belong on square plates.

Theory #2
Horseradish: This heady root is the cure for all. People think we serve shaved Parmesan next to our raw oysters, when in fact it's a snowy mound of pungent, freshly grated horseradish. While it's a seemingly small part of the meal, horseradish is a key part of our *mise en place*. A pile on a steak gives your appetite a shiver. We simply peel the thick, phallic root; cut it into chunks; store it in water and a bit of vinegar in the fridge; and then grate it with a fine rasp at the very last minute. Try it in a piping hot broth when you suffer your next cold.

Theory #3
The four seasons of lardons (sliced bacon): We cut our bacon according to the season. There are times of the year when the warm, fatty piece is a big part of the flavor and texture of the dish.

Winter lardons are big, thick, and long. During the dark days of January, when your beach body is a distant memory, toss your sorrows and your potatoes with a handful of large lardons, 1/4 inch (6 mm) thick and

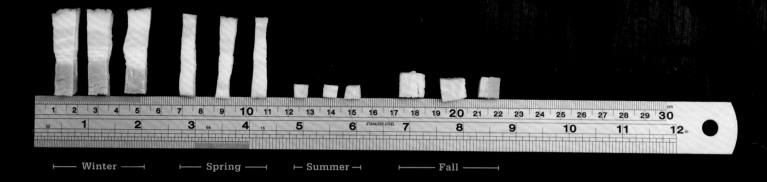

Winter — Spring — Summer — Fall

1 inch (2.5 cm) long, for when your latitude leaves you hanging with cellared roots, far-fetched greens, and melting pork neck. In spring, you're getting tired of bacon but still want to taste slivers in the spaghetti lobster. This is a detox from winter, not quite summer, and the lardons' matchstick figure does justice to snow morels, fiddleheads, or dandelions. In summer, you want just a hint, the tiniest dice, like a square from a matchstick. It seems only logical when you're serving perfect little vegetables and barely touched sea goods, and they don't assault the flavor of great summer libations like the Francois Cotat Sancerre Rosé. And in the fall, we cut thickish (¼-inch/6-mm) cubes, a clue of what's to come. The faint summer lardons would get lost in autumn's mushrooms, game, and roots. Such fare requires the companionship of a more substantial heft.

Theory #4

Greasy vegetables: When you cook vegetables and they look greasy, it's never because you've used too much fat. It's because you didn't use enough water. The "undercover" fat is somehow less repugnant than the blatant, oily fat. When you finish sauce in a pan, or you have a braised dish that seems split or greasy, scoop out a couple tablespoons of the fat and replace it with a few drops of cold water. The sauce will become more satiny, matte, and appetizing.

Theory #5

Hangovers: Whenever someone in our business comes to work saying he or she is in "top shape," he or she is extremely hung over. To alleviate said hangover, nothing beats a glass of ginger juice, a few B vitamins, a bottle of Pedialyte, and some Spam and American processed cheese prepared with three bunches of kale, wilted.

Theory #6

Fancy knives: People have too many knives these days. The classic chef's knife and, on the smaller side, a slicer and a butcher knife, are all you really need. We have a friend who is somehow a traveling salesman of Damascus steel knives. He drops in once in a while to tempt the kitchen staff with his newest imported beauties, promising "you can pay later." It's too tempting for a couple of knife passionistas like Frank and Marco. It's an easy sale, like a herring in a seal tank. That said, our favorite knives are carbon steel from E. Dehillerin, near Les Halles in Paris. They're black beauties: easy to sharpen and you know that Dumaine, Chapel, and Bocuse have cooked with them. Another great brand is Dexter-Russell, with carbon-steel blades and beech handles. They are cheap and dependable, and still made in America.

Theory #7

Customers as friends: When you are a chef, some of your customers become friends. They may ask you to cater (see box above), or you may get invited to parties with people who are different from those in your regular social circle (which is awkward). This gives us a *Pretty Woman*–type vibe. Not in a whorish way, but because most of us are from modest, ordinary backgrounds and suddenly we find ourselves in this blue-blooded patch of life. It's weird and seldom enjoyable, yet we know we were invited with the nicest intentions. Perhaps this is more of an admission than a theory.

Theory #8

Perks: It's always seemed funny to us that a restaurant will go out of its way to offer special treatment to people with millions in the bank, yet the couple who saved for months to eat at the same place on a special occasion is somehow lucky to be there. If we notice a passionate student-type or a couple on a first date eating in one of our restaurants, we will give them the world. They will have the entire menu for thirty bucks. It's our pleasure to give them a complimentary bottle of good wine. Of course, this is not a habit, but we do it once in a while.

Theory #9

Manners: Never wear your hat in an Irish pub.

Theory #10

Not everything is meant to be seen: An animal being slaughtered is not funny or pretty, but it's necessary, and most people who do it, do it with care. We don't have to witness every process in the universe. Waiters run their asses off, but should show up to your table cool, calm, and collected, treating you like you're the only customer. That's service.

Theory #11

Le Creuset cookware: We're not hawking kitchenware here, but if you've gotten this far in the book, you probably realize that having a proper enameled cast-iron pot is crucial. They'll fit a chicken, a shank, a soup, lentils, everything. They stay hot and they stay shut, plus they work on induction plates. We suggest having a few sizes: a braiser, a baking dish, and a few individual stoneware pots (ramekins). Stay with the original brand; you can obtain spare parts and the guarantee is unreal. The other alternatives are more contemporary, not as fluid or elegant. We also like how these pots are steeped in tradition: on their honeymoons, our parents rode sleds down the cobblestone streets in the old cities of Portugal, eating pineapple with Madeira and thinking about the wedding gifts of fondue sets and Le Creuset pots back home.

TASTE

In college, Fred dreamed he was composing a recipe for soup on sheet music, with the chords and scales representing salt and temperature: the soup was the song, the ingredients were the notes. This isn't just a peek into Fred's psyche, but rather a nice way of explaining how taste can be expressed in both the way we enjoy food and the way we create it. It's also a perfect setup for our last theory, which involves taste and the Big Mac.

The Big Mac has everything in the right amounts. The combination is so perfect that the whole becomes better than the parts. There is a great lesson to draw from the deliciousness involved here. You see, not only do you have salt, but you also have fat, then sugar and acid, and then the bite: pepper, chile, or whatever "the edge" is. At the intended serving temperature, it's irresistible and unstoppable. The Big Mac tricks our evolutionary upbringing because your mouth thinks it's great, yet you will not need that energy to labor in the fields, so to speak, for the day to come. Obviously, we're not using the example of a Big Mac for its political or nutritional value. I agree that we all have to eat better, so let's instead use the Big Mac as a model of optimal taste equilibrium. Draw from it to make your lentil soup taste right, your wine jus zingy.

Let's start: There is sweet, salty, fat, bite, and sour. When you add them to a dish to make something

$$T = |s_{ugar}| + |s_{alt}| + |F_{at}| + |B_{ite}| + |a_{cid}|$$

$$T = e_{su} + e_{sa} + e_F + e_B + e_a \ , \ T = \lambda$$

$$T = (e\pm T)_{su} + (e\pm T)_{sa} + (e\pm T)_F + (e\pm T)_B + (e\pm T)_a \ , \ T < \lambda$$

$$V = \frac{\{ |I_{su}| + |I_{sa}| + |I_F| + |I_B| + |I_A| \}}{5}$$

$$V = e \ , \ V = \lambda$$

$$V = e \pm T \ , \ V < \lambda$$

$$-T \qquad e \qquad +T$$

λ = OPTIMAL
T = TASTE   THE BIG MAC EQUILIBRIUM.

taste good, you don't add the same amount of each; instead, you add the same perceived amount, perhaps a pinch of something versus a teaspoon of another. When you season in small amounts, you barely perceive the change until you reach the threshold, at which point the effect becomes clear and the equilibrium becomes crucial. The point at which everything is in holy harmony is the optimal equilibrium. When you alter one of the five constituents, it alters the harmony and automatically triggers a need to increase the four others. So no one element can move independently. The accord remains coherent until the superior threshold, at which point harmony is no longer possible. Note that the movement is unidirectional and irreversible. For example, when I'm cooking lentils, I let them sit in the cooking juice and I start salting the broth. But salt alone will make the broth briny, so I add a couple dashes of vinegar, a pinch of sugar, then a

pinchette of cayenne (if I like it hot) and maybe a bit of butter, or, if the broth is cold, a bit of oil and a bit more of everything. The result is lentils that taste like lentils on steroids.

Anyone who has ever freewheeled a béarnaise or mayonnaise recipe knows what correcting flavor is all about, and that's the basis of the Big Mac Theory. It is an example of a precarious yet optimal equilibrium that exists between all of the taste actors. You can intervene with texture and/or temperature, but that's a whole other game. In France, a few years back, I had *oeufs en meurette*: it was more buttery and salty than I expected, yet because the dish had a healthy dose of vinegar, the whole thing was perfect (and memorable, as drag queens on stilts were handing out flyers in the Marais and looking at my eggs tenaciously as I ate).

The following recipes fit the Big Mac profile in taste, or are a simple, basic element of other dishes. **—FM**

ÉCLAIR VELVEETA

Serves 4

This recipe is a perfect illustration of the Big Mac Theory: It hits everywhere at the same time, it tastes perfect, and it's so rich but you barely notice it. It's a bit weird, a bit trashy, and very tasty. Awesome.

1 onion, thinly sliced

1 tablespoon canola oil

1 tablespoon sherry vinegar

1 tablespoon currants

½ cup (125 g) Velveeta cheese

⅔ cup (150 g) warm mashed potatoes

Salt and pepper

2 tablespoons chopped fresh chives, plus more for garnish

4 thin slices fresh foie gras, each about 3 ounces (85 g)

4 choux pastries for Éclairs (page 266), about 6 inches (15 cm) long

Flake salt

4 slices bacon, cooked crispy

1. In a sauté pan, cook the onion in the oil over low heat for about 5 minutes, or until caramelized. Mix in the vinegar and the currants, remove from the heat, and set aside.

2. In a small saucepan, combine the Velveeta and mashed potatoes and set over low heat. Cook until the cheese is melted, stirring occasionally. Season to taste with salt and pepper and then stir in the chives. Remove from the heat, cover the saucepan with foil, and keep warm on the stove top.

3. Set a sauté pan over medium-high heat and turn on your exhaust fan. Season the foie gras slices on both sides with salt and pepper. When the pan is hot, add the foie gras and sear for 1 minute on each side, until nice and brown. Remember to flip the slices away from you to avoid splashing your belly. Transfer the foie gras to a plate and let rest. Some extra fat will melt off the foie gras. It's pure yellow, it's good, keep it.

4. Cut the top off each pastry lengthwise, about two-thirds from the bottom (so the top is half the thickness of the bottom). Put a tablespoon and a half of the onion mixture in the bottom of each pastry. Divide the mashed potato and cheese mixture into four portions and place on top of the onion. Add a slice of foie gras, a pinch of flake salt, a sprinkle of chives, a slice of bacon, and the pastry tops. Serve warm.

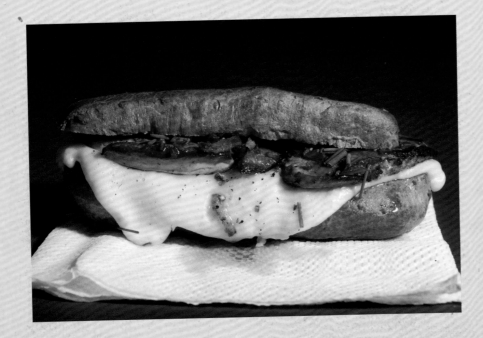

RICOTTA GNOCCHI with RICH and TASTY RED SAUCE

Serves 4

This red sauce is a steroid ingredient that we use to pump up wimpy dishes like gnocchi or in chicken gravy for a quick sauce *chasseur*. Most of our sauces are done this way, baked in a good French enameled cast-iron pot. We're not too fussy about the type of tomatoes we use, just canned and whole; San Marzano will do. If you cannot obtain pig skin from your butcher, then a pig's trotter, halved lengthwise, works, too. You could also add Smoked Baby Back Ribs (page 153) to the sauce before serving it with the gnocchi.

SAUCE
1 square pork skin, about the size of a sheet of printer paper
Salt and pepper
1 sprig rosemary
1 anchovy fillet
1 bay leaf
1 small fresh or dried chile
2 cloves garlic, roughly chopped
1 tablespoon fennel seeds
2 (28-ounce/796-ml) cans plum tomatoes
2 tablespoons olive oil
1 onion, finely diced
8-inch (20-cm) square Parmesan cheese rind (optional)

GNOCCHI
1 whole egg
1 egg yolk
2 cups (455 g) fresh ricotta cheese
1 cup (130 g) all-purpose flour, plus more for rolling and dusting
¼ cup (30 g) grated Parmesan cheese
Grated zest of ½ lemon
¼ teaspoon freshly grated nutmeg
Salt and pepper
8 quarts (8 liters) water
4 big handfuls ice cubes
¼ cup (60 ml) neutral oil

1. To make the sauce, preheat the oven to 350°F (180°C). Place the pork skin fat side up on a plate, and season generously with salt and pepper. Lay the rosemary, anchovy, bay leaf, and chile across the skin. Sprinkle the garlic and fennel seeds over the top. Roll the skin up tightly and tie it around and around with butcher twine, like you would a cheap sleeping bag for a college trip to Camp Lake Crystal. Set aside.

2. Open the cans of tomatoes and crush the tomatoes between your fingers over a large bowl.

3. In a Dutch oven, heat the oil over medium heat and sauté the onion. When it is translucent, after about 5 minutes, add the tomatoes. Nestle the sleeping bag in the tomatoes. Add a tablespoon of salt and the Parmesan rind.

4. Cover the pot and bake for 2 to 2½ hours, or until the skin pierces effortlessly with a fork.

continued

5. In the meantime, to make the gnocchi, whisk together the whole egg and egg yolk in a small bowl. On a vast and clean work surface dusted with flour, drop the ricotta and the flour and mix. Make a well in the ricotta mixture and add the eggs, Parmesan, lemon zest, nutmeg, a teaspoon of salt, and a pinch of pepper to the well. Mix in the sides of the well, first with the tips of your fingers, gathering together all the ingredients, and then with your hands. Cautiously and briefly knead to form a uniform dough. It should be firm but not hard.

6. Press the dough into a rectangle ¾ inch (2 cm) thick and cut into strips 1 inch (2.5 cm) wide. Between flat, floured hands, roll each strip into a serpent. Each serpent should be about ½ inch (12 mm) thick. Cut each serpent into pieces 3 inches (7.5 cm) long and carefully transfer to a floured tray. Refrigerate the gnocchi for 15 minutes so they will firm up and keep their shape.

7. Meanwhile, in a large pot over high heat, salt 6 quarts (6 liters) of the water and bring to a boil. Prepare an ice bath with the remaining 2 quarts (2 liters) water and the ice.

8. Working in batches of 12 gnocchi, gently slide the gnocchi into the boiling water with the help of a spatula. Once they float to the surface, they will need 2 to 3 minutes to cook through. Test one to see if it is ready. With a wire skimmer, transfer the gnocchi to the ice bath and leave for 1 minute. Then transfer them to a tray and oil them lightly.

9. Returning to the sauce, remove the rolled skin and the cheese rind from the oven. Discard the rind. You can snip the twine, unroll the skin, toss away the seasonings, and then dice the skin and serve it with the gnocchi. That's what we do, but we agree that it doesn't look appetizing.

10. Strain the sauce and keep it warm. (If you don't want to use it right away, it will keep for up to 7 days in the refrigerator and even longer in the freezer. You'll notice it becomes slightly gelatinous when you refrigerate it because the skin was cooked in it.)

11. To serve, add 2 tablespoons oil to a sauté pan set over medium-low heat. Add the gnocchi and cook for a minute or two, then carefully flip and cook for another minute or so, until warmed through. Top the gnocchi with the sauce and serve with a few thin slices of parmesan.

JOE BEEF DOUBLE DOWN

Makes 2, serves 4

Dear World,

We're sorry food has come to this. Like Richard Pryor said, more or less, the double down is God's way of telling you that you have too much money. But it's also really delicious.

CRUST

2 cups (260 g) all-purpose flour

1 tablespoon brewer's yeast (optional)

2 teaspoons baking powder

2 teaspoons crushed pepper

2 teaspoons powdered sage

2 teaspoons salt

2 teaspoons Old Bay seasoning

1 teaspoon garlic powder

2 cups (500 ml) buttermilk

MAYONNAISE

2 tablespoons mayonnaise

1 teaspoon Sriracha sauce

½ teaspoon Maggi sauce or marmite

4 slices fresh duck foie gras, each 3 ounces (85 g) and ¾ inch (2 cm) thick

Canola oil for deep-frying

2 slices good-quality Cheddar cheese

4 slices bacon, fried until crisp

2 tablespoons maple syrup

Sea salt and pepper

1. To ready the crust, sift together the flour, brewer's yeast, baking powder, pepper, sage, salt, Old Bay, and garlic powder into a bowl. Keep the buttermilk in the fridge.

2. To make the mayonnaise, in a bowl, mix together the mayonnaise and the Sriracha and Maggi sauces.

Put the sauce in the fridge until serving.

3. Put the foie gras in the freezer 30 minutes before you are ready to cook it.

4. Pour the oil to a depth of 3 inches (7.5 cm) into your deep fryer and heat to 350°F (180°C). To set up the crust assembly, put the bowl holding the flour mixture on your countertop. Pour the buttermilk into a second bowl and put it alongside the flour mixture.

5. To coat the foie gras slices, one at a time, dip them into the buttermilk and then into the flour mixture. Repeat the dips a couple more times. Keep the coating soggy—you don't want it too dry—and resist the urge to pat the slices.

6. Drop 2 coated foie gras slices into the hot oil and cook for exactly 3 minutes and 20 seconds. Drain briefly on paper towels and pat them dry. Repeat with the remaining 2 slices.

7. Lay a slice of cheese on 1 "patty," place 2 slices of bacon on top of the cheese, and spread half of the mayo on top. Top with a second patty, then plate. Repeat to a build second stack. Top each stack with a drizzle of maple syrup and a pinch each of crispy sea salt and pepper.

CHICKEN SKIN JUS

Makes about 2 cups (500 ml)

Our favorite sauce is made from chicken skin. It is a delicious gravy that we use for a lot of dishes at Joe Beef—more than we would like to admit. It's like an extraction of the deliciousness of crispy chicken skin. Ask your butcher for the chicken skin. More skinless chickens are sold out there than skin-on birds, so the skins must be somewhere other than at a schmaltz factory. Serve this on its own or as a sauce on guinea hens or other poultry.

2 pounds (900 g) chicken skins
1 carrot, peeled and cut into chunks
1 celery stalk, cut into chunks
1 onion, cut into chunks
1 sprig rosemary
1 clove garlic
Pinch of salt
2 bay leaves
4¼ cups (about 1 liter) water
2 cups (500 ml) dry white wine

1. Preheat the oven to 375°F (190°C). In a large enameled cast-iron pot, combine the chicken skins, carrot, celery, onion, rosemary, garlic, salt, bay leaves, and ¼ cup (60 ml) of the water. Place in the oven and cook, uncovered, for 2 hours, stirring and flipping the chicken skins occasionally.

2. After the 2 hours, the skins should look like the skin of a roasted chicken. Drain off the fat and add the remaining water and the wine to the pot. Return the pot to the oven, lower the temperature to 300°F (150°C), and cook for 1 hour.

3. Remove from the oven, strain, and serve right away or cool and refrigerate for later use. It will keep in the fridge for up to a week, or a month in the freezer.

THE ART OF LIVING ACCORDING TO JOE BEEF

CHICKEN SKIN TACOS

Makes 8 tacos

We made this dish because we like the "potato" de gallo idea. (In fact, you can make only the rub and eat it on almost anything, especially eggs.) Make certain that the potatoes are tiny and crisp, so you get that salt-and-vinegar potato chip taste.

About 1½ pounds (680 g) chicken skins
2 tablespoons canola oil
Salt and pepper

RUB
2 teaspoons salt
2 teaspoons sugar
1 teaspoon pepper
1 teaspoon red chile powder
1 teaspoon ground cumin
1 teaspoon ground coriander
1 teaspoon achiote powder (optional)

POTATO DE GALLO
1 cup (140 g) minutely diced peeled potato
¼ cup (60 ml) canola oil
⅓ red onion, very finely diced
1 jalapeño chile, seeded and diced superfine
1 tablespoon Mayonnaise (recipe follows)
¼ cup (10 g) chopped fresh cilantro
3 tablespoons fresh lime juice
Salt

8 small corn tortillas, warmed
8 hard-boiled quail egg yolks (optional)
8 sprigs coriander

1. Preheat the oven to 425°F (220°C). Cut the skins into 4 or 5 pieces, each roughly 1 inch (2.5 cm) square. With your hands, combine the skin pieces and canola oil in a roasting pan and season with a pinch each of salt and pepper.

2. Roast the skins for 1 hour, stirring and tossing them every 15 minutes with your trusty tongs.

3. While the skins are roasting, make the rub. In a small bowl, stir together the salt, sugar, pepper, chile powder, cumin, coriander, and achiote powder.

4. When the skins are ready, they should be crispy, golden, and delicious looking. Remove from the oven, drain, and pat dry with paper towels. Chop finely while still lukewarm, and season to taste with the rub. Keep warm. (The remaining rub will keep well in a tightly capped jar in a cool, dry cupboard.)

5. Just before the skins are ready, make the potato de gallo. In a non-stick frying pan, fry the potato in the oil for about 6 minutes, or until they have a French-fry color and are crispy. Transfer to paper towels and pat dry. Just before you are going to serve the tacos, combine the potato, onion, chile, mayonnaise, coriander, and lime juice and season with salt. Don't mix the ingredients any sooner; it is important that the "salsa" tastes fresh.

6. Now, build each taco: warm tortilla, some skin, some spud, a yolk (as dressing), and a coriander sprig.

MAYONNAISE

Makes about 1 cup (250 ml)

A classic mayo.

1 egg yolk
1 tablespoon Dijon mustard
1 cup (250 ml) canola oil
Salt and pepper
Juice from ½ lemon
Purée de Fines Herbes (page 176), optional

1. In a large bowl, whisk together the egg yolk and mustard. Pour in the oil in a steady, fine, slow stream and whisk, whisk, whisk. Always have a glass of water nearby in case the mayonnaise starts splitting and you need to thicken and mend. Season with salt, pepper, and lemon juice to taste. Mix in some of the puréed herbs if you want to add a bit of flavor.

2. Use right away, or cover and refrigerate for up to 2 days.

PURÉE DE FINES HERBES

Makes 2 cups (500 ml)

This is part of our *mise en place* at the restaurant. We mix it with mayonnaise (page 175), serve it straight up with potatoes or fish, or use it to punch up sauces, soups, stews, or anything raw like tartare. Do not use woodsy herbs like rosemary, thyme, or sage in this purée, and be sure to wash all of your herbs well.

1 bunch chervil
1 bunch chives
1 bunch flat-leaf parsley
1 bunch tarragon
1 bunch watercress, blanched and
    chilled in an ice bath
Squeeze of fresh lemon juice
2 teaspoons neutral oil
½ cup (125 ml) water
Pinch of salt

1. In a food processor, combine the herbs, watercress, lemon juice, oil, and water and process until smooth. Season with the salt.

2. Store in a tightly sealed container for up to a week.

MUSTARD

Makes about 2½ cups (625 ml)

Most Dijon mustard that is shipped to North America from France is made with seeds from Saskatchewan, Canada. Hence, it makes sense that we make our own mustard. Feel free to experiment with the types of vinegar and flavorings (tarragon, horseradish, dill).

½ cup (90 g) mustard seeds
5 tablespoons (75 ml) water
2 tablespoons maple syrup
Scant 2 tablespoons neutral oil
1¼ cups (300 ml) white wine vinegar
1 tablespoon ground turmeric
Pinch of cayenne pepper
1 teaspoon salt

1. In a powerful food processor, combine the mustard seeds, water, maple syrup, oil, one-third of the vinegar, the turmeric, the cayenne, and the salt and process on high speed. (If it is not powerful, you will end up with more whole seeds, which is okay but not ideal.) Once you start, the seeds will bounce around like money in a money cage.

2. When the seeds stop bouncing around, slowly add the rest of the vinegar. When the blade stops spinning well and the mustard is thick, it's ready. Transfer to a tightly capped jar and store in the fridge for up to a month.

BBQ SAUCE

Makes about 2 cups (500 ml)

This is our infamous rib sauce.

One 8-ounce (237-ml) bottle Coca-Cola
1 cup (250 ml) ketchup
¼ cup (60 ml) cider vinegar
2 tablespoons molasses
1 tablespoon Sriracha sauce
1 teaspoon instant coffee crystals
Salt and pepper

In a saucepan, stir together the Coca-Cola, ketchup, vinegar, molasses, Sriracha, and coffee. Season liberally with salt and pepper, place over low heat, and cook for 30 minutes. The sauce will keep for up to 2 weeks in a tightly sealed container in the fridge.

AN EASY HOLLANDAISE

Makes ½ cup (180 g)

We use this for our Scallops with Pulled Pork (page 30) recipe.

7 egg yolks, at room temperature
1 cup (225 g) unsalted butter
Pinch of cayenne pepper
Salt
1 tablespoon fresh lemon juice

1. Put the egg yolks into a 1-quart (1-liter) pitcher large enough to contain the head of your hand blender.

2. In a small saucepan, melt the butter over low heat and bring to exactly 245°F (119°C), then remove from the heat.

3. As you start blending with the hand blender, carefully but steadily pour the hot butter into the egg yolks, and keep mixing. You should obtain a smooth emulsion.

4. Season with the cayenne and salt, then mix in the lemon juice. Keep at room temperature until serving.

SOUR CRUDITÉS

Makes about 3 cups (600 g)

This is a staple in pretty much every professional kitchen, and with this easy method, it could be in yours, too. We like to eat the crudités with our Zesty Italian Tartare (page 245).

½ cup (70 g) chopped celery
½ cup (55 g) matchstick-cut carrot
½ cup (55 g) chopped cauliflower florets (try to maintain tiny shape)
¼ cup (30 g) sliced red onion
¼ cup (55 g) kosher salt
½ cup (125 ml) red wine vinegar
½ cup (125 ml) water
½ clove garlic
1 Thai bird chile

1. Combine the celery, carrot, cauliflower, and onion in a colander. Add the salt and massage into the vegetables. Let stand for 5 minutes, then rinse and place in a bowl.

2. In a small saucepan, combine the vinegar, water, garlic, and chile and bring to a boil. Immediately remove from the heat and pour over the vegetables.

3. Cover the bowl and refrigerate right away for a minimum of 1 hour—or as long as you can wait.

TRUFFLED EGGS with EVERYTHING BISCUITS and WATERCRESS

Serves 4

It's true, at least for Fred, that an egg cooked in meat is the best. So much so that when we make *braciole*, he's known to dig like a gopher to reach the eggs inside, leaving a hollow meat box to crumble on itself. The following is a short recipe where the egg gets that *viande* taste that Fred loves.

6 *oeufs mollets* (in case you break a couple) from the recipe for Oeufs en Gelée (page 57)

SAUCE
2 teaspoons chopped French shallot
1 tablespoon plus 1 teaspoon unsalted butter
1 cup (250 ml) Chicken Skin Jus (page 174)
Salt and pepper

4 Everything Biscuits (recipe follows), warmed and buttered
Truffles, the amount to your liking
1 bunch fresh watercress, tough stems removed
Aged Cheddar cheese for shaving

1. To make the sauce, in a small saucepan, sweat the shallot in 1 tablespoon of the butter over medium-low heat until tender. Add the jus and the remaining 1 teaspoon butter, bring to a simmer, and season with salt and pepper.

2. Carefully put the eggs in the simmering sauce and cook for 2 to 3 minutes. Gently poke the eggs to make sure they are not hard. They are ready when they are coated in the sauce, are still soft, and are warm to the touch.

3. Put a biscuit on each plate. With a spoon or your fingers, create a little depression in the middle of each biscuit. Carefully spoon an egg into each depression. Divide the sauce evenly among the plates and then shave some truffles over the eggs.

4. Put the pan back over medium-low heat, add the watercress, and leave it for just a few seconds so it loses its cold from the fridge. The tops of the sprigs will wilt slightly.

5. Top each serving with a few shavings of the cheese and serve right away with the watercress on the side.

> *"There's nothing better than* un oeuf cuit dans la viande.*"*
>
> —Frédéric Morin

EVERYTHING BISCUITS

Make 12 biscuits

½ cup (110 g) rendered bacon fat,
  at room temperature plus more
  for greasing baking sheet

2 cups (240 g) sifted all-purpose flour,
  plus more for dusting

1 tablespoon baking powder

1 tablespoon sugar

1 tablespoon salt

1½ cups (375 ml) buttermilk

3 tablespoons whipping cream
  (35 percent butterfat)

1 tablespoon sea salt

1 tablespoon dried onion flakes

1 tablespoon poppy seeds

1 tablespoon sesame seeds

1. Preheat the oven to 375°F (190°C). Grease a rimmed baking sheet.

2. In a large bowl, stir together the flour, baking powder, sugar, salt, buttermilk, and bacon fat. The mixture should come together in a thick, sandy dough.

3. On a floured work surface, flatten the dough to get an even thickness. It should be about 8 by 11 inches (25 by 28 cm) and about 1 inch (2.5 cm) thick. Dust with flour if sticky.

4. Using a wineglass or a biscuit cutter 3 inches (7.5 cm) in diameter, dip the rim in flour and cut out the biscuits. Place on the prepared baking sheet. Gather the scraps, pat flat again, and cut out more biscuits, or form them by hand.

5. Brush the tops of the biscuits with the cream, then sprinkle evenly with the sea salt, onion flakes, poppy seeds, and sesame seeds. Bake for 12 minutes, or until the tops are golden.

PURÉE DE POMMES DE TERRE

Serves 4

David has an Irish friend called Jerry O'Regan who always triple checks whether or not his main course is served with mashed potatoes. In fact, Jerry doesn't understand why all food isn't served with potatoes. Sometimes we send him a side of lentils instead of potatoes and he looks at it as if it were alien food. We don't want to make an "Irish guy potato" stereotype here, but after cooking for Jerry for ten years, we get it. At the end of the meal, Jerry doesn't say thank you, he says "Feels good to have some potatoes, hey Davey?".

2 pounds (900 g) fingerling potatoes, unpeeled
Salt and pepper
½ cup (125 ml) milk
½ cup (110 g) cold unsalted butter, diced, plus more if needed

1. Place the potatoes in a saucepan. Add water to cover by 1 inch (2.5 cm) and 1 tablespoon salt, and bring to a boil over high heat. Lower the heat to medium and cook for 15 to 20 minutes, or until you can press against the potatoes with a spoon and feel them crush.

2. Just before the potatoes are ready, in a small saucepan, bring the milk to a boil and remove from the heat. Drain the potatoes and pass them through a potato ricer into a large bowl. Add the butter and half of the milk. Using a wooden spoon, incorporate gently until silky. Add the rest of the milk and more butter if you deem necessary. Rectify the seasoning.

3. Serve immediately as is, or push through the ricer again (if you're going for that look) straight onto the serving plates.

POLENTA

Serves 4

A note on ricers: For a young boy, a potato ricer is akin to magic. It's more impressive than planes or satellites; it's up there with fire trucks, guns, and large breasts. We use ricers a lot at Joe Beef—for potatoes, Madeira jelly for foie gras, fruit preserves, and polenta.

One day, a hungover vegetable cook produced a plate of clumpy, amateur polenta. It was on the menu, so we couldn't send out carrots and apologies. Instead, we just pressed it through the ricer. It came out freaking perfect, the clumps gone and the polenta shaped like rice, slowly falling in the butter. There we were, four grown-ups, as fascinated as ever with the potato ricer.

The general rule for polenta is four parts water to one part cornmeal.

2 cups (500 ml) water
Salt and pepper
½ cup (110 g) cornmeal
¼ cup (55 g) unsalted butter
½ cup (55 g) grated Parmesan cheese
2 bay leaves
1 clove garlic, smashed

1. Bring the water to a boil over high heat and add a pinch of salt. Take the pot off the burner and whisk in the cornmeal in an even stream. Put the pot back on the burner, reduce the heat to medium-low, and cook, stirring occasionally with a wooden spoon, for about 30 minutes, or until the mixture pulls away from the sides of the pan and no longer tastes grainy. You would rather overcook polenta than undercook it.

2. Mix in 2 tablespoons of the butter and half of the Parmesan, correct the seasoning with salt, and pass the polenta through a ricer. Then cover with plastic wrap to keep it warm, and set aside.

3. In a small pan, melt the remaining butter, a turn of pepper, the bay leaves, and the garlic over high heat. Cook for 2 to 3 minutes, or until the butter bubbles and smells delicious.

4. Remove the butter from the heat and drizzle it along with the bay leaves and garlic over the polenta. Sprinkle with the remaining Parmesan and serve right away.

The only time I ever skipped school was to tend my garden. And I must have been really ashamed of my hobby because the excuse I gave was that I had eaten rye (enabling my gluten issue) and had gas. Gardening has a lot of memory and meaning for many Joe Beefers, too. If you have ever been to our backyard, you know that we're keeping a garden for reasons other than production. While we try to wring as much produce as we can from our one thousand square feet (ninety-three square meters), we garden more for the joy and enlightenment than anything else.

CHAPTER 6
BUILDING A GARDEN IN A CRACK DEN

Ours is not an environmental statement, either. We can't offer anything new on that front; for that purpose, there is Chez Panisse or River Café. Our prime motivation at the beginning was to replace the pop cans, plastic bags, and cigarette butts that littered our yard with tomatoes, kale, and turnips.

Obviously, when we took over the space, there was no garden. There was barely a backyard. And although we wanted to begin planting right away, we had other problems to deal with first, like getting alcohol licenses and keeping the same dishwasher for more than a few days. And so our garden didn't become a reality until a bunch of old Italian contractors who were making sidewalks on our street dumped a pile of dirt in our backyard. In that dirt, we planted two rows of tomatoes. Winter came, and the following summer we decided to build raised beds. From there, we were hooked, and our garden grew rapidly.

This is not a chapter on failproof gardening. It's just a story about how we turned a junkyard into a space that's ever changing and truly alive.

The Joe Beef garden is located in growth zone 5a—we're not arctic tundra, but we're sure not Virginia, either—on the plant hardiness chart developed by Natural Resources Canada (www.nrcan.gc.ca). It's a standard by which you measure what plants, flowers, and shrubs can survive in your zone. The Web site is a great resource (and time waster) for gardening nerds like us: if you want to know if radishes can grow in Kuujuaq, or kale will bloom in Sept-Îles, this is where you find the answer.

In Quebec, growing and caring for tomato plants year-round is a feat, compared to gardening in, say, California. Our growing season is short, so you have to know what plants can handle subzero temperatures. A great book on growing in climates similar to Quebec is Harrowsmith's *Northern Gardener*, which we routinely use as a reference. Our garden is both northern and urban: it's situated between three brick walls (one side of Joe Beef, the back of McKiernan, and the shop beside us) and opens onto a back alley facing a baseball field in the summer and an ice rink in the winter. We would have loved to have

a garden behind Liverpool House, but the backyard is very open, noisy, and vulnerable to the alley, and it's quite a bit smaller than the Joe Beef backyard. We would simply be gardening for our own enjoyment and creating a place for the staff to enjoy before and after service (but they have the Burgundy Lion Bar across the street for that). What follows is a month-by-month description of what the garden produces.

THE JOE BEEF GARDEN CALENDAR YEAR

January: We usually have our seed catalogs by this time. I order from two main sources, Johnny's Seeds in the United States and Stokes Seeds in Ontario. I also get lots of seeds on the spur of the moment from the outpost of Birri et Frères at Jean-Talon Market and at Pépinière Jasmin garden center. I tend to order way too many seeds, a practice of mine that, according to my wife, is also common at restaurants, markets, and bars. I don't start my own peppers, cabbages, or tomatoes, but if you wish to, January is the time to start.

When my seeds arrive in the mail, I open the packages and lay the seeds on my dining room table just to look at them. As I start to envision the garden, I'm paralyzed by all the choices, a feeling I've experienced before in the aisles at Toys "R" Us and when I've tried to DJ at a party. I usually make several drawings of

the ultimate garden, a painful stage that is full of what ifs and what happens if my partners don't like it. I pay attention to these cautionary voices as, left to my own devices, I could end up living in a tent trailer behind Joe Beef, wearing lederhosen and calling myself Helmut.

I love the idea of heirloom vegetables; they look great and taste even better. But recently, they have taken over. An heirloom is an ancient, stable, nonhybrid variety; in fact, an heirloom is the opposite of a hybrid. Bruno Birri, one of the brothers of Birri et Frères, said to me once, "The opposite of hybrid is inbred." Most of the foodie customers like their ingredients to be artisanal and homemade, however, and heirloom vegetables are part of that picture.

Once I determine what will go where, I wait for the snow to melt. Then I plan a train trip (see page 86). And then I wait for the snow to melt some more.

February: By this time, we have already started a legal grow-op in the Joe Beef basement. Two 400-watt metal halide lamps and an ebb-and-flow table permit me to start growing most of my lettuce and herb seedlings, as well as maintain a weekly crop of peppergrass (Cressida variety) and radish leaves (Cherry Belle variety). I start the seedlings in Jiffy-7 compressed peat pellets. They are clean to work with (in our context, this is crucial); you simply soak them in water and they expand into a netted mass of rich soil that you can plant directly.

Montreal residents pretty much agree that February is the worst month of the year. The snow in front of Joe Beef is cleared on both sides of the street at once, so it is cast to the side like giant waves. Often you can only see the roofs of the cars passing by. Our alley remains mostly uncleared, and our valiant team of cooks and waiters rolls garbage bins over ice caps to get to the garbage trucks.

We're telling you this because it's the thought of harvesting radishes in the balmy days of June that gets us through a month of the mercury stuck at −4°F (−20°C). Quebec is a land of extremes, and we have to plan for both extremes. That means we need a powerful air-conditioner to make the sweltering days of August bearable, and a megafurnace for January through March.

March: This month at Joe Beef, the ever-willing Frank (François Côté) has most likely shoveled the snow off the patio and thought of a novel way to clear the garden beds. March is the start of the worst time of year for food: nothing grows, the East Coast oysters are thin and smelly, and New Jersey has nothing in the fields. It seems like all there is to cook is mushrooms and hare: delicious but very brown. We adhere to the ideology of eating locally as much as possible. But if you want to truly stick to local eating throughout the winter,

anyone north of Seattle has to swear allegiance to the potato and learn to deal with scurvy.

By this point in the year, I have transformed both my house and the restaurant's basement into high-yield seedling farms. Covered plastic trays are filled with various lettuces in the process of germinating. I find that when you buy seeds from a reputable source, you only need to sow two or three seeds, then you can pick out the runts and keep the most vigorous seedlings. Within a

week or ten days of sowing, you can have uniform germination for pretty much all of the leafy stuff. Only do long-germinating seeds like chervil, parsley, and sweet cicely take up to a month. I plant lots of nasturtiums, too. We use the leaves, seeds, and flowers, and they grow fast, even under artificial lights, which is good for the green ego.

In Quebec, we are blessed with an "interesting" (a diplomatic descriptor) system of government control on alcohol sales that is a holdover from La Grande Noirceur— "The Great Darkness"—a period (the late 1930s, then from 1944 through the late 1950s) in Quebec politics when conservative policies ruled. The government applies a little stamp on each bottle of alcohol that deems it government controlled, government approved. Then, once a year, the officers come by to make sure every bottle has that little

stamp. Luckily, the officers in charge are usually very nice and chatty (wolves in sheep's clothing).

One year, just after I had installed my grow lights, the government officers dropped in for their annual visit. Intrigued by the glow from the basement, they asked to see what was happening down there. The look on their faces was pure horror until they realized I was growing lettuce. (That still doesn't beat the time that they thought they spotted a hashish brick wrapped in plastic, which turned out to be a nice fruity Manjari chocolate slab from Valrhona.)

April: If we're lucky, we get to start working the outside raised beds soon after Easter. Raised beds offer better drainage than in-ground gardens, and there is less risk of the soil becoming compacted, which deters growth. I religiously do an annual

soil test to check the pH level and assess the balance of the main elements, nitrogen, phosphate, and potassium. Our soil is often on the acidic side due to our compost pile and the tree leaves that fall every year. I correct the pH as necessary with gypsum to alkalinize the soil. I order a good load of horse manure to top the bed (never more than 10 percent), and use seaweed, blood, and bonemeal for fertilizer. I also use a little soluble fertilizer in the smaller containers, but no herbicides or pesticides, so the garden is organic. The last year we sowed and planted lettuce along a line that spread across five containers. It worked well and gave a soothing sense of togetherness: the compact garden we had imagined.

This is the month we plant peas, spinach, and radishes, unless there is still snow on the ground. If a heavy frost threatens, we finely mist our plants overnight. It is a simple procedure, but it is usually enough to prevent terrible damage.

It's a bit more fun to cook, but we're not quite there. We are still using vegetables purchased from Andy Boy or cellared Jerusalem artichokes; we have not yet started our true growing part of the season. This is when Montrealers start to crave hot weather. If it's above 60°F (15°C), people rapidly cram onto terraces to drink cheap-ass sangria. Then a week later, you slip on the icy sidewalk on your way to Gibbys or Moishes deli.

THE ART OF LIVING ACCORDING TO JOE BEEF

The hairy month of **May:** By now we have rows of young lettuces, herbs, and radishes. The soil looks fresh and clean, like a toddler after his wet hair is combed. We plant our cabbage seedlings at this time; we don't start them ourselves, because the guys at Birri et Frères do it better.

We also plant Swiss chard now, the easiest plant to grow and the hardest one to sell, unless you cook it in cream with bacon and Cheddar. Served al dente, Swiss chard tastes a bit like licking the cellar floor in my east European cottage dreams. I once read in an old French book that the best way to prepare Swiss chard is to blanch it for two minutes, chill it, chop it, season it with a good sherry vinegar, and then throw it in the garbage. (Nowadays, I eat it every week, largely overcooked, drained, and quickly dressed in olive oil with garlic and lemon.)

We leave the more delicate plant seedlings like peppers, tomatoes, and eggplants outside at night until the end of May, when we will transplant them. It's still too early to plant basil and cukes. Now is when I begin to appreciate my smartphone as a quick source for frost alerts and gardener-farmer forecasts.

June: This month, we cut lettuce at a rate that would make the crew at Andy Boy ashamed. Some days we have to make lettuce soup (*potage Choisy*) to use it all, but it's never

a big hit in the dining room. Think about it: salad soup.

We clear the seedlings for beets, turnips, and radishes, meaning that we need to make room for the fast-growing tomatoes and prepare for another batch of lettuce seedlings.

We recently harvested green bunching onions for the first time, which was nice.

I spray soapy water everywhere to get rid of the aphids that seem to fall from the sky. If it's a cool and humid year, I plant most crops

COMFREY TEA

COMFREY (*Symphytum officinale*) is a treasure trove of goodness for the organic garden. We make this easy "tea" to give a little boost midseason. You need to have planted comfrey or have access to lots of leaves. Fill a 5-gallon (20-liter) bucket with leaves. When they rot and decrease in volume, cover them with a board and top off the bucket with more leaves and let them rot. When you have half a bucket of rotten leaves, mix them together well. Take that slurry, mix it with three parts water, and use the mixture in your watering regimen, a little on the leaves, a little on the ground.

farther apart to prevent fungal diseases. I pour a bit of comfrey tea (an old recipe; see page 187) here and there to nourish the soil, and water religiously. The plants' roots will go where the water is, so you want to water well less often, rather than watering a little bit more often.

The half month of **July:** We are closed for two weeks twice a year, so this is only a half month for us—from the beginning we chose not to run a tyrannical restaurant with tyrannical hours. While Allison and I are traveling like the Griswolds to beautiful Peachland, British Columbia, we have former Joe Beefer Krissy Longtin water and weed the garden. Krissy does a great job keeping the garden nice and productive.

In July, radishes and upland cress taste like muriatic acid; they burn but make a nice pickle. Tomatoes start to give an odd fruit here

and there. And although I planted my Kentucky Wonder pole beans a bit late in 2010, once they started, they went nuts.

With July temperatures soaring above 113°F (45°C), tons of strawberries and corn are filling the market, people are skinny again (after six months of hibernating), and the cooks are mad. Sitting in the garden behind Joe Beef at night facing the "field of cream"—fat people playing slow-pitch softball—we smoke Cuban petit cigars (because we can) and dip into a vat of Campari: that's the essence of summer here.

August: This is a giant crops month. Tomatoes and peppers are no longer elusive, and there is a friendly customer who brings me his "biggest zucchini ever" each week. (Giant vegetables are the reason every household with a garden should have a house pig.) Now is when we do great

big aioli with *bagna càuda*: what a good way to use every little fancy vegetable that you planted. Raw, cooked, and some pickled—this dish is healthy until you hit it with what is basically a quart of mayo.

August is the hottest month of the year and is followed by the *avant gout* (buffet of seasons) of fall. If you watch carefully, some greens will start to turn red, which is why you let radicchio grow through the cold fall night before you harvest it.

The cooks are happy because they've had two weeks off, during which they reenacted in their own ways the festival of Woodstock and have returned to work with bags under their eyes the size of Hubbard squashes (gratuitous heirloom mention). And we're all happy because the food doesn't come from Holland, South Africa, or California, and because "greens" means more than rapini, and there are two more months of the bounty.

September: It's unanimous among the cooks I know that September is the best month in the garden. It takes on yellow hues and the tomato leaves shrivel. The rain falls cold but the sun still warms. We are done planting by now; it is crop time here, and at nearby Atwater market, field tomatoes and peppers are fifteen dollars a bushel. I wish I had a bigger love and less fear of canning. Freezing is not bad; if you freeze whole tomatoes, you have pulp by the time they thaw.

Last year we harvested carrots: very sweet Boule and Touchon carrots, varieties appreciated in France. We forgot that we had climbing beans, so we harvested the dried legumes and made a killer soup with smoked pig shoulder. The chard gets sweeter as the nighttime temperature drops. We also planted Bionda di Lyon, a great chard variety with a thin green stem. It tastes less like "vintage tent stored wet" than other varieties.

Tons of apples are coming in. Not long ago, I bought a health-nut juicer and now juice a half case of apples every day. A glass of fresh apple juice with Canadian rye and crushed celery leaves puts homemade bitters to rest—clean, crisp, and simple. I love the juicer; it gives the bar that seasonal thing.

I also made wine at home like every Italian household in Montreal. I started with a lot of good intentions and clean hands, but it's up to Mother Nature to reward you or beat the crap out of your ego with vinegar. In my case, 35 gallons (134 liters) of vinegar.

October: The rain is colder, but the sun ain't warmer. The garden provides pumpkins, squashes, and the best apples. Ziggy, the German painter, delivers bolete and chanterelle mushrooms on his bicycle. (If you hunt for birds, October is good for ducks, pheasants, partridges, and woodcocks. I don't hunt, but our

friend Elvio Galasso does; that's all he talks about.)

Some kale and Brussels sprouts are still holding on in the garden. If you have kids, plant Brussels sprouts. The sprouts form in the armpits of the bigger leaves, which make the plants look like palm trees with a trunk full of gremlins.

Cabbages don't fear the snow, and leeks will grow even in winter under snow. If you harvest them early (before they bear a flower), they are really sweet.

Krissy is now ripping the garden apart. We might turn in some unfinished compost in a few beds, but the freeze and thaw will finish the job.

November: After realizing that pumpkin pie is, in fact, squash pie, you let the remains of your jack-o'-lantern decompose on your porch.

We harvest all that's left in the garden, and enjoy the temporary peace between the inferno of summer and the dark and slushy days of winter.

December: We close for the last ten days of the month, so you will find me mumbling again about spending two weeks with the in-laws (I love them, but I didn't invent the age-old dissensions between in-laws). The garden is dead, the greenhouse is dead, and the only things that remain are the trusted old hibiscus that survives every year in a dark corner and one or two cabbage plants.

The following recipes can be found on the menu sometime between May and October. —**FM**

PARC VINET SALAD

Makes 1 large salad

This is only a Parc Vinet salad when the garden is lit with the flood-lights of the Parc Vinet ballpark directly behind all three restaurants and we're harvesting enough greens to fill a bowl. Although this light salad seems a bit un–Joe Beef, it is in fact the best partner to a browned-out meal of wine reductions, marrow, and other consorts. We use whatever herbs and greens we have to make it, and this is what you should do, too. Let's say 40 percent bitter greens, 40 percent sweet greens, and the rest in *fines herbes*. Just don't go and put in rosemary. If it's got woodsy stems, keep it out of the bowl. And do not use commercial salad mix. That's not the point of this salad.

1. Regardless of the amount of greens you have—let's say the cutting-edge foodie in you bought frisée, oak leaf lettuce, small green radicchio, Boston lettuce, watercress, chervil, and nasturtium flowers, and you have chives, mint, and flat-leaf parsley in your garden—gently wash them in cold water. Then gather a few leaves at a time in a clean cloth and spin like a biblical sling (rapidly, like in David and Goliath). Keep the greens in a freezer bag in the fridge. Tear the big leaves right before serving, and then add the fresh herbs and flowers to them. Nowadays, food is often presented in rather rustic ways, which is fine, except when pieces are bigger than your mouth and you and your cute date end up looking like ruminants. (Easy, we haven't called anyone a cow yet!) That's why you need to *adapt* the big leaves.

2. We dress the salad lightly and evenly with our Apple Vinny (page 196). If you bite into the salad and dressing squeezes out between your teeth, that's gross, and it means you have used way too much dressing.

3. We also finish the salad with a handful of toasted pumpkin seeds, which are easy to make. Here is how to toast a big batch for finishing off quite a few salads: Preheat the oven to 400°F (200°C). In a bowl, toss together 2 cups (130 g) raw pumpkin seeds, 2 tablespoons canola oil, and 1 tablespoon sea salt, coating evenly. Spread the seeds out evenly on a rimmed baking sheet and toast in the oven for about 10 minutes. They can burn quickly, so keep a close eye. That means a timer and a rubber band on your thumb! When they smell good and are popped up and light brown, transfer them quickly to a wide bowl. Let cool before using.

THE ART OF LIVING ACCORDING TO JOE BEEF

PICKLED RHUBARB

Makes 1 quart (1 liter)

If you want long sticks of rhubarb, peel the rhubarb first. If you want ½-inch (12-mm) chunks, don't bother peeling it. This is pickle in a small amount, so don't bother canning it, either. But do keep it in a proper (sparkling clean, tight cap) container in the fridge, where it will keep for up to a month. We serve this pickle with charcuterie and cheeses.

4 cups (570 g) chopped rhubarb (½-inch/12-mm pieces)
1 teaspoon salt
2 cups (500 ml) distilled white vinegar
1 cup (250 ml) water
1 cup (200 g) sugar
1 tablespoon mustard seeds
2 sprigs tarragon

1. In a bowl, mix together the rhubarb and salt, coating the rhubarb evenly. Let stand for 20 minutes, then drain quickly and return to the bowl.

2. In a small pot, combine the vinegar, water, sugar, mustard seeds, and tarragon and bring to a boil, stirring to dissolve the sugar. Remove from the heat and immediately pour over the rhubarb.

3. Let cool completely, then cover tightly and refrigerate. Serve the pickle after a few days in the fridge.

SALADE D'ENDIVE

Serves 4

Back in the day, when there was Sally Wong, when there was yellow pepper, and when there was tuna, David was doing endive salad and roast chicken. Although nonrevolutionary, this salad is always delicious. It's on the menu often, especially in the winter when the garden is under a snowbank and the Parc Vinet Salad (opposite page) is a distant memory. Use Stilton in this salad; it works much better than other blues.

About 36 walnut halves
2 tablespoons canola oil
1 tablespoon salt
4 heads Belgian endive, white and plump
2 hard green apples, cored and cut into matchsticks
8 ounces (225 g) Stilton cheese
¼ cup (10 g) chopped fresh chives
Apple Vinny (page 196)
Pepper

1. Preheat the oven to 400°F (200°C). In a bowl, toss the walnuts with the oil and salt. Spread the walnuts in a single layer on a rimmed baking sheet, place in the oven, and toast for about 15 minutes, or until they take on color. Let cool.

2. Separate the endive leaves and divide them among 4 plates. You can place them casually or stack them like a game of Jenga. Next, add a handful of the matchstick-cut apples to each salad, followed by a handful of the walnuts. Crumble the Stilton and sprinkle it on top. Finally, add the chives, some dressing, and a twist of pepper.

BAGNA CÀUDA and AIOLI

Serves 4 to 6

The best image we have of *bagna càuda* is in the Time-Life Book, *Cooking of Italy*: a few stocky men and their elegant wives, towels around their necks, are sitting solemnly around a table in a brick vault. You would think they are about to eat ortolans or monkey brains, but no, they are enjoying long sticks of celery dipped in a warm butter-oil-anchovy bath. It's a strange image, and we were inexplicably inspired by it. *Bagna càuda* is peasant yet elegant—the essence of Italian food. We love the flavor and the process of trimming the vegetables, and we (bittersweetly) think most people like *bagna càuda* because it tastes like Caesar salad. We serve our *bagna càuda* with a dip or aioli and have provided both options below.

VEGETABLE SUGGESTIONS

Small crisp cucumbers, quartered crosswise and halved

Small carrots, peeled and quartered lengthwise

Celery hearts, split lengthwise

Small ripe tomatoes, quartered

Radishes with leaves attached, halved if you like

Little Tokyo White turnips, thinly sliced

Small zucchini, halved lengthwise

Young kohlrabi, peeled and thinly sliced

Small beets, peeled and sliced

Small new potatoes, cooked and chilled

Young sweet peppers, seeded and slivered

Cauliflower florets, blanched for 10 seconds in boiling salted water and refreshed in ice water

AIOLI

1 cup (250 ml) grape seed oil

1 cup (250 ml) olive oil

1 potato, boiled until tender, peeled, and diced

4 egg yolks

1 egg

3 to 5 cloves garlic, roughly chopped

Salt and pepper

Juice of ½ lemon

DIP

1 cup (250 ml) whipping cream (35 percent butterfat)

Two 2-ounce (55-g) cans anchovy fillets in olive oil

3 or 4 cloves garlic, finely chopped

1 cup (250 ml) olive oil

1 cup (225 g) unsalted butter, cubed

1 or 2 ice cubes, if needed

Salt and pepper

GARNISHES

2 soft-boiled eggs (boiled for 5 minutes)

3 or 4 bread sticks

Poached salt cod, chilled

Poached lobster meat and shrimp, chilled

continued

FRED'S ANECDOTE ON GARLIC

I AM FORTUNATE TO SPEND A FEW WEEKS of each summer in the small town of Keremeos in the Similkameen Valley, in the interior of British Columbia. It is beautiful and hot, and has good wine and great farms. Not too hippie, not too "the man," but just right. A guy named Yuri and his wife farm there, growing (among other things) the best Russian garlic: big, red, and curved like the roof of the Kremlin. It's what I imagine opium must feel like to touch, sticky and rich. You can shave it like you would a truffle. I buy a few hundred bucks' worth of it every year and I keep it at home and not at the restaurant as I don't think I have the self-control needed to politely explain to a cook that you don't half-assly fill your stockpots with it. I don't get high like that on produce often; in fact it irritates me when others do it. So I guess I'm using my wild card here.

1. First, figure out how many vegetables you need to serve your guests. Then, for the vegetables, sit down in a garden chair with a bottle of rosé or pastis, a cutting board on your knees, and a good paring knife. Throw the peels straight into the garden.

2. To make the aioli, combine the oils in a measuring pitcher. In a food processor, combine the potato, egg yolks, egg, and as much of the garlic as you like and process until smooth. (Potato is added to the traditional aioli for texture; you can also use bread that has been soaked in milk.) With the motor running, slowly drizzle in the combined oils. The mixture should emulsify with no problem. Keep a glass of warm water handy, however, in case the mixture splits. If it does, immediately add a spoonful or two of the water, pulsing as you add. When all of the oil has been added, season with salt and pepper. To finish, add the lemon juice. Refrigerate until serving.

3. To make the dip, in a small saucepan, combine the cream and anchovies and simmer over medium-low heat until the cream is reduced by one-third. Bring the heat down to low, and, using a hand blender, blend in the garlic and oil. Using a hand whisk, delicately whisk in the butter a few cubes at a time. The mixture may break and split. If it does, add an ice cube and whisk again. Season generously with salt and pepper and serve warm. If the weather is chilly, keep the dip warm on a fondue warmer on the very lowest setting.

4. Serve the vegetables along with the garnishes of your choice in a nice bowl or arranged on a platter along with the dip and aioli.

JERUSALEM ARTICHOKES with KETCHUP

Serves 4

Fred's mom is from Belgium, and like most Europeans who lived through the war, she can't bear the smell of Jerusalem artichokes, which, along with rutabagas, were the readily available vegetables in those years. Supposedly, they are a miraculous food, with some claiming they cure diabetes, and pet-food makers thinking about putting them in cat food so used kitty litter would remain odorless. Says Fred: "I still couldn't stomach them, until I tried a batch at Toqué! during a staff meal. They were killed in coarse pretzel salt and dunked in ketchup. Another case of the sum being light-years from the parts!"

2 tablespoons rendered chicken fat, unsalted butter, or olive oil

8 large Jerusalem artichokes

3 tablespoons water

Big handful coarse salt

Pretzel salt

Pepper

Leaves from 3 sprigs thyme

Ketchup for serving

1. Preheat the oven to 400°F (200°C). Smear the chicken fat onto a non-stick rimmed baking sheet.

2. Put your artichokes in a large, heavy-duty lock-top plastic bag and pour in the water. Add the coarse salt, seal the bag closed, and shake the bag well. Now open the bag and rinse the artichokes well. This is a great way to clean Jerusalem artichokes. You're getting all the dirt and debris off better than your hands would.

3. Halve the artichokes lengthwise and arrange them, cut side down, in a single layer on the prepared pan. Season them generously with the pretzel salt and pepper. Strew the thyme leaves evenly over the top.

4. Place in the oven and cook for 45 minutes. Turn the artichokes over and cook for another 30 minutes, or until browned and slightly shriveled.

5. Take the artichokes out, let cool, and serve with ketchup.

APPLE VINNY

Makes about 1¹/₃ cup (330 ml)

This is a great dressing. We use it on our Parc Vinet Salad (page 190), and it's also the best with Belgian endive and blue cheese (page 191). Plus, it works to pimp any sauce that needs a sugar-vinegar hit, it's great on top of cold crab or lobster, and it doubles as a verjuice when you need to acid-ify a jus. If you have easy access to great apples (that is, you live somewhat close to an "apple belt," as we do), this dressing will become a staple. Just mix it up and pour it into a plastic squirt bottle.

2 cups (500 ml) unfiltered apple juice
¼ cup (60 ml) olive oil
2 tablespoons cider vinegar
Salt and pepper

1. Pour the juice into a saucepan, place over high heat, and boil until reduced by half. The best way to do this is to mark the level of the full amount on the pot with a Sharpie, then let it reduce to half of where you marked, watching the sides of the pot. Scrape with a rubber spatula to prevent any burning.

2. Take off the heat when reduced and add the oil, vinegar, and a pinch each of salt and pepper. Mix well and chill before using. The dressing will keep for up to a week in the refrigerator.

CIDER TURNIPS

Serves 4

Boil turnips for too long and you'll have socks juice soup. Cook them just right and you're being Richard Olney for an instant. Do not confuse turnips with rutabagas; here in Quebec, they hold the same name in French. And if you have some rendered duck fat on hand, please use it in place of the oil and butter.

2 tablespoons canola oil
12 to 16 Tokyo White turnips (each the size of a golf ball), halved lengthwise, keeping a few leaves intact and reserving the remaining leaves
Sea salt and pepper
1 tablespoon unsalted butter
2 tablespoons maple syrup
1 tablespoon cider vinegar
1 fresh sage leaf, torn

1. Heat the oil in a sauté pan over medium-high heat. Sprinkle the turnips with the salt and pepper and cook, tossing them so they don't burn, for 4 to 5 minutes, or until light brown.

2. Add the butter, maple syrup, vinegar, and sage leaf and reduce for 2 to 3 minutes, or until shiny. Toss in a few of the reserved turnip leaves.

3. Transfer to a serving dish. Finish with a pinch of sea salt on the sheen of the syrup.

CARROTS with HONEY

Serves 4

You can use any type of carrot for this dish: perfect bunching carrots in midsummer, Touchons in the fall, or large carrots to feed livestock in the winter. Use anything but the dreary, bagged mini carrots carved from larger, less valuable specimens (they have more in common with sea monkeys than food). It's simple: if the carrots look shitty that day, buy spinach. If not, cook them up like this.

¼ cup (60 ml) olive oil

1 bunch thyme

1 bay leaf

1 clove garlic, lightly crushed but whole

12 carrots, not too big, peeled

1 tablespoon honey

2 tablespoons crunchy sea salt

Pepper

Grated pecorino cheese for dusting

1. Heat a large frying pan over medium heat. Add the oil, thyme, bay leaf, and garlic. When the oil is hot, add the carrots and cook, tossing often, for 7 to 9 minutes, or until tender.

2. When the taste test is conclusive, add the honey, coat the carrots, and transfer to a serving dish. Sprinkle the sea salt evenly on the carrots, making sure it sticks to the honey. Lastly, add a couple of cranks of pepper and some pecorino.

BAKED MUSHROOMS with NEW (OR OLD!) GARLIC

Serves 4

Here is a simple way to enjoy big Paris mushrooms. I like chanterelles, morels, and even matsutakes, but these common white mushrooms—the kind you see in supermarkets—remind me of culinary school; they smell like *la bonne cuisine française*. We use banker watch–size mushrooms—as big as you can find. If you're looking for an upscale alternative, porcini will also work.

This dish is best prepared in a cast-iron frying pan, served family style at the table. Bring it out hot and bubbling.

16 large white mushrooms, stem ends trimmed
¼ cup (55 g) salted or unsalted butter
1 tablespoon olive oil
Salt and pepper
¼ teaspoon smoked paprika (pimentón de la Vera)
2 garlic flowers or garlic cloves
6 sprigs thyme

1. Preheat the oven to 450°F (230°C). Score each mushroom cap with shallow cuts about ⅛ inch (3 mm) deep. Spread the butter and oil in the bottom of a heavy ovenproof pan. Season the bottom of the pan with salt, pepper, and the paprika. Place the mushrooms, cap down and side by side, in the pan. Tuck the garlic flowers and thyme among them.

2. Bake the mushrooms for 18 to 20 minutes, or until the pan juices are bubbling and the mushrooms have shrunk and roasted. Serve bubbly.

HERBES SALÉES

Makes 1 large jarful

Every year we buy a large jar of *herbes salées* in Kamouraska. It's a typical Bas Du Fleuve product that lets you enjoy the taste of garden fresh herbs when the temperature is −4°F (−20°C) and your backyard is under a blanket of snow. It is essentially a big spoonful of herbs with carrots and onions that stay fresh because of the brine. You can use this traditional northern condiment with anything: potatoes, soups, seafood, lamb, gravies, terrines, and meat pies.

1 cup (40 g) chopped fresh chives
1 cup (40 g) chopped fresh savory
1 cup (40 g) chopped fresh flat-leaf parsley
1 cup (40 g) chopped fresh chervil
1 cup (55 g) grated carrots
1 cup (40 g) chopped celery leaves
1 cup (85 g) chopped green onions
½ cup (115 g) coarse salt

1. In a large bowl, combine one-fourth each of the chives, savory, parsley, chervil, carrots, celery leaves, and green onions. Top with one-fourth of the salt. Repeat the layering three times, using up all of the ingredients. Cover and refrigerate for 1 week.

2. At the end of the week, a brine will have formed. Uncover the bowl and pour the herbs into a large jar with a tight-fitting lid. Store in the fridge for up to a year.

KALE FOR A HANGOVER

Serves 4

We can't explain why this helps cure hangovers, but it does. It's like a vitamin with a sugar coating (the coating being the bacon and butter).

Salt

1 bunch kale, stems removed and roughly chopped

4 slices bacon, thick fall lardons (see Theory #3, page 166)

1 small onion, chopped

1 clove garlic, chopped

¼ cup (60 ml) dry white wine

Pepper

1 tablespoon unsalted butter

Small squeeze of fresh lemon juice

1 egg (optional)

1. Bring a large pot of salted water to a boil. Add the kale and cook for 10 minutes, or until soft. Drain well and squeeze lightly. Transfer to a cutting board and chop finely. Set aside.

2. In a frying pan, fry the bacon over medium-high heat for about 6 minutes, or until crisp. Add the onion and cook, stirring, for 3 to 4 minutes, or until translucent. Lower the fire to medium-low, add the garlic, and sweat for 1 minute. Add the kale, wine, and a pinch each of salt and pepper and cook for 3 to 4 minutes to blend the flavors. If the mixture looks really shiny, scoop out a little of the fat and add a bit of water (see Theory #4, page 167), and then add the butter. Mix in the lemon juice.

3. Move the bacon and kale mixture to a plate and fry an egg in the same pan. Serve the egg on top of the bacon and kale. Go to bed.

CAULIFLOWER GRATIN

Serves 4 to 6

The mimolette cheese in this dish makes it look like a favorite Kraft product and will have your kids chomping at the bit to eat cauliflower.

SAUCE

1½ cups (375 ml) milk

1 bay leaf

1 clove garlic, chopped

¼ cup (40 g) chopped ham hock or prosciutto trimmings

3 tablespoons unsalted butter

3 tablespoons all-purpose flour

¼ cup (30 g) grated young mimolette cheese

¼ cup (30 g) grated Gruyère cheese

Salt and pepper

Salt

1 head cauliflower, a little lighter than 1 pound (455 g), cut into large florets

¼ cup (15 g) *panko* (Japanese bread crumbs)

¼ cup (50 g) grated aged mimolette cheese

1. Preheat the oven to 400°F (200°C). To make the sauce, in a saucepan, combine the milk, bay leaf, garlic, and ham hock and bring to a simmer over medium-high heat. Turn off the heat and let cool for about 10 minutes. Toss the bay leaf.

2. In another saucepan, melt the butter over medium-high heat. Slowly whisk in the flour and then cook, stirring, for 1 minute to remove the raw flour taste. Slowly add the hot milk mixture, bit by bit, whisking constantly. Then continue to whisk until thick. Stir in the young mimolette and the Gruyère until melted, season with salt and pepper, and keep warm over the lowest heat setting.

3. Bring a large pot of salted water to a boil. Add the cauliflower and cook for 3 to 4 minutes, or until al dente. Drain well.

4. Toss the cauliflower with the sauce and pour into a large enameled cast-iron baking dish. Scatter the *panko* and the old mimolette over the top.

5. Bake for about 15 minutes, or until bubbling and golden. Serve hot.

SPRING BEETS

Serves 4

Fred once threatened to reveal Monsier Jean Charest's dislike of beets to the world, along the lines of President George Bush's broccoligate. "He stared at me while his goons were considering my removal—not funny, not funny at all."

This way of making beets is delicious. Fred prefers red beets; he finds the yellow ones taste like house-brand diet soda.

8 small beets with leafy tops

1 tablespoon unsalted butter

Salt and pepper

1 teaspoon cider vinegar

Smoked Cheddar (page 164) for finishing

Chopped fresh parsley, dill, or chives for garnish

1. Rinse the beets under cold running water, then cut off the leafy tops, leaving 1 inch (2.5 cm) of the stem intact. Roughly chop the beet tops into 1-inch pieces and set aside. Put the beets in a saucepan, add water to cover, and place over high heat. Bring to a boil, then reduce the heat to medium and simmer for about 30 minutes, or until the skins slip off easily. Drain and slice the beets.

2. In a small saucepan, melt the butter over medium heat. Add the beets and cook, turning as needed, for 5 minutes, or until slightly brown and roasted. Add the reserved leaves, season with salt and pepper, and then add the vinegar. Cook for another 2 minutes, or until the leaves are wilted.

3. Transfer the beets to a serving plate. Garnish with the herbs, grate a little of the cheese over the top, and serve.

PETITS FARCIS

Serves 4

We remember falling in love with a photograph of *petits farcis* in an old issue of *Cuisine et Vins de France*. We're sure that most chefs our age who had dreamed of cooking professionally since childhood feel the same when they open a vintage copy of *Cuisine et Vins de France*, or of Georges Blanc's *De la Vigne à l'Assiette*. There is no greater food era than when Michel Guérard, Bernard Loiseau, Paul Bocuse, Alain Chapel, Georges Blanc, and Roger Vergé were at the top.

Petits farcis are vegetables stuffed with sausage mix, then baked and eaten lukewarm. We make them in the summer when the growers show up with pattypan squashes. What else are you supposed to do with those little squashes other than admire them? The stuffed vegetables are awesome with a mâche salad and partner perfectly with a nice rosé or pastis. Get the smallest vegetables you can find, about the size of a golf ball.

4 small new onions, with tops attached

4 small pattypan squashes

4 small tomatoes

4 small eggplants

4 bell peppers

4 small zucchini

STUFFING

1 small onion, finely chopped

1 tablespoon neutral oil

8 ounces (225 g) ground veal

8 ounces (225 g) ground pork

1 egg, lightly beaten

1 slice white bread, crust removed, crumbled and soaked in 2 tablespoons milk

¼ cup (30 g) grated Parmesan cheese

1 teaspoon finely chopped fresh thyme leaves

½ teaspoon fennel seeds

¼ teaspoon finely chopped garlic

¼ teaspoon dried chile flakes

Salt and pepper

Olive oil for drizzling

1. Cut the top one-third off the onions, squashes, tomatoes, eggplants, and peppers, and set aside to use as caps. Cut the zucchini in half lengthwise. With a melon baller or an espresso spoon, scoop out the inside of each vegetable the best you can. Leave the walls about ¼ inch (6 mm) thick. Set the vegetables aside.

2. Preheat the oven to 400°F (200°C). To make the stuffing, in a small frying pan, sweat the onion in the oil over medium heat for 4 to 5 minutes, or until translucent. Remove from the heat.

3. In a bowl, combine the veal, pork, cooked onion, egg, bread, Parmesan, thyme, fennel seeds, garlic, chile flakes, and a pinch each of salt and pepper. Mix together using your hands; it should have the texture of a raw meatball.

4. Divide the meat mixture among the vegetables, stuffing it carefully and deeply inside each one. Stand the vegetables, without their caps, in an oiled gratin dish or cake pan. Bake for 20 minutes, or until the meat is cooked but not colored. Remove from the oven, top each vegetable with its cap, and return to the oven for another 10 minutes, or until the tops are getting crispy and the meat is sizzling.

5. Remove from the oven and drizzle olive oil on top. Serve lukewarm.

*E*ach night I stand at the end of the bar at Joe Beef or Liverpool House and dictate wines and booze to customers all evening. After twenty years of buying wine, I know what I like and why. It took me twenty years to love Ricard. And it was Campari that brought me into loving Ricard. And California Pinot made me love cheap Burgundy. And cheap Burgundy made me love great Burgundy. So what follows are strictly my own opinions, observations, and rants on wine and booze.

CHAPTER 7

A WORD ON BOOZE

If you bring your partner into the restaurant and spend all of your time talking to your waiter about wine (which I see all the time) instead of focusing on the conversation, you're a jerk. A restaurant meal is a precursor for the acts of business, friendship, and lovemaking. Leave your wine OCD at home. Once you choose the wine and taste it (this should only take three minutes, not twenty), *there is no more talking about wine*. Then it's time to talk about how pretty your date's dress is or how nice your date smells, how well you're doing this quarter, or how many widgets you've sold.

ON WINE

That said, the wine list at Joe Beef is an opinionated one. With only thirty seats in the restaurant, we can't afford to choose a bit of everything and appease en masse. Instead, the list is a reflection of my work of twenty years of purchasing, tasting, and reading voraciously about wine. Even though you may disagree with what our direction is (and some people do), our wine list is truly ours.

At Joe Beef, I work the wine list with the mysterious Vanya Filipovic, a true Burgundy fanatic and the best

"I love red Burgundy wine so much I want to pour it into my eyes."

—David McMillan

waitress I've ever had the pleasure of working with. Her exuberance and her pinpoint accuracy of what people want to drink astound me. She is the only person who can sell Morgon to Cabernet-drinking alpha-male golfers and make them love it. In fact, she is loved by all.

At Liverpool House, I work the wine list with Ryan Gray, who has given himself the tongue-in-cheek title of Director of Wine (*sommelier* is a dirty word around these parts). Ryan challenges me to open my mind to wines I would otherwise (loudly and rather obnoxiously) say that I hate, which happens often, like every day. He is humble, which is to say he makes people feel good about wine, without pretension.

OUR WINE LISTS

The direction of our lists is mostly Burgundy, Beaujolais, Loire, Alsace, and some American and some Canadian wines. We try (as much as possible) to buy from family-owned wineries and the people we've met, drank with, visited with, people who work as hard as we do in our restaurants. We have a lifetime to study

and discover the few regions that we feature on our list, and so far we've only barely scratched the surface. When I look at a wine list, I want to see wines I've never heard of, that I can't get, and, ultimately, that I want to learn about. Is it organic? Biodynamic? From a winemaker who owns the vineyard with his son and wife? If I could drink wine only from small family wineries, I would. I can taste the corporate lab coat in wine and I don't like that flavor.

Fifteen years ago, I couldn't wait to get my hands on Australian wines. And I remember a period three years before that when the only California wines available to us were Ridge Geyserville Zinfandel and a wine called Cherry Block (what ever happened to that wine?). Although I had at my disposal all the Old World wines I could possibly want, New World wines were forbidden fruit. I was amazed to learn that Pinot Noir was growing in other parts of the world. I read about Pinotage from South Africa, Malbec from Argentina, and Riesling in Australia. How badly I wanted a bottle of Cloudy Bay Sauvignon Blanc from New Zealand!

But after tasting (and sometimes getting drunk) on these wines many times, something was always missing. The Rieslings were too sweet and yellow, and the Sauvignon Blanc reeked of fresh-cut grass and cat pee. In general, the wines were always a little too sexy, with too much oak, too much sugar, and too much alcohol; cost too much money; and were too contrived. The new winemakers seemed like speculators; they weren't born into wine, and if the next gold rush were in, say, peaches, they would pull out all the vines and plant peach trees. Don't

get me wrong, I'm not slamming all New World wines. I taste New World wines all the time that I love (see box opposite page).

The air in Quebec is sweet and old, however, and we've been drinking French wine with French food here for more than three hundred years. Cornas with braised beef, Meursault with truffled eggs on biscuits—the flavors and food combinations with French wine are countless and can and will suffice for the rest of my life. Classically, Montreal has always preferred French wine. There is a core Quebec crowd that

has, for many historical reasons, cemented this province with a *vin français toujours* policy. I have many customers who won't even acknowledge any wine other than French wine. Italian wine is exotic, and Spanish wine, well, they just shrug and look bewildered.

Our dining room at Joe Beef looks much different from other dining rooms (such as big American restaurants where hundreds of English-speaking people sit down to dinner at seven o'clock, or even at the ungodly hour of six). Here, half of the customers are French. They read the newspaper in French, go to work in French, listen to the radio in French, and go to French school. Many have lived here all of their lives and know what they like. "Bring me a Sancerre," "bring me a Chablis," "bring me a Gevrey" are phrases I often hear. Dining out is an art that is learned at a young age. It's not something you discover watching the Food Network. For Montrealers, there have always been oysters and Muscadet at Christmas, or foie gras and Jurançon or Sauternes, a Burgundy and a Bordeaux at the table. Our dining rooms reflect the spirit of Montreal dining. When I see two men sharing a magnum it excites me. When I see two women dressed in high heels and new jeans treating themselves to a bottle of Champagne, well, I mean, it's like, yes! That is the point! With only thirty seats, Joe Beef feels like a festive

celebration even on a Tuesday night. Food and wine are about having fun. The wines that we serve by the glass are usually the wines that we want people to try. They are mostly French, with some oddities from Slovenia or Hungary thrown in.

Following is a tour of the very simple makings of our wine list. The list is really about what Montrealers want, what is available to us, and what we ourselves are usually drinking.

Drink wine, it's a healthful beverage.

WHITES

Our white-wine list is about half the size of the red. And because it is basically all that Ryan, Vanya, and I ever drink, there is no logic to it, except that it's what we love and/or believe to be exceptional.

Champagne

Champagne is not a festive beverage. Champagne is a wine that should be drunk every day for no apparent reason. Life is short, hard, and can often suck.

When I visited Champagne, I hated it. I was in Reims and thought the town was cold and the people annoying. I realized just how much I hated it when I got into the electric tram at Mumm's and they bragged about how they had over eighteen kilometers (eleven miles) of underground cellars. There are millions upon millions of bottles in that cellar. I guess I would be impressed if I were a soft drink magnate!

I remember standing at the top of a hill, looking over the vineyards somewhere near Cramant, and asking the person beside me, "Why is the soil glittering in the sun?" I was shocked to see (and smell) an

inorganic mulch of broken glass, shredded plastic bottles, and orange and green garbage bags mixed into the soil to stop erosion. The supposedly noble Champagne grapes were growing in trash!

After visiting more Champagne factories, I had my fill of big producers. Drink small-grower Champagnes. It's easy! If you want to find out which bottles are made by growers who harvest the grapes, work the land, and make the wine, look for initials before a number on the bottom of the wine label. The initials you want to see are RM for *récoltant-manipulant*. This roughly translates to small growers who harvest and bottle their own crops.

Our favorite wines to serve at Joe Beef consist of these small, site-specific producers. They are, among others, Vouette et Sorbée, Jacques Lassaigne, Cédric Bouchard, Egly-Ouriet, and Gimonnet. These are serious Champagnes, and they are possibly five to ten dollars cheaper than your regular mass-market stuff. It's the real deal. We would also *like* to sell Jacques Selosse, but it's so expensive, we don't really even know what it tastes like.

We have three profiles of Champagne on the menu: Champagne with sugarosity, like it's been dosed with a sweeter wine, or *liqueur d'expedition*. Vouette et Sorbée is a good example. Then, of course, there's bone-dry Champagne, such as Larmandier-Bernier or Jacques Lassaigne, that will cut through butter or oyster fat. And finally, there is the best of both worlds, like Cédric Bouchard.

And that's just Champagne. There are also amazing sparkling wines. I love Crémant de Bourgogne, Crémant d'Alsace, Montlouis-sur-Loire, all of them true-quality-for-price sparklers.

We've also tasted wonderful wines out of California, such as Schramsberg, Roederer, J, and Deutz's California branch, Lateita. The big sparkling wine producers in California sometimes do a better job than those in France and for half of the price. Their bottles are a deal.

Chardonnay

You can't time your watch to California Chardonnay like you can with French Chardonnay. If we're in California and you're my neighbor, you could make a completely different wine than I do. So, if there are fifteen winemakers in our town, there are fifteen different wines, with different degrees of alcohol-sugar, oak, and toast. Sadly, in the last few years, the reputation of Chardonnay has been sullied by double oak, high alcohol, and critter wine, that is, wines named for children: little penguins, dancing goats, yellow tails, toasted bears. But don't hate on Chardonnay. It's still the king. At Joe Beef we always have a few solid Chardonnays on our list:

Chablis: This is the Phillips screwdriver of Chardonnay. From Petit Chablis to Grand Chablis, I prefer a gunflint vibrant acidity, mouthful of gravel, and stainless steel. Drink it with vigor with steamed clams, hot oysters, or (my favorite) *Oeufs en Gelée* (page 57). Billaud-Simon (all cuvées), Droin, Pacalet, Raveneau, Tribut, and Picq are some of our favorite producers.

Côte de Beaune: This region turns out the "elbow grease" wines, which are always fat, buttery, and perfect for winter meals on the cozy banquettes at Joe Beef. Alain Gras, Pierre-Yves Colin-Morey's simple cuvées in Auxey-Duresses, Meursault, and Saint-Aubin (he makes a dozen wines) are all amazing. Vincent Dancer is my go-to favorite producer in the area. Amateur photographer and the man most in love with wine making, Dancer doesn't pontificate on his wines, so we will honor him by not getting into it, either. We also love Sauzet, Roulot, Jobard, and Bouzereau. Drink white CDBs with rotisserie chicken, sea salt, and mashed potatoes to get the full effect. Also, they are a perfect fit with sautéed mushrooms with onions and Époisses cheese on toast.

We are trying to bring more Canadian Chardonnays to the list, but our SAQ (the crown-run-and-operated alcohol governing system) gives no breaks to Canadian wines outside of Quebec. The prices are too restrictive for now. Norman Hardie and Tawse from Ontario and Cedar Creek and Kettle Family from British Columbia produce some real standouts that we wish we had the freedom to stock in quantity. (I'd like to take this opportunity to tell the SAQ to open up the Canadian market with "grown in Canada" tax breaks.)

Sancerre

On the Joe Beef blackboard, you'll see three profiles of Sancerre: There's the classic Sancerre, usually nameless, nothing great, but still noble. There's the perfect, clean Sancerre, such as Reverdy, Bourgeois, Jolivet, Lafond, and Bondelet. And then there is my favorite, the

Sancerres from Chavignol, in the Loire.

With good Chavignol producers, I can smell the rind of a goat cheese and a straw floor in the wine. I can smell the grass that the goat eats in the wine. The winemakers of Chavignol are absolutely magnificent, so rustic, and authentic. Pascal Cotat, for example, is both an auto mechanic and a winemaker. Chavignol is full of that type: true, natural winemakers, people like Edmond Vatan and Gérard Boulay, who are ordinary citizens by day, wine gods by night. A lot of people set out to make natural wine, whereas Chavignol always just has.

Other Loire Whites

The Loire is a fascinating place, and I like everything there. It is also one of the most intriguing French wine regions. You can easily overlook a lot of the villages, because they are often overshadowed by their bigger brothers, Sancerre and Pouilly-Fumé. Seek out the excellent and better-priced Sauvignon Blancs from Menetou-Salon, Quincy, and Reuilly.

The Muscadet area, in the west of the Loire, is experiencing a resurgence, with Domaine de la Pépière and Domaine Pierre Luneau-Papin among its stars. And let's not forget the delicious wines of Saumur, Vouvray, and Montlouis, where Chenin rules with its three incarnations of dry, off-dry, and sweet. A nice off-dry Vouvray with Joe Beef scallops is delicious, and I can't imagine anything better than a cheap bottle of Pépière Muscadet with a trout shore lunch, when the wine is the same temperature as the water from which you pulled the fish.

I also want to mention the microscopic appellation of Cour-Cheverny, home of Romorantin, a grape with which we have a torrid love affair. Ryan ordered a case of Philippe Tessier without telling me, and when we received it on a Tuesday, I blasted him, asking why he would buy such an oddity. I drank one glass that night and proceeded to finish the case by Saturday. For me, it's like a mix of all of my favorite wines. It makes me feel like fighting.

Other Whites

I always like to throw in a dry Alsatian Riesling, Marcel Deiss or Schueller, just in case a jellied ham or cold crustaceans have been ordered. Nothing goes better with Riesling than cold canner (small) lobsters or the Joe Beef smorgasbord (see insert). Indeed, I dream of eating the smorgasbord with a mid-range Zind-Humbrecht.

The rest of our list is composed of new Old World wines. We've recently been obsessed with the wines of Slovenia, Serbia, Hungary, Croatia, and Greece. And let's not forget the white wines of Italy. There is a period during the summer in Montreal, when, sadly, it's too hot to drink anything with even a hint of oak in it. All we want to serve then are the Italian whites of Trentino–Alto Adige (Colterenzio) and Campania (Mastroberardino).

REDS

Our red list comprises about two hundred wines, as that is all the chalkboard will permit. For the thirty patrons dining at any one time, it is actually way too much choice.

Burgundy

Every time I drink Burgundy wine, I feel like I'm part of a secret club of people who know things. The best things. Like Star Trek things. Did you know that Burgundy was drunk in space? Yep, it was. Nuits-Saint-Georges to be exact.

If I scrape my knee, I immediately consider pouring Burgundy on it. I'm sold on its healing qualities. If I'm at home sick with a cold, I think to drink it. If I see someone with acne, I want to rub it on his or her face. I want to bathe my daughter in it. Red Burgundy—Pinot Noir in its purest form—goes with absolutely everything: breakfast, lunch, and dinner. It goes with fast food, birthday food, food that other chefs cook for you, and fries. At Joe Beef, we've never met a bottle of Burgundy that we didn't like; even the ones that apparently suck. My judgment is so flawed that I can even say positive things about the worst Burgundian battery acid.

COTAT PASCAL
MECANIQUE
CARROSSERIE
VIDANGE PNEUS
TEL. 02.48.54.15.91

The Burgundy drinker is a great lover, is well-read, and has impeccable style. He or she loves woodland animals and is the kind of person who might have a miniature bear as a pet (like Charles McKiernan). He likely owns several tweed coats and partitions his garden with stone walls. Her prized possession may be a mechanic's nightmare of an old Peugeot. When drinking any other wine, the Burgundy drinker typically says insane things like, "this Sancerre is quite Burgundian," or "this Bandol reminds me of why I love Burgundy!" Drinkers of Burgundy scold themselves for overlooking (abandoning!) certain villages: "We really do not drink enough Pernand-Vergelesses," or "I simply must rediscover Saint-Aubin!" Of course, this is all fiction, but I always seem to find something in a bottle that expresses a rural sense of pensiveness. For me, it's like drinking archeology.

It is said that Celts grew vines in Burgundy as early as 51 B.C. Later, Benedictine monks and Cisterians set about the task of separating vineyard plots because they believed certain areas provided consistently different wines. They set up the system of *crus* and the notion of terroir. I can feel the mystical presence of these snail eaters when I walk through Burgundian vineyards that are just off the beaten path. Sometimes when wine reps want us to try a $58 Oregon Pinot Noir, the answer is an understandable, "No thanks."

New World Pinot, out of respect, shouldn't be more expensive than true noble Burgundy. Hundreds of years ago everyone agreed that this bacon strip–shaped piece of land that runs just south of Dijon is the best place on earth for these grapes to exist. It's a World Heritage site, meaning the laws are so strict that you can't irrigate—in other words, you can't just run the hose into a vineyard.

In my dream-world restaurant, I would serve only red and white Burgundies. From Dijon all the way to the Beaujolais, each village in Burgundy is a treasure. Each day in Burgundy, people ask, "What did you eat for breakfast?" Then, "What did you eat for lunch?" Like Montrealers, these people are obsessed with food and wine. (Wouldn't you love a Romanée Conti or Meursault Perrières sweatshirt? Or, a "My parents came back from Burgundy and all I got was this shitty Clos Vougeot" T-shirt?)

A plethora of French winemakers visit Montreal on a regular basis—Étienne de Montille, Pierre-Yves Colin-Morey, the Muzard brothers—and most seem to have the impression that Quebecers are a bunch of cowboys riding around on skidoos, fishing giant salmon, and shooting grizzly bears. This isn't true, of course (though I have to say, I didn't see one bird for two years while living in Burgundy; they've eaten every fucking thing that moves there). Always seen as the exotic cousins to the French, Quebec may very well be the last frontier of moose hunting, angling, foraging, and sugar shacks.

On the Joe Beef board, we have three profiles of red Burgundy. First, we sell village wines more than anything else. Marsannay Ladoix-Serrigny, Pernand-Vergelesses, and Beaune are easy, inexpensive, and the best value for your money. It's also interesting to find the different villages on the map (if you're geeks like Vanya, Ryan, and me). These are great wines to start off a meal or to end one, as no one objects to going down a few notches after a big wine to have a bottle of Marsannay.

The second profile is the premier cru. There are 562 premier cru vineyards in twenty-eight villages in Burgundy. These are site-specific, heritage plots. I love the Clos du Val in Auxey-Duresses, Clos du Chapitre in Fixin by Méo-Camuzet, and Forêt in Chablis by Raveneau. Okay, I could go on and on about this and that, but premier cru vineyards and their wine are personal affairs. The three I mentioned, I drank in a particular time and place with a "special" friend when everything seemed perfect. At any given time we carry 25 to 30 premiers crus at Joe Beef.

Grand cru Burgundies, the third profile, are for special occasions and should be cellared properly, served at the right temperature, carried carefully to the table, and treated as the geographical blood of the earth that they are. As a restaurateur, I prefer not to sell them to just anybody. And the truth is that most folks who can afford to spend three hundred dollars for a bottle at a restaurant are not the people who will really savor it. Such is life. If you're lucky enough to get your hands on a grand cru Burgundy, drink it at home with your friends, your family, and your favorite music. We would rather see you for a great meal and a decent bottle. Cheers.

Beaujolais

We love Beaujolais. Vanya coined the term for our favourite producers: "The Beaujolais Beatniks." They are, in no particular order: Métras, Foillard, Pacalet, Chamonard, Brun, Descombes, Theuvenet, Thivin, and Breton. And, of course, there is Marcel Lapierre (RIP), who will always remain King in our eyes. This group tries as much as possible to keep their wines clean, low alcohol, and low sulphur.

Rhônes are the roast beef of wines. When you braise a whole lamb shoulder in a cast-iron pot, au natural with carrot, celery, and onion, the jus that results is nectar and is made to go with Rhône wines. I like Côte-Rôtie; it's festive for me. If I'm drinking Gevrey-Chambertin and I want to kick it up a notch, Côte-Rôtie is my go-to. I have three words for you in the Rhône: Gaillard, Cuilleron, and Villard. These men are legends.

They formed a partnership, Cuilleron-Villard-Gaillard, and a

company, Les Vins de Vienne, so they could work together. But each has solo wine projects that turn out Rhône wines I want to drink for the rest of my life. In their solo wine projects, each of them makes the Rhône wines that I want to drink for the rest of my life. I would follow these three blindly. I think François Villard has a serious man crush on me, and I know that Yves Cuilleron is scared of me. I am scared of Pierre Gaillard, and I know one day it will come to blows. These men are supergood at drinking and deserve a trophy. I've been practicing for ten years to beat them, but sadly they consistently crush me. Of course, we're not forgetting the southern Rhône, where, for me, there is only one game in town, Vieille Julienne— the iron fist in the velvet glove.

WINEMAKER QUESTIONNAIRES

IF STRANDED ON A DESERT ISLAND, I'D WANT THESE SIX WINES . . .

NORMAN HARDIE (PRINCE EDWARD COUNTY, ONTARIO, CANADA)

- Krug Clos du Mesnil
- Hubert Lamy Saint-Aubin "Les Dents de Chien" 2005
- Evesham Wood Pinot Noir "Cuvée J" (Oregon) 2006
- Pommard Grand Clos des Épenots 1998
- Clos Blanc de Vougeot 1999

I love Riesling and want to bring one, but it would be finished in about eight seconds. If there were such a thing as an endless bottle of JJ Prüm Wehlener Sonnenuhr, that would be my number 1. Alas . . .

EMMANUEL LASSAIGNE (MONTGEUX, FRANCE)

- Chardonnay, Jura, J.F. Ganevat
- Sainte Epine, Côte du Rhône, H. Souhaut
- Les Terres Chaudes, Tavel, E. Pfiferling
- Le Champ des Oiseaux, Alsace, B. Schueller
- Fleurie, Beaujolais, Y. Métras
- Morgon, Beaujolais, J. Foillard.
- (Et du Champagne . . . et tout ça en magnums)

ÉTIENNE DE MONTILLE (VOLNAY, FRANCE)

- 2 bottles of La Tâche 1971
- 1 bottle of Vina Tondonia 1964 (Rioja)
- 1 bottle of Volnay Taillepieds 1971
- 1 Romanée-Conti, any vintage
- 1 bottle of Krug, any vintage

THIBAULT LIGER BELAIR (NUITS ST. GEORGES, FRANCE)

I'd leave the best bottles in my cellar for my friends and family to enjoy and bring some simple whites. Chablis, Picpoul de Pinet (amazing with crustaceans!), maybe old vintages of Champagne. I'm not a Champagne fan, but with age it can be magical. If I had to pick some crazy bottles, I'd bring an Hermitage 1961—this wine is filled with emotion for me; one of the best things I've ever tasted. Also a La Tache 1919, the best DRC vintage in my opinion. Honestly, there is so much less pleasure in drinking these bottles alone on a deserted island . . . great wines are meant to be shared!

DAVID CROIX (BEAUNE, FRANCE)

So difficult to pick just six! I'd try to take bottles that bring back memories to distract myself from the loneliness. I recently purchased a wine called Triple Zero made by Jacky Blot. It's a phenomenal *pétillant naturel*. I always crack a bottle or two with friends as an *apéro* . . . I'd definitely bring one of those. It's so refreshing! I love Riesling. In my opinion, it's one of the noblest grape varietals on the planet. I'd bring an old bottle of Trimbach Clos St. Hune. I'd also bring a nice white from Burgundy—maybe a Saint-Aubin from Olivier Lamy. I really admire the way he makes white wine. One of my closest friends, Maxime Graillot, makes stunning Crozes-Hermitages. I'd surely bring one in his honor. As a showstopper bottle, I'd bring a Musigny from Mugnier. Any vintage, young, old, doesn't matter. It's always breathtaking. I'd also pack a Vosne-Romanée from Mugneret-Gibourg.

JULIEN LABET (ROTALIER, FRANCE)

Magnums of Morgon Lapierre to remind me of my first time at Joe Beef! I tried making Cerdon last year from Savagnin grapes. The result was incredible—so refreshing! I'd bring a few of those and maybe some old vintages of Ramonet whites.

ARIANNA OCCHIPINTI (VITTORIA, SICILY)

- Pinot Grigio, Dario Princic
- Ageno, Az. Vitivinicola La Stoppa
- Mâcon-Villages Quintaine, Domaine Guillemot-Michel
- Brunello di Montalcino, Il Paradiso di Manfredi
- Arbois Pupillin Ploussard, Overnoy
- Barbaresco, Roagna

WINEMAKER QUESTIONNAIRES

NORMAN HARDIE (PRINCE EDWARD COUNTY, ONTARIO, CANADA)

If you weren't making wine in Prince Edward County, where else would you like to make wine?
Saint-Aubin. Sure, the reds would be shitty, but the whites would make up for it.

If you weren't making wine in general, what would you do?
Cook and play tennis.

What do you love about your job?
Taking something from the ground and being able to polish it and put it in a bottle.

EMMANUEL LASSAIGNE (MONTGEUX, FRANCE)

What are your favorite cocktails?
I don't drink booze, just wine.

What do you hate about your job?
Nothing.

What do you love about your job?
The complexity, the diversity.

ÉTIENNE DE MONTILLE (VOLNAY, FRANCE)

What's your take on Quebec?
This land is nonsensical in such a positive way. It has all of the good spirit of France without the arrogance of the French. Cool attitude, amazing energy, and a business mind of the New World. Completely unique.

What's your favorite band?
Bach.

What do you hate about your job?
Drinking wine all the time.

What do you love about your job?
Drinking wine all the time.

THIBAULT LIGER BELAIR (NUITS ST. GEORGES, FRANCE)

What's your favorite car?
Old cars! I'm a collector—the 1960s and 1970s. That era is where the last collectible cars can be found. They have such soul. A classic smell. I love it. I hate new-car smell. Cars today are made of plastic and are practically disposable. It makes me so happy to know my cars have a story to tell. I just bought a Peugeot 403 Panhard from the 1970s. It's all aluminum! I love it.

What's the best tractor?
The horse! I was the first to bring the horse back in Burgundy. It's an eight-hundred-kilo engine—what could be better? I also have a gorgeous tractor—a red Caval that I brought here from Mâcon. It's amazing. It's a quad-wheeler and can cover three rows at a time. It's super-lightweight and doesn't crush the soil. This is essential for me. It lets oxygen circulate.

DAVID CROIX (BEAUNE, FRANCE)

Where do you like to eat?
At my parent's place, family style. My mother is a great cook, and I really appreciate being back home in the Loire Valley around a big table full of food, wine, family,

and friends. I also have many close friends in the Morvan, and I love escaping to their villages for the weekend and hunting. We cook what we catch. It's amazing.

If you weren't making wine in Burgundy, where else would you like to make wine?
Probably in the Loire Valley, where I'm from. I love Burgundy, but the Loire is where my roots lie, as well as my heart. I'd also love to make wine in California. The best Pinots aside from Burgundy are made there, and it would be a great challenge. The lifestyle there is also very appealing.

What's your favorite cocktail, aperitif, or digestif?
Cognac. It's a wonderful way to end an evening.

JULIEN LABET (ROTALIER, FRANCE)

What's your take on Quebec?
People are so open. It's fantastic. There is a great sensibility in Quebec, which must be why wine is such a big part of the culture. People are very excited to try new things. It's lovely.

What's your favorite car?
I've been known to drive very fast. I love it. I'm not materialistic and don't care about brands or looks, but I like a car that can handle speed.

What's the worst part of your job?
I have a lot of anxiety. So much work goes into winemaking, but nature is the real worker. It's all up to Mother Nature, and that causes unbelievable stress. Every year, I lose at least five pounds during the *vendange* season just stressing over the quality of the grapes harvested. It's crazy.

ARIANNA OCCHIPINTI (VITTORIA, SICILY)

Who is your favorite singer or songwriter?
It is an Italian singer, Vinicio Capossela.

If you weren't making wine in general, what would you do?
I would like to have a big farm in Sicily with cattle, horses, and crops. I know winemaking is what I always want to do, though, so I would eventually plant vines!

Cats or dogs?
Dogs, and particularly PACO, my dog.

ON BOOZE

The cocktails we serve at Joe Beef and Liverpool House often are based on the time of year and the weather—and up here the weather is drastic, ranging from plus 30°F (−1°C) to minus 30°F (−34°C). When it's hot and humid, there's a general consensus to make lemonade-based drinks, perhaps with tea or Campari or Suze.

Around Christmastime, we want clementines or satsuma tangerines in our beverages. In January, after all the eating and parties, artery-cleansing grapefruit juice makes an appearance. Throughout the darkness of winter, cocktail making grinds to a halt. Brown booze—Bourbon, Islay Whisky, and Irish

Whisky—seem to be the only drinks that will quiet the dogs barking in our heads (see box opposite page).

March is a trying month on a restaurateur, that's why god made gin: Daddy's little helper. Soon spring is here and all is good again, which means simply Campari and Ricard all summer. And then the cycle starts again.

Here are our random thoughts on booze.

Vodka

Blindfold us and we can't tell the difference between one vodka and another, and neither can you, really. If you think you can, come to the bar at Joe Beef and we'll line up six glasses and taste blind. If you can tell the difference, we'll gladly buy you dinner. If this sounds like a challenge, that's because it is.

Years ago when I lived in Dijon, a sommelier that I worked with told me about the "lesson of humility" day at the Institut Oenologique et Agronomique de Bourgogne in Dijon. A teacher sat him, blindfolded, in a room and put ten wines in front of him, five white and five red. The lesson was simple: reds to the left, whites to the right. It goes without saying that he failed and apparently no one (at the time of writing) has passed. The point? When served wines at the same room temperature, the best sommeliers in the world often cannot tell the difference. The only time vodka makes sense to me is if you're on a diet. Reyka vodka from

Iceland is what we serve at Joe Beef, and people love it.

Campari and Ricard

Now here is something we love. I don't know why we don't sell more of it. A couple Camparis in the afternoon is a great thing. Bicyclette: white wine with a splash of Campari. A Molson Export with a drop of Campari brings more bitterness to the beer. Same idea with Ricard: when I drink Ricard, it's like an invitation to the best party. Nothing that I can drink opens up my appetite more. I have a weakness for women who wear hats and who drink Ricard and Campari. Girls who drink Ricard have really good stories.

OTHER BROWN BOOZE

A few of particular note.

Cognac

Our friends represent the Tesseron Cognac collection, which we carry exclusively. Drinking Cognac has always been big in Quebec. From December until April, it's often no more than 14°F (−10°C), or lower. And if it's not the extreme cold, it's the giant snowstorms. Either way, it won't stop a Montrealer from going out to eat. In fact, quite the opposite. Cognac in the winter is the best. It's a contemplative beverage, which aids in digestion and warms the soul. I like to drink it after a walk on a frozen lake or out of a silver Mickey while riding a chairlift.

BROWN BOOZE: THE JEKYL AND HYDE EFFECT

IS IT JUST US, or do you also notice that drinking brown booze makes you exceptionally drunk? Not "a few glasses of wine" drunk, more "where are we and how did we get here?" drunk. At Joe Beef, brown booze has turned many situations from great to really bad. We asked our friend and (fine brown liquor) distributor, Paul J. Coffin of LCC wines, to answer the question: Does brown booze make you crazy?

All distilled spirits come off the still as clear liquids, so what we now recognize as brown liquors are spirits that have gained color through the aging process in wood barrels. The aging of spirits is a fairly recent practice, as it was not deemed necessary in the past. Alcohol as it was produced was considered quite satisfactory by those who consumed it. Through necessity and experimentation, though, the virtues of barrel-aged spirits eventually became apparent.

Aged spirits get their color from the time they spend in wood barrels, usually oak. The color comes from the chemical exchange with the wood and the oxidation that takes place during aging. Aging also introduces the development of rich and complex flavors, a gradual reduction in alcohol volume through evaporation, and a certain filtering effect due to contact with the charred inner staves of the barrels.

The ill effects of alcohol consumption are caused by a combination of the toxic by-products of alcohol metabolism (acetaldehyde), dehydration, and vitamins A, B, and C depletion caused by the chemical action of alcohol on your system. While it is the ethyl alcohol (ethanol) that gets you drunk, amyl alcohol, butyl alcohol, methyl alcohol, propyl alcohol, and isopropyl alcohol are also found in most drinks to varying degrees, and the concentration of these congeners will go a long way in determining the aftereffects of too many drinks. Congeners are most present in brown liquor*, though they may also exist in smaller doses in clear liquors. While they have a down side, they also contribute to the flavor, smell, and appearance of the alcohol. It is possible through meticulous filtration to rid the alcohol of most congeners, resulting in a clear liquor. The filtration will also eliminate color and eventually flavor as well.

It is now scientifically proven, however, that aged spirits, such as whiskeys, rums, and brandies, can contain up to thirty-seven times more toxic compounds than vodka does, including organic molecules such as acetone, acetaldehyde, tannins, and furfural. That's one potential reason for the symptoms following the consumption of brown liquor.

The brown liquor of yesteryear was mostly poorly distilled alcohol carelessly transported in wooden barrels aimed for hasty consumption in excessive quantities. It is thus likely that the brown liquor of the 1700s and 1800s did, in fact, make you crazy.

Most of the knowledge we now have on the topic of bacteria, germs, and prevention of disease stems from Louis Pasteur's work in the mid-1800s. Coincidentally, many of his most important discoveries came as a result of work commissioned by distilleries and breweries. Prior to this, the medicinal properties of alcohol were apparent through observation, but the practices surrounding its production and consumption were still lacking. The sanitary conditions of the barrels exemplify this point. Even though the practice of charring the inside of a barrel to "clean" it is quite old, it is unlikely that this practice was carried out with much rigor on repurposed barrels that had once transported pickles or fish. Today, we can appreciate how far we have come in the craft of distilling and aging spirits, and we can surely enjoy brown booze for all the character and flavor it has to offer, in moderation of course.

*We thought so.

Brandy

Marc de Bourgogne is a pomace brandy and is *not* subtle in taste or the opinions it provokes. It's like rocket-fuel "hooch" made with the remnants from the winemaking process. It's amazing in espresso, and the kind of stuff that if you drink too much of, you start yelling at stop signs, barking at dogs, or hugging trees. Some marcs are pedigreed, such as the Domaine de la Romanée-Conti Marc de Bourgogne or (my favorite) Guy Roulot. Marc is also what is used to wash the rind of the famous Époisses de Bourgogne cheese. It's made all over viticulture France, and watch out, as it is legal rustic moonshine. It should have a pickled snake or reptile in the bottle, but the Burgundians probably ate them all. This is the kind of boys' night out, nail-in-the-coffin drink that I give to customers who need to be pushed off a cliff into the abyss.

Scotch Whiskey

Michel Couveur is a seventy-six-year-old oddity in the world of scotch whiskey. He is a Belgian living in Bouze-lès-Beaune, Burgundy. He's like a mad professor of whiskey, importing whiskeys and sherries and aging them in ancient sherry casks in his cellars. We're proud to sell his single-malt as well as some of his blend whiskeys and cask-aged sherry, as I fear that someday soon these products may be gone.

Islay Whiskey is a scotch whiskey made on Islay, the southernmost

"Chartreuse, the only liquor so good they named a color after it."

—Quentin Tarantino as bar owner Warren in *Death Proof*

island of the Hebrides, off the coast of Scotland. The whiskeys of Islay have a medicinal flavor—like medicine, peat, and seaweed. They are food whiskeys and they go well with the products we use: Cheddar, trout, scallops, and oysters. It seems like the *terroir* of Islay is similar to that of eastern Quebec, where the Saint Lawrence meets the ocean. The island's everyday bread basket is similar to ours. The air, the soil—it's like the island was broken apart from Quebec.

DIGESTIFS

Digestifs are the most important thing to get you through the marathon of dining. At Joe Beef, the four most popular digestifs are Chartreuse, amaro, slivovitz, and Calvados.

Chartreuse

Made from some 130 plants and extracts, a bottle of Chartreuse is like a giant multivitamin. It's a very peculiar drink that makes you feel strong (and drunk). First concocted by Carthusian monks at the Grande Chartreuse monastery in Voiron, France, Chartreuse was originally

known as the "elixir of long life." Served alone or on ice, it's a medicinal drink that speaks for itself, literally. (The Carthusians were essentially hermits who didn't speak, and they certainly didn't have a marketing department.)

Amaro

Lawyers, bankers, and golfers—in other words, rich guys—love amaro. I'm lucky to have a lot of these guys as customers, and when they are drunk, they all develop a big ego, a kind of Godfather complex. The other people who drink amaro are hipsters—in other words, poor people. And then, of course, there is the third group, the people who truly understand the digestive qualities of this elixir. All of these reasons are good enough for me. Our favorite amaro is Nardini.

Slivovitz

A straight shot of slivovitz (also known as plum brandy or plum eau-de-vie) the first thing in the morning took some gray out of communism for a lot of East Block friends.

Calvados

For the last three years, we've been selling Michel Beucher's Calvados, which is made from and tastes like organic apples. Calvados followed by a short espresso is the ultimate way to finish a meal. Some people say, "I don't like the taste." It's not about the taste. It works: it's cleansing and digestive. If you don't believe me, try drinking two bottles of 15 percent red and having sex. Go ahead. Everyone will be disappointed.

Punch Abruzzo

Years ago, Fred showed up at the restaurant with Punch Abruzzo. We all stared at the bottle like it was Christmas. The label sports a winter scene, with deer pulling sleighs full of happy people wearing tuques. Feels like Christmas, smells like Christmas, tastes like Christmas. We sell it like it's going out of style (which it did about forty years ago). Awesome hot or cold.

THE BEST OF THE JOE BEEF COCKTAIL LIST

Our cocktail recipes are the drinks we've been serving since the beginning. They're tongue-in-cheek and extremely tasty. We hope you enjoy them. **—DM**

THE VIJAY SINGH

Serves 1

Our alternative to the Arnold Palmer. Serve it in a julep goblet.

1 ounce (30 ml) green tea syrup
1 ounce (30 ml) gin
¼ ounce (7 ml) Chartreuse
Squeeze of fresh lemon juice
Ice
Tonic to top up

Pour the syrup, gin, Chartreuse, and lemon juice over ice. Stir and top up with the tonic.

ROMAN COKE

Serves 1

We like to plow through these heady drinks with a stack of cheap Genoese salamis. Chinotto, for anyone who hasn't sipped the bittersweet nonalcoholic soda, looks like Coca-Cola but is made from a citrus fruit grown primarily in central and southern Italy and some secret herbs. Serve in a highball glass.

¾ ounce (20 ml) cheap grappa
Dash of Fernet Branca
Ice
Chinotto to top up

Pour the grappa and Fernet Branca over ice. Stir and top up with the chinotto.

SAUSAGE MARTINI

Serves 1

Why did the olive meet the martini, the onion the Gibson? It just seems to make sense that if you want a snack in your liquor, you should make it a sausage. Give a new life to those pesky little Vienna wieners, or buy good-quality knackwurst and pickle them in a brine of equal parts vinegar and water. Serve in a small martini glass.

2 ounces (60 ml) vodka
½ ounce (15 ml) white vermouth
Dash of canned Vienna sausage juice
Drop of Tabasco sauce
1 canned Vienna sausage

Freeze a martini glass. Shake together the vodka, vermouth, sausage juice, and Tabasco. Serve in a chilled glass with a Vienna wiener on a skewer. Add more juice and it's a dirty sausage martini.

Clockwise from left: The Master Cleanse, Bock Tomate, Gin 'n' Jews

THE MASTER CLEANSE

Serves 1

A few years ago, we had a server and a bartender who were in the middle of a "cleanse." We tried their sordid-looking "drink" and decided to make our own, with booze, of course. Serve in a lowball glass.

½ cup (150 g) maple syrup
½ cup (125 ml) fresh lemon juice
Pinch of cayenne pepper
1 ounce (30 ml) bourbon
Soda water to top up

In a small, heavy pot, combine the maple syrup and lemon juice and bring to a boil. Add the cayenne, remove from the heat, and let cool. Measure 1½ ounces (45 ml) and mix with the bourbon; reserve the remainder in the fridge for more drinks. Pour over ice and top up with soda.

GIN 'N' JEWS

Serves 1

People are always complaining about Manischewitz. We think it's tasty and has applications at the bar. This is our tribute to our financiers Jeff, Ronnie, and David. Serve in a Champagne coupe.

1 ounce (30 ml) Manischewitz
1 ounce (30 ml) gin
1 egg white
¾ ounce (20 ml) fresh lemon juice
Ice

Combine the Manischewitz, gin, egg white, and lemon juice and shake extremely well to froth the mixture. Serve over ice.

BOCK TOMATE

Serves 1

Mixing beer and tomato juice is classic; some people call it a "soup." This is an overlooked drink perfect for brunch, lunch, and hot summer afternoons. Molson brewing has been in the Old Port since 1786. It's the beer we grew up on. It's a beer for the tavern, Sundays, camping, and hockey. We love micro-breweries, but a cold Molson Export, the Habs, and a hockey-arena smoked meat sandwich is the holy trinity. Serve in a tavern glass.

½ glass Molson Export
½ glass tomato juice
Salt

Pour the beer on the juice or the juice on the beer. This is a classic of the era when tavern windows where opaque to wives and priests. Add a pinch of salt when the carbonation fades. Serve with a pack of saltines or BBQ chips in the soothing haze of a du Maurier king size.

ROBERT ROY

Serves 4 to 6

This drink started as a vinaigrette for razor clams, and it still is. But with scotch, really cold, it's awesome. If you have a juicer, it's the best. If you don't, a blender and a sieve will do. Chervil is one of those herbs that you can't cook, and if you buzz it in syrup, for example, you will end up with something more akin to soup Florentine than a cocktail component. Serve in a lowball glass.

3 green apples, the more sour the better
1 bunch superfresh chervil
Juice of 2 small limes
¼ cup (85 g) honey
Scotch (we use Balvenie 12-year-old single malt)
Ice

Juice the apples, alternating with the chervil and lime juice. Mix the honey into the apple-chervil-lime juice. For each serving, combine ½ cup (125 ml) of the juice and 1 ounce (30 ml) of the scotch over ice.

THE RAW BEEF

Serves 1

Here's a short, delicious, and lethal concoction. Good when you're in search of instant numbness. Serve in a lowball glass.

2 ounces (60 ml) cheap sake
2 ounces (30 ml) vodka
Ice
Dash or two of Worcestershire sauce
1-ounce (30-g) piece perfect raw beef (from the tenderloin), on a skewer and well chilled

Freeze a lowball glass. Shake the sake and vodka with ice and strain into the glass. Serve *piscine* (with ice) with the Worcestershire dash sinking, and stir with the skewer of beef.

JOE BEEF CÉSAR

Serves 1

This is more of an appetizer than a cocktail. What's the reason behind the size? Hunger, gluttony, and insecurity are but a few. Serve in a large glass or a Mason jar.

Lemon wedge
Old Bay seasoning
Ice
1½ ounces (45 ml) vodka
Dash of Worcestershire sauce
Dash of Tabasco sauce
Finely grated fresh horseradish
Salt and pepper
Mott's Clamato juice to top up
Suggested garnishes: fresh shucked oyster, fresh shucked clam, lobster claw, cornichons, poached shrimp, BBQ ribs

Rub the lemon wedge around the rim of a large glass, then set the wedge aside. Dip the damp rim in the Old Bay to coat. Add a good amount of ice to the glass, then add the vodka, Worcestershire sauce, Tabasco, horseradish, some salt and pepper, and a squeeze of juice from the lemon wedge. Top up with the Clamato and garnish excessively.

BURDOCK ROOT WINE

Makes 4 cups (1 liter)

When we opened Joe Beef, we didn't have a patio. We had a patch of wasteland where only burdock grew. Not many people know what burdock is, though they may have seen or eaten the roots in vegan or Japanese restaurants. Its Latin name is *Arctium lappa* and it is a biennial plant, which means that the first year it makes a long taproot and hairy rhubarblike leaves. It survives the winter because of its reserve of food, and then the second year, it bears flowers, then fruits. These itchy little clingers stick to your pants.

It's a treasure chest of medicinal virtue for lungs, hair, and bowels. We didn't know what to do with it. But the four leathery-skinned Italian men who came to lay our concrete slab knew what to do with it. In fact, it took them four hours to lay the slab, half of which was spent carefully pulling and collecting the burdock roots. They said they would wash it when they got home, then steep it in red wine and consume it as a tonic.

So now every year, we send the newbies to dig for burdock in the fertile grounds of the Liverpool House backyard and make a few bottles of that tonic.

1 or 2 burdock roots, peeled

Peel of 1 orange, in one piece

2 whole cloves

About 1½ bottles (1.1 liters) of no-frills red table wine

1 cup (200 g) sugar

Put the burdock, orange peel, cloves, wine, and sugar in a 2-quart (2-liter) Mason jar. Cover tightly and shake well. Strain the mixture into a clean bottle and cap. Store the tonic in the fridge for 2 months, then enjoy.

COLD MULLED WINE

Makes 3 cups (750 ml)

This recipe, aka *Kälte Glühwein trinken für Freunde im Sommer*, was inspired by a box of German mulled wine: it depicted a blond, deliriously happy family sitting down to a few cups of this mulled tea. Serve in highball glasses.

1 bottle (750 ml) not-so-crappy-yet-not-too-good red wine

4 orange slices

4 whole cloves

2 cinnamon sticks

1 star anise

1 bay leaf

½ cup (100 g) sugar

Ice

Brandy in desired amount (we like Magno; it's Spanish, cheap, and sweet tasting)

Soda water to top up

In a saucepan, combine the wine, orange slices, cloves, cinnamon sticks, star anise, bay leaf, and sugar and bring to to a slow simmer over medium heat, stirring to dissolve the sugar. Simmer for a minute or two, then take off the heat, let cool a bit, and refrigerate. When cold, strain about 3 ounces (90 ml) into each glass, pouring it over a lot of ice. Add about 1 ounce (30 ml) brandy to each glass and top up with soda. If you have one of those nifty carbonation devices, run the wine through it. It will be even better.

MAKING YOUR OWN ABSINTHE

Makes about 6 cups (1.5 liters)

On the first year of the garden, we planted six tomato plants, one smallish row of lettuce that bolted overnight, and, just for fun, a dozen wormwood plants (*Artemisia absithium*). Of course, by then the absinthe craze had faded and the silver-slotted spoons were long gone. It didn't take much for us to soak way too much of those plants (in our houses, of course) in a jug of alcool (grain alcohol), then correct the awful taste of wormwood with a full bottle of pastis. Man, it was strong, and it worked, too.

A few years ago, we gave Martin Picard at Au Pied de Cochon a pickle jar full of absinthe; when we later visited the restaurant, about a thousand dollars in cash was sitting in the liquid and people were drinking it right out of the jar. Disgusting. Picard would add more booze when the level dropped. So you have this huge jar of plants and money just sitting there with the top on.

Every season we try to concoct a better mix—at home, of course. You'll need a gram scale for this recipe.

MIX A
30 g dried wormwood
45 g fennel seeds
45 g aniseeds
10 g dried angelica root
12 g coriander seeds
10 g dried lemon peel

MIX B
10 g dried hyssop
10 g dried lemon balm
10 g dried peppermint

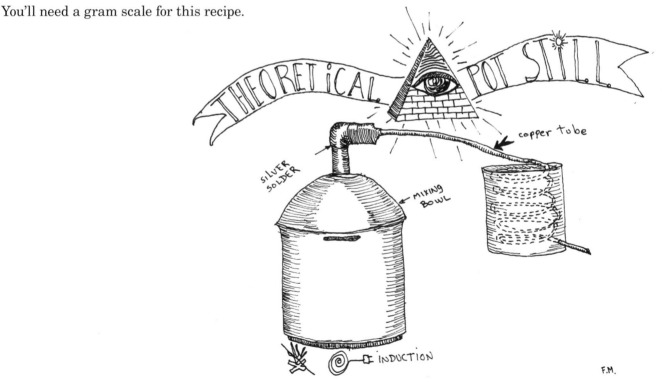

In reality, you should macerate Mix A for a few days in a 1 quart (1-liter) bottle of 190 proof (95 percent) clear alcool, then dilute and distill it. But since it is dangerous and mostly illegal, we don't suggest it. After you get a clear distillate, you would macerate Mix B in it for a few days to impart the greenish tinge (though not the fake mouthwash color) and a light herbaceous tone. Then you would add clean water and strain it through a coffee filter to bring down the alcool content to 90 proof (45 percent). So if you're bottling in old wine bottles, it should be half mixture, half water. Cork, shake, and serve.

Another option (that purists would find disturbing) is to put Mix A in a muslin bag and tie it closed. Soak the bag in 190 proof clear alcool for 3 days in a dark, cool room. Remove the Mix A bag, add Mix B in a muslin bag, and leave again for 3 days, same process. Then remove the second bag and filter the liquid through a series of coffee filters. Add an equal amount of clean water. Or, you can substitute simple syrup (equal parts sugar and water; dissolve the sugar in the water) for part of the water.

Note: *Here is how to find our herb man, a one-stop shop for absinthe ingredients: Herbarôme-la Bottine aux Herbes, 3778 A Rue Saint Denis, Montreal, QC H2W 2M1, (514) 845-1225; labottineauxherbes@bellnet.ca.*

round the time of our second year, a Florida steak-house owner came in for dinner. When we checked on him at the end of the meal, he couldn't get over the taste of the strip loin. "This is delicious beef," he said. "Where is it from?" "It's Alberta strip," we replied, reiterating what we had been assured of by our distributer since the beginning. "Can I see a strip, unopened, in the bag?" he asked.

CHAPTER 8

PUTTING THE "BEEF" IN JOE BEEF

We resurfaced with the goods and the diner took a look at the code on the side of the meat. "I know this code, this meat is from Western Australia!" he said, grinning. We were furious. We had not only been (unknowingly) lying to every customer about the origin of the beef, but we had also not been buying beef in accordance with our own values. Alberta was a bit far but passable, at least until we could find something better closer to home. But Western Australia? That's way out of line with our whole "as long we can drive there in an afternoon" mantra. And "beef" is in our name. What would Charles McKiernan think? Needless to say, we looked like complete assholes, standing at the table with our Australian beef.

The next day, heads rolled, and we began what seemed like our one hundredth exploration for the elusive strip loin. The biggest dilemma—and the weakest link—of our restaurant lives has been the beef we sell. It is our Achilles' heel. This is not a joke: we simply could not get it right. I cannot tell you how many times we've been lied to over the years, by packers, by food-service vendors, even by famous Montreal butchers.

If the strip loin was Canadian, it was often a bit "un-special" in both taste and distribution. If it was not commercial, it was undependable hippie beef handled by purveyors who never showed up on time and left you serving a table of businessmen guinea hen and trout.

We can tell you who traps our eel, where the *magrets* of duck are farmed, in which bay the Malpeque oysters are tonged. But with strip loin, "Canada" was our lame (and incorrect) answer. We've always had a good handle on our rib steak, but in general, beef is an issue. So why not just scrap any cut other than rib steak? Because beef has no equal.

As problematic (and in some cases, downright disgusting) as the industry is, we still want to find, and

eat, that perfect cut. Fred is the first to tear into a rib steak. He's a regular at the city's steak houses. And even though I find the thought of steak on the blackboard numbingly boring, a lean strip loin is my go-to when I'm ordering. As Mark Schatzker says in *Steak: One Man's Search for the World's Tastiest Piece of Beef*, "No one celebrates a bonus at work by ordering chicken."

We have three very small restaurants with high food costs, which means we need to sell wine. And beef is the product responsible for the biggest wine sales. Whenever we sell big wine, it's followed by big beef. Often the behemoth corporate food distributors come to us and say, "Isn't it annoying to make one call for ricotta, one call for carrots, one

call for Coke, one call for water, and one call for sirloin steaks? Why not a one-stop shop?" To this, our answer is, "Yes, it's annoying, but we want to buy things from real people."

Nowadays, some products are even packaged in ways that make you believe they have come from small producers. Big brewers make microbrews, cheese conglomerates package artisanal cheeses, and Pepsico owns San Pellegrino. Knowing that "Industrial Organic" exists, we want to be damn sure that we've met the people who are raising, slaughtering, hanging, and cutting our beef. We work with many likeminded individuals in Quebec. One person we'd love to work with operates outside of Quebec—Stephen Alexander at Cumbrae's—and is our model of a good beef farmer.

Stephen is a third-generation butcher who started hanging out in butcher shops in Melbourne, Australia, when he was nine years old. He wasn't even allowed to touch a steak until his second year working at the shop, at the age of seventeen. At the same time, Alistair Roberston, a Scot from the Isle of Cumbrae, was working for a large agricultural company in Toronto. In 1987, Alistair, then fifty-one, went back to his farming roots. Stephen met Alistair by chance when he was visiting his girlfriend (now wife), Bella, in Toronto. All that was in Toronto at the time butcherwise was the old-school Portuguese guy, the Italian guy, the neighborhood guys. And thank god for them. Everything else was your basic grocery store (Maple Leaf) generic meat wrapped in cellophane and Styrofoam.

Alistair was the farmer, Stephen was the butcher, and it just made sense: "In 1994, we started a shop downtown on the then-grungy Church Street. We had the old farmer, the old shop. We worked it hard. All livestock was from Alistair and his neighbors in Haldimand County (southern Ontario, just outside of Hamilton). It was one of those situations where Alistair's neighbors were raising lambs and someone else had pigs, so they became an unofficial co-op of sorts. We grew and grew and grew until we became a full-service butcher shop. We did everything. I dealt with abattoirs and with farmers. I was obsessed with getting the raw ingredients I wanted. I would have to deal with genetics."

Stephen grew up on 100 percent grass-fed beef and the cows from Cumbrae's eat grass, with a bit of hay, alfalfa, clover, and grains. They eat five to ten pounds (2.3 to 4.5 kilograms) of it in the morning and the same at night. They don't require antibiotics, as the hay pushes the grass through the digestion tract. The meat goes from the fields to the abattoir, where it can swing for seven to fourteen days. Then the beef goes to the Cumbrae's shop, where it is broken down. It's then tagged and put into the drying rooms, where the dry-aging process begins.

How long it is aged is up to the chef. Dry aging is a huge cost for sellers and buyers. A massive amount of waste and rot happens when you age beef. As mass is lost, the rot imparts a pleasing blue cheese–foie gras taste to the muscle and fat, a lot of which is thrown out. Cumbrae's is able to customize rib steak with a long bone (about eight inches/twenty centimeters). The purpose of this is mostly bragging rights, but not ours. That long bone is also just aesthetically pleasing. Stephen figures these rib steaks are the best 5 to 10 percent of beef the farm produces, which is why it's what he uses for his own personal stash.

Each Cumbrae's cow costs between $200 and $250 more per head than commodity cattle. More time is taken with each animal and all of the feed is grown on the property. On selling to restaurants, Stephen says, "It's a nice break from retail, but I mostly do it because it ignites my passion for dealing with likeminded people. I'm not saying we lose money, but we don't make much. Overall, Cumbrae's is about the relentless pursuit of great meat."

The same goes for us with our Quebec producers. It's not cheap for us to bring in rib steak from small farms, but it's the right thing to do. It makes us feel comfortable. We would rather be proud than rich when we wake up in the morning. Farmers now have a choice; they don't have to grow the commodities crops like in the 1980s and 1990s. It's coming full circle. There's a huge demand for nonindustrial-farmed products. Traditional family-farmed beef is a good compromise for us between Cargill and organic meat.

Here are the recipes that put the "beef" in Joe Beef. —**DM**

STRIP LOIN STEAK

Serves 1

When we first started cooking, beef was like tuna is today: incorrect to buy and incorrect to sell. But over the last couple of years, beef is finding its place again, especially with the burger *courant* sweeping the continent. We've used sirloins from large companies, but doing so feels a bit like cheating on my wife with a lady boy: part guilty, part disgusting, and yet I still buy it. Since we began purchasing more carefully aged and selected strip loins, this is now one of our favorite cuts. It is tasty, the perfect size, monolithic.

The method here is specific to this strip loin, cooked medium-rare. Check the temperature chart (see page 242) for different levels of doneness. Remember that dry-aged meat tends to cook much faster because of its lower moisture content, so act accordingly. And when it comes to cooking, the weight of the steak does not matter as much as the thickness (our steaks each weigh about 21 to 22 ounces/610 to 640 grams), which is why you see only the thickness here. Also, the middle of the steak is where you can see doneness, not on the tip, so insert an instant-read thermometer through the side to the center to verify it is ready. If you must, you can also cut the steak in two to check doneness. Remember, though, you can always cook longer, but not "de-cook."

1 strip loin steak, 1½ inches (4 cm) thick

1 teaspoon kosher salt

Pepper (optional)

3 tablespoons canola oil

Pat of unsalted butter

Montreal Steak Spice (page 250), optional

1. Take the steak out of the fridge and let it rest at room temperature for 3 hours. This is crucial and makes this method what it is. The meat should almost be at room temperature.

2. When you are ready to cook, heat a thick cast-iron frying pan over medium-high heat. It should get very hot. Season your steak liberally with the salt and some pepper.

3. Add the oil to the hot pan, carefully add the steak, and lower the heat to medium. Cook for 5 minutes on one side and then 3 minutes on the other for medium-rare.

4. Transfer to a plate, add the pat of butter and steak spice to the top and let the steak rest on the counter for 3 to 7 minutes before serving.

continued

THE JOE BEEF TEN VARIATIONS FOR STRIP LOIN

MIRABEAU

On each steak, crisscross 8 anchovy fillets and 8 olive halves. Add Joe Beef Sauce Vin Rouge (page 250), a sprig of thyme, and a pinch of cayenne.

HORSERADISH

Grate a heaping tablespoon of fresh horseradish onto each steak.

PICKLES AND MONTREAL STEAK SPICE

Add a sliced dill pickle on top of the steak spice.

TOMATOES AND GREENS

Sprinkle a thick tomato slice with salt and pepper. Serve with a handful of wilted greens, a bit of butter, and Joe Beef Sauce Vin Rouge (page 250). Most of the time when you order a steak, it looks like this, our classic.

SLAB OF STILTON

Put a 2½-ounce (75-g) piece of Stilton cheese on the steak with Joe Beef Sauce Vin Rouge (page 250).

GREEN PASTURES (VERT-PRE)

Serve with a watercress salad, matchstick potatoes, and a disk of beurre mâitre d'hôtel. To make the butter, in a small pan, combine ⅓ cup (80 ml) dry white wine and ⅓ cup (40 g) chopped French shallots over medium heat and cook for 6 to 8 minutes, or until the pan is just dry but the shallots are not colored. Remove from the heat and let cool. With a rubber spatula, combine 8 ounces (225 g) room-temperature unsalted butter, 3 tablespoons Dijon mustard, the shallots, a handful of chopped fresh parsley, and a little salt and pepper. On plastic wrap, shape the butter mixture into a cylinder the diameter of a silver dollar and refrigerate until firm.

STEAK AU POIVRE

Use the Duck Steak au Poivre recipe (page 61) for the sauce, and coat the meat in smashed peppercorns on one side (the one that's facing up) prior to searing.

THE MAIN

At The Main restaurant on Boulevard Saint Laurent, across the street from Schwartz's, the kitchen serves a steak with a side of liver and franks. And if you're nice, they'll drape a slice of smoked meat on it.

CHINATOWN

If you're willing, just make the sauce for Oysters #37 (page 123) and use it on your steak. Or, serve the steak with an oyster topped with the sauce and some Chinese broccoli.

ZESTY ITALIAN

Use the dressing for Zesty Italian Tartare (page 245) on a steak.

TEMPERATURE DONENESS CHART FOR BEEF

This is the temperature *before* you let the meat rest for 3 to 8 minutes. (The temp will continue to rise a bit as the meat rests.) Larger pieces of meat can rest longer than small pieces.

Doneness	°F	°C
Rare	105°	40°
Medium-rare	115°	45°
Medium	125°	50°
Medium-well	130°	55°
Well done	140°	60°

CÔTE DE BOEUF

Serves 3, 2, or (on rare occasions) 1

1 côte de boeuf, 2½ pounds (1.2 kg) and 2½ inches (6 cm) thick

1 tablespoon salt

Pepper (optional)

3 tablespoons canola oil

3 tablespoons unsalted butter

Montreal Steak Spice (page 250), optional

Joe Beef Sauce Vin Rouge (page 250)

Roasted marrowbones, cooked according to Marrowbones Cultivateur (page 23), omitting the soup

Good Fries (page 154)

Parc Vinet Salad (page 190)

1. Temper the meat for 3½ hours prior to cooking it. That means take it out of the fridge and set it on a clean cutting board or plate.

2. When you are ready to cook, turn on the oven to 375°F (190°C). Season the meat with the salt and some pepper. Remember, you are salting meat over 2 inches (5 cm) thick.

3. Heat the oil in a large, thick oven-proof pan over medium heat. Add the meat and sear it on the first side for 12 minutes, and on the second side for 8 minutes.

4. Drain the fat out of the pan, add the butter and the steak spice, and then send the pan to the oven for 8 minutes.

5. Remove the pan from the oven, flip the meat onto a plate, and let it rest for 8 minutes for medium-rare. Serve on a hot plate with the sauce, marrowbones, and fries or a salad.

We owe it to Riad Nasr and Lee Hanson at Balthazar for the revival of the *plat pour deux* in restaurants. It's great for the passionate cook, and great for the passionate diner, as it denotes a more willing, yet easygoing approach. Nicolas Jongleux used to do a guinea hen for two, the breast on the bone with *jus truffé*, in fine china; vegetables in a silver casserole dish; and a second service of legs with squash gnocchi and mimolette cheese. It was beautiful food made perfect by the antique tableware. Alain Ducasse once said that if you go with a date to the cinema, you don't go to different movies; the same applies to dining. If you and your companion agree, it can be heaven.

Why another book with a *côte de boeuf*? Because this is the Joe Beef *côte de boeuf*. A *côte de boeuf* is a majestic cut. It is 2½ pounds (1.2 kilograms) of natural, aged, carefully butchered steer good-ness. In our mind, a *côte de boeuf* has to be cut by hand, leaving the bone intact. (One, if not the main, difference between European and American butchery is the use of the meat saw. In North America, the cuts are based on sawing parts; in Europe, the cuts are made by knife, every muscle separated.)

At Joe Beef, the side dishes keep coming when you order a *côte de boeuf*: green salad, fries, horseradish, red wine sauce, and marrow-bones. This, in addition to the quality of the meat, is why we cannot justify lowering the price.

ZESTY ITALIAN TARTARE

Serves 4

At Joe Beef, we mix up the tartares on the menu, sometimes offering the classic French recipe and other times the zesty Italian. This is the one we prepare at home the most. A nice alternative to carpaccio, it's a great summer tartare.

DRESSING

1 pimiento-stuffed green olive, chopped

1½ teaspoons chopped fresh flat-leaf parsley

1½ teaspoons chopped fresh basil

½ teaspoon finely chopped garlic

½ teaspoon finely chopped red onion

2 anchovy fillets

1 tablespoon grated Parmesan cheese

2 tablespoons red wine vinegar

3 tablespoons canola oil

3 tablespoons olive oil

1 teaspoon brown sugar

1 teaspoon Dijon mustard

1 teaspoon water

1 pound (455 g) top sirloin

Salt and pepper

4 slices country bread, brushed with olive oil

1 or 2 cloves garlic (optional)

4 anchovy fillets (optional)

Sour Crudités (page 177)

1 tablespoon fresh flat-leaf parsley leaves for garnish

Thin shavings of Parmesan cheese for garnish

1. To make the dressing, in a large measuring pitcher, combine the olive, parsley, basil, garlic, onion, anchovy fillets, Parmesan, vinegar, the oils, the brown sugar, mustard, and the water. Emulsify with a hand blender and set aside.

2. To prep the meat, cut the sirloin into ½-inch (12-mm) cubes, making sure there is no silver skin or gristle. Using a small blender or food processor, grind the meat until it has that steak tartare consistency. Place the ground meat in a bowl and season with salt and pepper. Add the dressing and mix well. We recommend starting with half and adding more to taste.

3. Toast the oil-brushed bread slices. If you want to get crazy, rub the toast with a garlic clove, and place an anchovy fillet on top of each slice.

4. Place the tartare on a plate, arrange the toasted bread slices on the side, and spoon the pickled vegetables alongside the tartare. Garnish the tartare with the parsley and Parmesan shavings. Serve right away.

DAUBE DE JOUES DE BOEUF CHAUDE (HOT)

Serves 4

Hot, it's beef stew. Cold, it's jellied beef stew.

4 nice-size beef cheeks, about
    10 ounces (280 g) each, trimmed

Salt and pepper

2 tablespoons canola oil

½ cup (100 g) winter lardons
    (see Theory #3, page 166)

½ cup (70 g) finely chopped onion

2 anchovy fillets

1 tomato, halved, seeded, cut into
    rough chunks

Leaves from 4 sprigs thyme

2 cloves garlic

Zest of ½ orange, in one piece

1 bay leaf

Pinch of cayenne pepper

2 cups (500 ml) dry white wine

½ cup (125 ml) water, more or less

¼ cup (40 g) black olives (pitted or not)

¼ cup (60 g) green olives (pitted
    or not)

Purée de Pommes de Terre (page 180)

1. Preheat the oven to 375°F (190°C). Pat the cheeks dry and season with salt and pepper.

2. Place a 3-quart (3-liter) cocotte or other heavy ovenproof pot over high heat and drop in the oil. When the oil is hot, add the cheeks and sear on both sides until you get the color you would get on a nice steak. This should be roughly 4 to 5 minutes on each side.

3. Remove the cheeks and set aside. Add the lardons to the pot and cook for 4 to 5 minutes, or until crispy. Add the onion, anchovy, tomato, thyme, garlic, orange zest, bay leaf, and cayenne. Sweat for 3 minutes.

4. Now put the beef back in the pot and add the wine. The wine shouldn't cover the meat; top it off barely with the water. Bring to a simmer, cover, and place in the oven. Cook for 2½ hours, or until the cheeks are no longer bouncy when pressed with a fingertip.

5. Add the olives, re-cover, and cook for another 30 minutes. Remove and correct the seasoning before serving. Serve hot with the potatoes.

DAUBE DE JOUES DE BOEUF EN GELÉE (COLD)

This recipe is identical to the hot daube, with the exception of the addition of gelatin and the fact that no olives are used in the stew. Oh, and it's cold.

Cook the daube as directed, omitting the olives. When it's ready, remove and discard the bay leaf, crush the cooked garlic, and correct the seasoning. Add more salt than usual, because when the beef is cold, the salt is less obvious. Remove the cheeks and set aside.

Meanwhile, bloom 12 gelatin sheets in a bowl of cool water to cover for 5 to 10 minutes, or until they soften and swell. Gently squeeze the gelatin sheets and add to the daube jus. It should be hot enough to dissolve the gelatin. Shred the cheeks roughly with a fork and mix well with the jus. Line a medium-size

terrine mold with plastic wrap, allowing it to overhang the edges. Transfer the cheeks and then the jus to the terrine. Fill in the gaps with the warm jus, cover with the plastic wrap overhang, and refrigerate for at least 8 hours or up to overnight.

To serve, remove the jellied beef from the mold by pulling gently on the plastic wrap. Cut into slices ¾ inch (2 cm) thick. Serve the slices with olives, olive oil, black pepper, and rough peasant bread. The beef will keep for 1 week max. If you get tired of cold jellied meat, you can gently melt it in a pan and toss in a few rigatoni. It's good like that.

DEVILED KIDNEY and HANGER ON TOAST

Serves up to 4

This is what we imagine old Scots at the turn of the century in the Montreal's famed Golden Square Mile neighborhood ate for breakfast: steak, kidneys, kippers, and a few eggs. After a gin festivity, it would be exactly what it takes to get you back on your feet. It's delicious with a little watercress salad.

DEVIL SAUCE

1 tablespoon red wine vinegar

¼ cup (60 ml) Beef Shank Stock (page 249)

¼ cup (30 g) diced French shallots

¼ cup (60 ml) Worcestershire sauce

2 pinches of cayenne pepper

2 tablespoons ketchup

4 large white mushrooms, finely chopped

4 teaspoons chopped fresh flat-leaf parsley

2 teaspoons Colman's dry mustard

¼ cup (60 ml) water

Salt and pepper

HANGER AND KIDNEY (PER PERSON)

2 oz (55 g) veal kidney, diced the size of half a marshmallow

2 oz (55 g) hanger steak, diced like above

2 big white mushrooms, diced like above

Salt and pepper

1 teaspoon olive oil

Pat of unsalted butter

1 slice country bread, toasted, per person

1 egg, fried over easy, per person

1. For the devil sauce, in a saucepan, stir together all the ingredients. Bring to a low simmer for 5 minutes and correct the seasoning.

2. Season the kidney, steak, and mushrooms with salt and pepper. Heat a frying pan over high heat and drop in the oil and butter. When hot, add the goods and sauté together for 4 minutes. Add some devil sauce to taste.

3. For each serving, place the hot toast on a plate, top with the sauté, and then with the just-fried egg. Serve right away.

FILET DE BOEUF: THE POSTMODERN OFFAL!

Serves 2

If you're a fervent practitioner of the nose-to-tail thing, you probably scoff at tenderloin, favoring instead oxtail or udders. In a hypothetical dystopian foodist nation, animals will be bred in humane ways to produce more spleens, livers, and guts than loins and legs. No joke. The meat business wanted pig with more bacon and less shoulder a few years ago, a disturbing enough thought. It's a common dichotomy and funny somehow. The rich feast on what was once peasant food. Think about it: risotto, polenta, offal, eggs are everywhere. Once again, we don't omit ourselves from the criticism. In fact, it's the stuff that keeps us up at night.

The fillet comes from the small end of the tenderloin, from a muscle inside the ribs called the psoas major, which reportedly has the function of providing the quadruped with an efficient humping motion. We put filet mignon on the blackboard, get sick of it, and a week later put it back on the board. Cut into thick chunks, hog tied, and roasted, tenderloin is great. One of my favorite dishes, beef Stroganoff, is also best made with tenderloin (I omitted it from this book for fear of being ostracized by the cool chef gang). Also, the River Café Raw Beef (tenderloin, too) is still one of my favorite cookbook recipes.

1-pound (455-g) piece tenderloin, about 2½ inches (6 cm) thick, untrimmed and tied

3 tablespoons canola oil

1 teaspoon kosher salt

Pepper (optional)

1 tablespoon unsalted butter

2 crosscut marrowbones, each about 2 inches (5 cm) high, prepared according to Marrowbones Cultivateur (page 23), omitting the soup (optional)

Gentleman Steak Sauce (page 251)

Good Fries (page 154)

1. Take the tenderloin out of the fridge and let it rest at room temperature for a minimum of 3 hours.

2. In a cast-iron frying pan, heat the oil over medium heat. Season the tenderloin generously with the salt and pepper. When the oil is hot, place the tenderloin in the pan. (Always remember the splash risk and drop away from you; your genitals and bystanders will thank you). Lower the heat to medium-low, so there is just a slight sizzle, and cook the top side for 4 minutes, the bottom side for 4 minutes, and each of the other three sides for 4 minutes each, for five sides total at medium-rare.

3. Remove the tenderloin to a plate, top with the butter, and let rest for 4 minutes before serving. Serve with the marrowbones, the sauce, and some fries.

BEEF SHANK STOCK

Makes 4 cups (1 liter)

A great way to maintain matrimonial bliss is *not* to make classic stock in your house. Do this one instead. It's another one-Creuset wonder where everything goes in the oven. It's enough for a few recipes, plus you can eat the meat with pickles and mustard for a classic French snack. You can use a bit more meat if you have it. This is more of a guideline than a recipe. Remember that when you make a stock, it has to look like you would *want* to eat the meat at any stage—that is, don't use old meat or lean cuts. You want that marrow taste and that thick jelly feel.

2½ to 3 pounds (1.2 to 1.4 kg) beef shank, sawed crosswise into 1-inch (2.5-cm) pieces by your butcher

Salt and pepper

¼ cup (60 ml) canola oil

3 celery stalks, roughly chopped

3 big carrots, roughly chopped

2 onions, roughly chopped

1 tomato, halved and seeded

2 cloves garlic

2 sprigs flat-leaf parsley

2 sprigs thyme

8 cups (2 liters) water

2 cups (500 ml) dry red table wine

1 tablespoon all-purpose flour

1. Preheat the oven to 325°F (165°C). Season the meat like you would a steak.

2. Put a large ovenproof pot over high heat. Add oil to a depth of ¼ inch (6 mm). When the oil starts smoking, it's ready. Sear the meat for 3 to 4 minutes on each side. When flipping sides, be sure to use long tongs and roll the steak toward the back, so if oil splashes, it's not toward you. And remember, just because it is meat for a stock, it doesn't mean you shouldn't give it the love and care you would if you were to eat it *comme ça*. It should look and smell delicious.

3. Remove the meat to a plate and drain off most of the oil from the pot. Turn the heat to medium, and add the celery, carrots, onions, tomato, garlic, parsley, and thyme to the same pot. Cook for 4 to 5 minutes, or until the vegetables have some color.

4. Pour the water and wine into the pot. Sprinkle the browned shank pieces evenly with the flour and add them to the pot. Bring to a boil, cover, transfer to the oven, and cook for 3½ to 4 hours. After 3 hours, check the progress. The stock is ready when the meat is very tender.

5. Remove from the oven. Scoop out the big pieces, then strain the stock through a fine-mesh sieve into a container. Let cool, cover, and refrigerate. The stock will keep for up to 1 week in the fridge or up to 1 month in the freezer. Before using, scoop off the fat that has congealed on top.

MONTREAL STEAK SPICE

Makes 2 to 3 cups (200 to 300 g), about 60 servings

Montreal institutions like Gibbys and Moishes have been selling their own classic steak spice for decades. Here's our take on the Montreal steak spice. This is an all-purpose seasoning used in many Montreal-style beef, pork, and steaky fish dishes.

1 onion, finely diced
10 cloves garlic, finely diced
3 small red dried chiles (such as Thai birds), minced
½ cup (115 g) kosher salt
¼ cup (50 g) packed brown sugar
Leaves from 1 bunch rosemary
½ cup (45 g) coriander seeds, cracked
6 tablespoons (40 g) cracked pepper
1 tablespoon dill seeds
1 tablespoon paprika

1. Preheat the oven to 225°F (110°C). In a bowl, stir together the onion, garlic, chiles, salt, sugar, and rosemary. Spread the mixture on a rimmed baking sheet and bake for 2 to 3 hours, or until the onions are dry. Keep an eye on the oven to make sure the onion pieces don't burn, and turn down the heat if they threaten to scorch.

2. When the mixture is nice and dry, remove from the oven and let cool, then transfer to a food processor and pulse just two or three times to break up the clumps.

3. Return the mixture to a bowl, add the coriander seeds, pepper, dill seeds, and paprika, and mix well. Transfer to a jar, cap tightly, and store in the fridge for up to 1 month. Or, freeze in a lock-top plastic bag for up to 6 months.

JOE BEEF SAUCE VIN ROUGE

Makes 2 cups (500 ml)

Sauce Vin Rouge is our mother-ship sauce, good on all matters of protein. When seasoning this sauce, or any sauce, keep in mind that it won't be consumed like a soup, so go ahead and be relatively liberal with the salt.

½ cup (55 g) sliced French shallots
1 small red beet, peeled and thickly sliced
2 cups (500 ml) dry red table wine
2 tablespoons cheap-ass balsamic vinegar
1 bay leaf
2 cups (500 ml) Beef Shank Stock (page 249)
3 tablespoons unsalted butter
Salt
1 teaspoon pepper

1. In a small saucepan, mix together the shallots, beet, wine, vinegar, and bay leaf. Bring to a boil over high heat and reduce by half. Add the stock and continue to boil until reduced by half.

2. Whisk in the butter and season generously with salt and with the pepper. Serve right away. Or, let cool, transfer to a tightly capped container, and refrigerate for up to a week or freeze for up to a month.

ONION SOUP SAUCE

Makes about 1½ cups (375 ml)

Here is another of our kitchen staples, which tastes like an extraction of the essence of onion soup. Awesome on liver, veal, beef, or even schnitzel, it's the taste of winter in Paris.

2 cups (200 g) thinly sliced onions
¼ cup (55 g) unsalted butter
1½ cups (375 ml) Beef Shank Stock (page 249)
2 tablespoons dry sherry (optional)
1 to 2 tablespoons sherry vinegar
Leaves from 4 sprigs thyme
1 bay leaf
Salt and pepper

1. In a thick-bottomed saucepan, sweat the onions in 2 tablespoons of the butter over medium heat until the onions are about one-third of their original volume and nicely colored. This should take about 15 minutes. Add the stock, sherry, vinegar, thyme, and bay leaf and season with salt and pepper. Simmer slowly for 20 minutes to blend the flavors.

2. Swirl in the remaining butter and correct the seasoning (with vinegar, too). Use immediately, or store in the fridge for up to 5 days.

GENTLEMAN STEAK SAUCE

Makes about 1½ cups (375 ml)

We champion this generalization: gentlemen eat their beef with steak sauce—the brown type, thick and sharp. Although we support Heinz ketchup and we think it calls for respect and pride, we don't use bottled steak sauce. Here is an easy and tasty alternative. It is delicious with *Filet de Boeuf* (page 248).

1 cup (170 g) pitted prunes, soaked in hot water to cover for 1 hour
1 cup (250 ml) ketchup
1 cup (250 ml) cider vinegar
¼ cup (60 ml) water
¼ cup (60 ml) Worcestershire sauce
½ cup (65 g) packed brown sugar
2 tablespoons molasses
4 green onions, roughly chopped
2 anchovy fillets
3 whole cloves
1 clove garlic
1 tablespoon Colman's dry mustard
1 tablespoon ground allspice
1 tablespoon black pepper
Pinch of cayenne pepper

1. In a small, thick-bottomed saucepan, combine all of the ingredients. Bring to a slow simmer and simmer gently for 30 to 45 minutes, stirring occasionally with a wooden spoon. If it reduces excessively, add a bit of water. You're looking for the texture of ketchup with chunks.

2. When it's ready, remove from the heat and carefully buzz with a hand blender (if you don't own one, pulse in a food processor).

3. Let cool, transfer to a container with a tight-fitting lid, and refrigerate. It will keep for up to 1 month.

efore we opened Joe Beef, David had a theory that the ideal menu anywhere would have ten mains, ten appetizers, and five desserts. Today, we overflow completely from those holy principles, except when it comes to dessert. We honestly rotate among twenty (max!) desserts per year, and have only three on the board at a time. The reason? Our kitchens are quite small, so whoever is working the cold station is also the token dessert guy or girl. Plus, our limited space dictates the kinds of desserts we can make. We don't have room for a pastry station or its appliances. This is good for you, the reader, as we don't have any appliances or resources that you don't have in your own kitchen. The *marjolaine*, meringue, and éclairs are time-consuming but not difficult, and they don't require any special tools.

CHAPTER 9

THE DESSERT CHARIOT

On the day we opened, dessert was a complete afterthought. We decided on Concord grape *panna cotta* at the last minute. It's a simple, traditional dessert, and like all of the recipes in this chapter, it is something we imagine seeing on a grand dessert chariot, those lauded dessert carts of yesteryear. One of the most amazing things about running a thirty-seat restaurant is that we don't always have to come up with clever interpretations: fresh, perfectly ripe fruit, delicious cheese from the Magdelan Islands, or a big wooden bowl of mixed nuts with crackers is always appreciated by the finest diners.

The following recipes are our staples, desserts that we imagine sitting proudly on a regal chariot. —**FM**

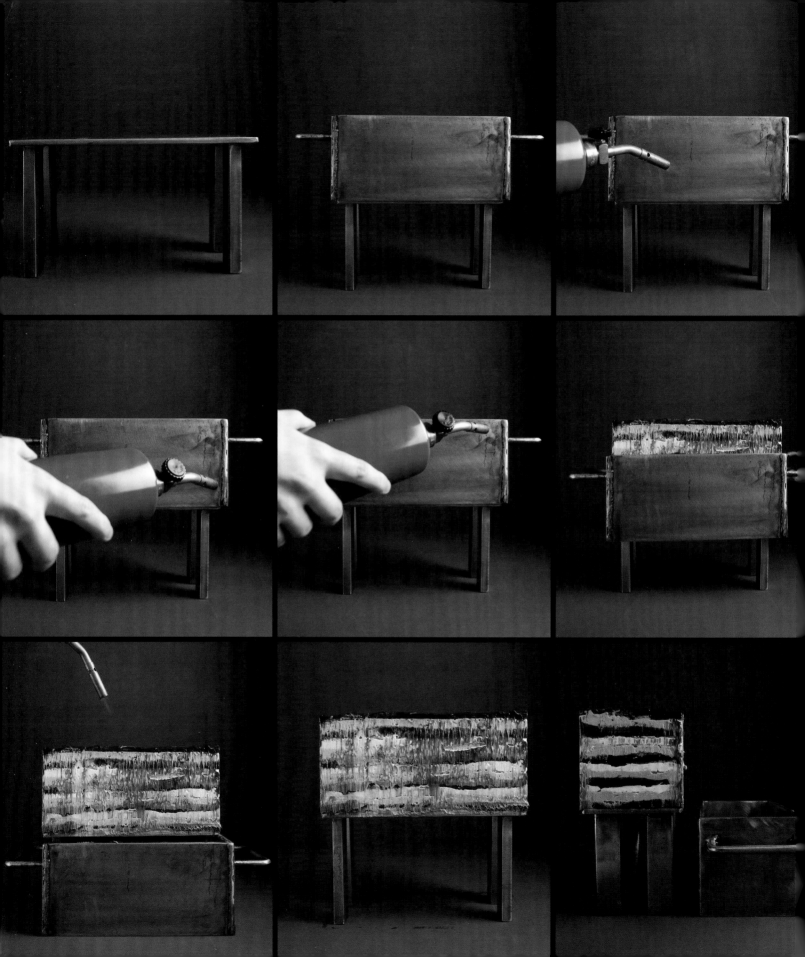

MARJOLAINE

Serves 10

Fred first learned of this cake from Brendon Vallejo, a friend of many and a real one-of-a-kind guy. He lived in an apartment with a stage in the living room. One night he passionately ripped out all of the electrical wiring for his kitchen stove, only to realize that gas was not an option. He had truly weird and original ideas that (sometimes) led to great things.

He told Fred about the *marjolaine* he made with marjoram and cream beaten into butter. It's odd, and not the Fernand Point way, but there is something about it that screams genius. A few years after hanging with Brendon, Fred fell upon a copy of *Ma Gastronomie* by Fernand Point. It's up there with Escoffier for him. And not only did it have the recipe for his signature awesome *marjolaine*, but it also had little anecdotes about drinking Champagne all day and getting the neighboring restaurant's fourteen-year-old apprentice wasted on vermouth lemonade. This book gave Fred a desire to have fun at work, to be like a gang of buddies in the kitchen. Sure, sometimes it's dictatorial and tyrannical, but most of the time it's goofy and fun.

Jackie Turotte, the former *garde-manger* at Liverpool House, was always vocally doubtful about Fred's new purchases or creations. And the stainless-steel mold with walls ¼ inch (6 mm) thick that Wally made for holding a *marjolaine* was no exception (especially after explaining the numerous layers of almond cake, cream, and butter cream). But after Fred's successful first *marjolaine*, she was convinced. It's a gorgeous dessert, and has not one but two buttercreams, which you don't see much of these days.

This recipe has three main parts: the cake, the buttercreams, and the ganache. The steel mold we use is worthy of a Mies van der Rohe miniature. Your mold doesn't have to be as labor-intensive, but its dimensions should be similar, at least volumewise: 9 by 4 by 3 inches (23 by 10 by 7.5 cm). If the mold is a springform type (that is, you can release a clasp and the sides fall away), your *marjolaine* will be a lot easier to serve.

continued

CAKE BASE

1½ cups (200 g) packed hazelnut powder

4 eggs

1⅔ cups (180 g) plus 5 tablespoons (40 g) powdered sugar

½ cup (60 g) sifted all-purpose flour

5 egg whites

¼ teaspoon salt

GANACHE

12 ounces (350 g) dark chocolate (65 percent cacao), finely chopped

1¼ cups plus 3 tablespoons (350 ml) whipping cream (35 percent butterfat)

VANILLA AND HAZELNUT BUTTERCREAMS

4 egg yolks

1¼ cups (240 g) granulated sugar

3½ tablespoons water

1½ cups (340 g) unsalted butter, cut into cubes and at room temperature

1 vanilla bean

2 heaping tablespoons Nutella

6 tablespoons (90 ml) dark rum

About ¼ cup (35 g) hazelnuts, toasted and skinned

1. Preheat the oven to 350°F (180°C). Line two 11-by-17-inch (28-by-43-cm) rimmed baking sheets with parchment paper.

2. To make the cake base, spread the hazelnut powder on another rimmed baking sheet, place in the oven, and bake for about 5 minutes, or until it smells like roasting nuts. Remove from the oven and pour into a bowl to cool.

3. In a stand mixer fitted with the whip attachment (or by hand with determination), whip together the eggs and 1⅔ cups (180 g) of the powdered sugar until white and creamy.

Using a rubber spatula, fold in the hazelnut powder and flour just until thoroughly combined. Transfer the mixture to a large bowl, and rinse the whip attachment and the mixer bowl.

4. Refit the whip attachment to the mixer, and put the egg whites, the remaining 5 tablespoons (40 g) powdered sugar, and the salt in the bowl. Beat until stiff peaks form. Gently fold the beaten whites into the egg-hazelnut mixture just until no streaks are visible.

5. Divide the batter evenly between the prepared baking sheets, and spread to level with a spatula, preferably an offset spatula. Place in the oven and bake for 11 minutes, or until lightly browned and set. Let cool in the pans on wire racks for about 10 minutes, then remove the parchment paper by lifting and peeling it slowly off the cakes. Let cool completely.

6. To make the ganache, put the chocolate in a bowl. In a small saucepan, bring the cream to a boil and pour it over the chocolate. Let sit for 3 minutes, then whisk until smooth. Let the ganache sit for 20 minutes at room temperature to firm up a bit.

7. To make the buttercreams, rinse the whip attachment and bowl again, then put the egg yolks in the bowl. In a saucepan, combine the sugar and water over medium heat and heat until the sugar melts. Clip a candy thermometer to the side of the pan. When the sugar mixture reaches 226°F (108°C), start whisking the egg yolks. When it reaches

239°F (115°C), remove from the heat while slowly pouring in the yolks and whisking constantly. Continue whisking until the mixture is at room temperature.

8. Add the butter a few pieces at a time to the cooled egg mixture and whisk until well incorporated. Scoop out half of the mixture into another bowl. Split the vanilla bean lengthwise and, using the tip of a sharp knife, scrape the seeds from the pod halves into one of the bowls and mix well. Add the Nutella to the second bowl and mix well. If you notice a shiny film forming as you are stirring the buttercreams, quickly add a few drops of cold water and continue stirring. The buttercreams are easiest to work with if used right away.

9. If you're unable to get your hands on (that is, build) a metal mold in the dimensions described in the headnote, you can use 2 half-gallon (2-liter) milk cartons with the top and one long side cut out of each one. Adjust to any desired length by sliding the sides of the two cartons onto one another. Tape the bottom of the mold so that it maintains a perfect rectangle, and line the inside of the mold with parchment paper. With your "mold" built, you are ready to build your cake.

10. Measure the width of the mold, then cut the cakes into slabs of the same width, minus ¼ inch (6 mm). Cut the slabs into even lengths to fit the mold. Place a cake layer, shiny brown side up, in the mold and brush a little of the rum over it. Top the cake layer with a layer of the Nutella buttercream, making it

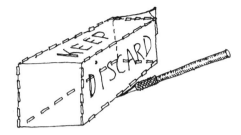

slightly thicker than the cake layer. Top the buttercream with a second cake layer, shiny brown side up, and brush with more rum. Top the cake layer with a layer of ganache, making it slightly thicker than the cake layer. Place a third cake layer, shiny brown side up, on the ganache layer and brush with more rum. Add a layer of the vanilla buttercream, making it slightly thicker than the cake layer. Repeat the layers, finishing with a cake layer topped with a layer of ganache. Then add the nuts.

11. Let the cake rest in the refrigerator overnight. The next day, cut the tape holding the mold together to release the cake. You may discover that the whole thing has sunk a bit, or that the cake has soaked the ganache excessively. No matter. You will have a delicious, silky brick of joy. To serve, cut into slices with a hot, wet knife.

O + G'S CARDAMOM BANANA BREAD

Makes 10 luscious muffin-size loaves

Our good friends Dyan Solomon and Éric Girard own Olive + Gourmando, a perfect luncheonette on Saint Paul West in Montreal's Old Port. Their little shop is what we expect the coffee shop in the afterlife to be like: they're detail fanatics and it's no contest the best place for lunch in the city. When they first opened, they were bakers, and the place was a bakery with a few seats. They still make bread, but mostly to use in delicious sandwiches. The front counter is displayed with brioches, croissants, brownies, and fruit pastries, and they're all killer. We thought they were insane when they decided to open in Old Port a decade ago. It was a barren ghost town of bombed-out buildings, seedy bars, and grow-ops. There were no *people,* much less hotels and tourist shops selling maple-sugar products and "raccoon" Daniel Boone hats actually made from Chinese skunks.

Like us, Éric and Dyan don't take anything too seriously (Dyan can tell you many stories of Fred's practical jokes when they used to work together: her showing up at 6:00 A.M. to a fake "dead man" at the bottom of the stairs; Fred putting a scraped lamb shank in his shirt, saying he may have hurt his hand. . . .) They're Montreal classics and were kind enough to hand over one of their most beloved recipes.

> **NOTE: BEFORE YOU BEGIN, KEEP THESE THREE TIPS FOR SUCCESS IN MIND:**
>
> **1.** Using unripened bananas for banana bread is a big no-no. As bananas ripen, their starch converts to sugar quickly. A black, spotty banana has more than double the amount of fructose of its "yellow brother." Also, do not mash the bananas so finely they liquefy. If you do, the muffins will take forever to bake and will be too crisp.
>
> **2.** Freshly grind the cardamom and cinnamon in a spice grinder. The difference in taste is phenomenal.
>
> **3.** As with most cake or cookie recipes, have the eggs, butter, sour cream, and any other liquids at the same temperature to ensure better emulsion.

½ cup (115 g) unsalted butter, at room temperature, plus more for muffin cups

½ cup (about 125 ml) sour cream, at room temperature

1½ teaspoons baking soda

4 very ripe bananas (spotted and black a must)

1 cup (200 g) packed light brown sugar

2 eggs, at room temperature

1 teaspoon vanilla extract

1⅓ cups (170 g) unbleached all-purpose flour

1 teaspoon salt

1½ teaspoons freshly ground cardamom

½ teaspoon freshly grated nutmeg

½ teaspoon freshly ground cinnamon

Handful of crushed walnut pieces (optional)

1. Preheat the oven to 350°F (180°C). Grease 10 standard muffin cups with butter.

2. In a small bowl, combine the sour cream and baking soda and set aside. It will puff up.

3. Peel the bananas, put them in a glass bowl, and put in the microwave for 5 minutes. This will allow them to release their liquid. Transfer the bananas to a fine-mesh sieve placed over a bowl and allow to drain, stirring gently. You should have ¼ to ½ cup (30 to 60 ml) liquid.

4. Pour the liquid into a small saucepan and place over medium heat until reduced by half. Add the liquid back to the bananas and gently "crush" the bananas by hand. *Do not liquefy or purée the bananas.*

5. In a stand mixer, or in a bowl with a handheld mixer, cream together the butter and sugar until smooth and fluffy, about 2 minutes. Add the eggs, one at a time, beating after each addition. Add the vanilla, mix well, and then scrape down the sides of the bowl, making sure the mixture is smooth. Add the fluffy sour cream and mix well. The same for the bananas.

6. In separate bowl, whisk together the flour, salt, and spices. Fold these dry ingredients into the wet mixture until just combined. Do not overmix.

7. Pour the batter into the prepared muffin cups, filling each one two-thirds full. Top each muffin generously with the walnut pieces (untoasted, or they will be burned by the time the muffins are cooked). Bake for 30 to 40 minutes, or until a toothpick inserted into the center of a muffin comes out clean. Let cool on a rack in the pan for 30 minutes, then turn out.

WARM BANANA CAKE WITH CHOCOLATE GLAZE AND COFFEE ICE CREAM

Makes 1 (10-inch / 25-cm)
Bundt cake

For an amazing puddinglike banana cake, substitute cake flour for the all-purpose flour. Add 1 cup (170 g) finely chopped Valrhona dark chocolate (Manjari is a good choice with fruity things) to the dry ingredients. Omit the walnuts. Bake the batter in a buttered 10-inch (25-cm) Bundt pan (or a buttered 11- to 12-inch/ 28- to 30-cm springform pan) in a preheated 350°F (180°C) oven for about 50 minutes, or until a toothpick inserted near the center comes out clean. Let cool on a wire rack.

This cake tastes best not long from the oven. Serve within 1 to 2 hours of baking.

Just before you are ready to serve the cake, make the chocolate glaze. Place 4 ounces (115 g) dark Valrhona chocolate (70 percent cacao), chopped, in a bowl. In a small saucepan, bring 1 cup (250 ml) whipping cream (35 percent butterfat) to a boil. Pour the cream over the chocolate and let sit for a few seconds, then stir with a wooden spoon until the chocolate is completely melted. Add 6 tablespoons (85 g) room-temperature unsalted butter, cubed, right away and stir until completely melted.

Pour the warm chocolate glaze over the cake just before serving. Top with toasted crushed pecans. Serve with Sanka Ice Cream (page 260).

ICE CREAM BASE

Makes 1 quart (1 liter)

This recipe calls for Carnation evaporated milk, which provides that neutral yet milky taste you want in an ice cream base. Suggestions for flavoring this all-purpose base follow. There is no way to get around making ice cream without having an ice cream maker— at least not if you want to get the best results.

1½ cups (375 ml) whipping cream (35 percent butterfat)

¾ cup (180 ml) homogenized milk

½ cup (125 ml) Carnation evaporated 2-percent milk

¼ cup (60 ml) light corn syrup

⅓ cup (65 g) sugar

½ cup (110 g) powdered milk

3 egg yolks

1. Fill a large bowl with ice cubes, and rest a medium metal bowl on the ice. You'll need it soon to do a rapid transfer and keep the mixture cool.

2. In another bowl, combine the cream, homogenized milk, evaporated milk, corn syrup, sugar, powdered milk, and egg yolks and mix well. (If you are making the Ovaltine or Sanka flavor, the flavoring goes in now.) Pour through a fine-mesh sieve into a thick-bottomed saucepan.

3. Place the saucepan over medium heat and heat, stirring constantly with a wooden spoon—including into the corners of the pot—until the mixture reaches 175°F (79°C). A thermometer is important here because the eggs will start curdling at about 183°F (85°C).

4. Immediately pour the mixture through the sieve into the metal bowl sitting on ice. (If you are making the *café brûlot* or Goglu flavor, it goes in now.) Let cool, stirring occasionally, for 10 to 15 minutes. Cover with plastic wrap and refrigerate overnight.

5. The following day, churn in your ice cream maker according to the manufacturer's instructions. Transfer to a container, cap tightly, and store in the freezer for 3 to 4 hours before serving.

ICE CREAM FLAVORS

OVALTINE ICE CREAM

Add 6 tablespoons (28 g) Ovaltine along with the sugar.

GLACE CAFÉ BRÛLOT

In a small saucepan, gently warm ¼ cup (60 ml) brandy, then ignite it to burn off the alcohol. When the flames die, add ¼ cup (35 g) dark-roast coffee beans, zest of 1 orange (in one piece), ¼ teaspoon freshly grated nutmeg, 2 whole cloves, 1 cinnamon stick, and 1 teaspoon Angostura bitters. Stir to combine. Add to the hot cream mixture on ice and let it steep. Cover and refrigerate as in the mother recipe, then strain and churn as directed.

SANKA ICE CREAM

Add 2 tablespoons Sanka instant-coffee powder along with the sugar. Serve the ice cream with a dusting of Sanka.

GOGLU ICE CREAM

Drop 16 Goglu (arrowroot) cookies into the hot cream mixture and blend with a hand blender. Then, cool, cover, and churn as directed. Serve the ice cream with chopped cookies on top.

FINANCIERS

Makes 4 to 6 (4-inch / 10-cm) round cakes

The *financier* gives you a failproof moist cake that will stand through the rigors of *pâtisserie de cuisine*. It is simple to make, which is a good thing for us at Joe Beef, with our limited space and no real pastry chef, and for the home cook. Keep in mind that baking is a science, and although we include volume measures here, weighing the ingredients is recommended.

We use ornate wax paper tartlet molds. If you don't have them or can't find them, you can just fill muffin cups half full and you'll get the same result. Serve the cakes with ice cream and sweet wine.

1 cup (250 g) almond powder

1⅔ cups (175 g) powdered sugar

⅓ cup (40 g) all-purpose flour (or cornstarch for a gluten-free option)

1 tablespoon baking powder

Pinch of salt

4 eggs, separated

¾ cup (170 g) unsalted butter, at room temperature

1 teaspoon natural almond extract (we use this, but it's optional)

1. Preheat the oven to 400°F (200°C).

2. In a bowl, sift together the almond powder, powdered sugar, flour, baking powder, and salt. Set aside. In another bowl, using a whisk or hand-held mixer, beat the whites until stiff peaks form. (Or, use a stand mixer fitted with the whip attachment.)

3. In a stand mixer fitted with the paddle attachment (or with a hand-held mixer or a wooden spoon and some stamina), beat the butter until creamy and soft. Add the egg yolks, one at a time, beating after each addition. Beat in the almond extract. Then add the dry ingredients, beating just until thoroughly combined.

The mixture will be a bit stiff. On low speed, slowly add half of the whipped whites, mixing just until combined. Using a rubber spatula, gently fold in the remaining whites.

4. Spoon the mixture into the molds. You want the batter in each mold to be 1 to 1½ inches (2.5 to 4 cm) deep. Bake for 20 minutes, or until the center is bouncy. If you stick it with a knife, it will always be greasy. The best way to test is to press the center with your finger. If it bounces back rather than sinks, it's ready. If you are using paper molds, leave and serve. If you are using metal molds, remove the cakes from the molds and let cool on wire racks. Serve at room temperature.

VARIATIONS

HAZELNUT

Subsitute hazelnut powder for the almond powder. You need to toast the hazelnut powder before using it. Spread it on a rimmed baking sheet, place in a preheated 350°F (180°C) oven, and set the timer for 5 minutes so you don't forget about it. Stir it with fork occasionally so it toasts evenly. It is ready when it smells like a Belgian chocolate store. Pour it into a bowl and let it cool completely before using, then sift with the other ingredients as directed in the recipe. This version is delicious with a few apricot halves gently pushed into the top of the cake batter before baking.

MUSCAT

When the big Italian grapes arrive in the market in their foam-padded wooden crates, it's an exciting time. Press them into the cake batter before baking, just like the apricots above.

ORANGE

Simmer thick orange slices in simple syrup (equal parts sugar and water; dissolve the sugar in the water) for 1 hour. Add ¼ cup (60 ml) Irish whiskey to the batter with the almond extract, and press the orange slices into the top of the cake batter before baking.

RED PEANUT

Whisk 2 tablespoons creamy peanut butter into the batter before adding the egg yolks. Sink 15 red candied peanuts (French burnt peanuts) into the top of each cake before baking.

PISTACHIO

Whisk 2 tablespoons pistachio paste into the batter before adding the egg yolks. Dust the top of the cake batter with chopped pistachios before baking.

GOLDEN RUSSET OR GOLDEN DELICIOUS APPLE

Peel, halve, and core apples. Place cut side up on a small baking sheet, top each half with a pat of unsalted butter and 1 teaspoon sugar, and bake in a preheated 400°F (200°C) oven for 15 minutes, or until browned and puffy. Gently press an apple half, rounded side down, into the top of each cake before baking.

ITALIAN LIQUOR STORE WEDDING NUTS CONFETTI

Take a handful of bold-colored, sugar-coated almonds and crush them with a rolling pin. Add ¼ cup (60 ml) Strega, anisette, or *alkermes* (sometimes spelled *alchermes,* a typical Tuscan liqueur) to the batter with the almond extract. Dust the top of the cake batter with the crushed almonds before baking.

PANNA COTTA

Serves 6

Here is the dessert we served on opening day at Joe Beef. You can use small foil molds or teacups for serving.

4 sheets gelatin

1⅔ cups (400 ml) whipping cream (35 percent butterfat)

6 tablespoons (75 g) sugar

1 tablespoon powdered milk

¾ cup (180 ml) sour cream (make sure it is full fat)

1. Have ready six 8-ounce (250 ml) foil molds or teacups. Bloom the gelatin sheets in a bowl of cool water to cover for 5 to 10 minutes, or until they soften and swell.

2. Meanwhile, pour half of the whipping cream into a small saucepan, add all of the sugar and powdered milk, and bring to a simmer. Gently squeeze the gelatin sheets and add to the cream mixture. Take off the heat and let sit at room temperature for 20 minutes to dissolve. Then stir in the sour cream.

3. Whisk the remaining cream until soft peaks form. Gently fold the two creams together.

4. Carefully spoon the mixture into the molds, then cover and refrigerate for at least 2 hours or up to a day.

5. If you want to unmold to serve, dip the bottom of each mold in warm water for a few seconds, then carefully flip over.

VARIATIONS

PANNA COTTA IN A YOGURT MAKER

Inoculate the mixture with yogurt culture, as per the directions for your yogurt maker, then let the mixture ripen in the yogurt maker. When it is ready, set it in the fridge as usual.

TAPIOCA

Drop 3 tablespoons medium-size tapioca into boiling water for 6 minutes and then drain. Substitute Carnation condensed milk for the sour cream and proceed as directed. Mix in the tapioca at the end, just before folding the cream into the molds.

RUM RAISIN

Soak 3 tablespoons golden raisins in boiling water to cover for about 2 minutes, drain, and then combine the raisins with ¼ cup (60 ml) rum and leave to soak for an hour or two, or more if you want a more boozy taste. Add the rum and raisins after you stir in the sour cream. If you like, substitute British treacle syrup for the sugar.

CONCORD GRAPE

In a saucepan, combine 2 cups (500 g) Concord grapes, 1 cup (200 g) sugar, and the juice of ½ lemon and cook slowly for 30 minutes, or until the grapes have shriveled. Strain through a fine-mesh sieve, reserving the syrup and discarding the solids. To serve, drizzle a tablespoon or two over each chilled mold. We like to top off the syrup with streusel.

For the streusel, in a bowl, combine 2 tablespoons each all-purpose flour and almond or hazelnut powder, 2 tablespoons room-temperature unsalted butter, ¼ cup (50 g) packed brown sugar, grated zest of ½ lemon, and a pinch of Maldon salt or *fleur de sel* and mix until crumbly. Spread on a rimmed baking sheet and bake in a preheated 425°F (220°C) oven for 7 to 9 minutes, or until hardened and delicious smelling. Let cool before using.

RISOTTO AND PUNCH ABRUZZO

In a saucepan, combine 4 cups (1 liter) water, 2 tablespoons Punch Abruzzo, 1 tablespoon fresh orange juice, 3 tablespoons Italian risotto rice such as Arborio, and 1 tablespoon sugar. Bring to a boil and simmer for 25 minutes (yes, overcooked). Drain, cool, and mix the rice with the cream mixture just before spooning it into the molds.

DARJEELING AND PRUNES

In a saucepan, combine 1 cup (170 g) pitted prunes, 3 cups (750 ml) water, 1 cup (200 g) packed brown sugar, 2 Darjeeling tea bags, juice of 1 lemon, 1 teaspoon ground ginger, and 1 cinnamon stick and bring to a boil, stirring to dissolve the sugar. Remove from the heat, transfer to a heatproof jar or plastic container, and let soak overnight.

To make the *panna cotta* base, add 3 Darjeeling tea bags to the hot cream mixture after removing it from the heat and before adding the sour cream. Let steep for about 15 minutes. Remove the bags and press on them to release the essence into the mixture. Proceed as directed in the recipe. At serving time, spoon a couple teaspoons of the prune mixture over each serving.

ÉCLAIRS

Makes 8 pastries

We love éclairs, even the soggy ones with a crusty fondant. This is a recipe with many parts: the *pâte à choux* (dough) and the pastry cream are the constants, and then come the variations of fillings and toppings. It seems confusing, but it's not; plus if you can handle the variations here, you're adding a whole new level to your dessert repertoire. In terms of assembly, it's best to make the pastry cream first, as it needs 2 hours to chill.

PASTRY CREAM

6 tablespoons (80 g) sugar
Scant ¼ cup (25 g) all-purpose flour
Scant ¼ cup (25 g) cornstarch
2 cups (500 ml) milk
3 egg yolks
1 egg
1 vanilla bean
¼ cup (55 g) cold unsalted butter, diced

CHOUX PASTRY

2 cups (500 ml) water
¾ cup plus 2 tablespoons (200 g) unsalted butter, cut into ½-inch (12-mm) cubes
Pinch of salt
2⅓ cups (300 g) all-purpose flour
7 or 8 eggs
1 egg yolk beaten with ¼ cup (60 ml) milk for egg wash

Filling and topping of choice (recipes follow)

1. To make the pastry cream, sift together the sugar, flour, and cornstarch into a good-size bowl. In a separate bowl, whisk together a generous 6 tablespoons (100 ml) of the milk, the egg yolks, and the egg, and then incorporate it with the dry ingredients, mixing well.

2. Split the vanilla bean lengthwise and, using the tip of a sharp knife, scrape the seeds into a saucepan with the rest of the milk (1⅔ cups/400 ml). Bring just to a boil, then remove from the heat and slowly add the hot milk to the egg mixture while stirring constantly. When all the milk has been added, pour the mixture through a fine-mesh sieve into a thick-bottomed saucepan.

3. Place the pan over medium heat and stir, watching it carefully. As soon as the mixture thickens and you see 3 bubbles boil up, lower the heat and cook for 1 minute. Take the pan off the heat and pour the contents into a clean bowl. Let cool to body temperature, then whisk in the butter until incorporated. Cover with plastic wrap, pressing it directly onto the surface of the cream. Refrigerate for at least 2 hours before using. You should have about 2 cups (500 ml).

4. To make the pastry dough, in a saucepan, combine the water, butter, and the salt, cover, and bring to a boil over medium heat. As soon as the butter has melted and the water is boiling, add the flour in one shot. Remove from the heat and mix vigorously with a wooden spoon until well combined—that is, no clumps. Return to the heat and continue to mix for 3 to 4 minutes only, or until the mixture is dry.

5. Transfer the mixture to a stand mixer fitted with the paddle attachment. On medium speed, mix for about 3 minutes, or until the mixture is at room temperature. Then, one at a time, crack the eggs into a little bowl (so you won't drop the shells in the mixer bowl) and add them to the mix. When you have added the seventh egg, check the consistency of the dough. It is ready if when you flip it with a wooden spoon, it drops neatly. If it is too stiff, add the remaining egg. You can refrigerate the dough at this point, but it will be very hard to pipe or manipulate, so it is best to use it right away.

continued

6. Spoon the mixture into a pastry bag fitted with a round, plain tip (an Ateco no. 806, about ½ inch/12 mm in diameter, is ideal). Line a large rimmed baking sheet with a silicone mat or parchment paper. Pipe 8 pastries onto the prepared baking sheet, forming a line about 6 inches (15 cm) long and ¾ inch (2 cm) wide.

7. Let the pastries rest for 20 minutes at room temperature. Meanwhile, preheat the oven to 425°F (220°C).

8. Brush the pastries with the egg wash, then slip them into the oven and bake for 20 minutes, or until you no longer see any white in the cracks. Lower the oven temperature to 325°F (165°F) and continue to bake for another 10 to 20 minutes, or until golden brown. Remove from the oven and immediately poke each pastry with a bamboo skewer to let the steam out (this prevents sogginess). Let cool on the pan on a rack.

9. Add fillings and toppings from the variations that follow. Using a serrated knife, cut the top off each éclair lengthwise, about two-thirds from the bottom (so the top is half the thickness of the bottom). You may also fill the éclairs without cutting off the tops. Poke two holes the size of a pen at each end of the bottom of the pastry, and fill using a pastry bag fitted with a small tip.

To make most of our éclair toppings, we use commercial fondant, which is nothing more than corn syrup and sugar. It is relatively easy to obtain. You can probably get your local pastry shop to front you a little, or you can find it in some groceries.

VARIATIONS

PISTACHIO AND GREEN TEA

Filling: We've tried to make our own pistachio paste, succeeding only in making a mortar with a very small amount of shamrock-green pistachio and 1 or 2 apricot kernels. It is easiest to use store-bought pistachio paste, of course, if you can find it. Add 3 tablespoons pistachio paste to the boiling milk when making the pastry cream, whisking well. The rest of the recipe process is identical.

Topping: Vigorously whisk 1 tablespoon green tea powder (*matcha*) into 1 cup (350 g) fondant until evenly distributed. Spoon about 2 tablespoons onto each éclair. Sprinkle chopped pistachios on top.

NUTELLA AND HAZELNUT

Filling: Add ¼ cup (80 g) Nutella to the boiling milk when making the pastry cream, whisking well. The rest of the recipe is identical.

Topping: Vigorously whisk 1 tablespoon Nutella into 1 cup (350 g) fondant until evenly distributed. Spoon about 2 tablespoons onto each éclair. Sprinkle toasted halved hazelnuts on top.

DOUBLE CHOCOLATE

Filling: Sift 2 tablespoons unsweetened cocoa powder with the dry ingredients for the pastry cream. The rest of the recipe is identical.

Topping: Vigorously whisk 1 tablespoon unsweetened cocoa powder into 1 cup (350 g) fondant until evenly distributed. Spoon about 2 tablespoons onto each éclair. Crushed chocolate Poky sticks are delicious on top, as great Japanese pastry chefs have shown us.

CORN, CARAMEL, AND EAGLE BRAND

Filling: Omit the sugar from the pastry cream recipe, and subtract 5 tablespoons (75 ml) of the milk. Mix the generous 6 tablespoons (100 ml) milk with the egg yolks as directed, then bring the remaining 1⅓ cups (325 ml) milk to a boil. Add 5 tablespoons (75 ml) Eagle brand sweetened condensed milk to the boiling milk. The rest of the recipe is identical. (Warning: Somehow the sugar helps the flour and cornstarch to disperse, preventing clumping. Because you don't have sugar, you will need to go heavy on the whisking to avoid as many clumps as possible.)

Topping: To make your own caramel, in a small, thick-bottomed saucepan, combine ½ cup (125 ml) water and 1¼ cups (250 g) sugar, place over high heat, and bring to a slow boil. Let simmer undisturbed for 10 to 15 minutes. It's important that you don't toss the mixture with a spoon or swirl the pan, or the caramel will crystallize. The mixture can go from a nice caramel to burnt quickly, so watch closely. Also, have your pastries filled and ready to be topped. When the mixture is a nice blond, take it off the heat.

Using a sharp knife, remove a flat side from an ear of corn (a few rows of kernels wide and about 6 inches/15 cm long), working as carefully as you can. Place the strip of corn kernels on top of a filled éclair.

Drizzle 1 to 2 tablespoons hot caramel over the corn. Be careful not to touch it before it sets or you'll leave a mark. Remember, too, hot caramel will burn the hell out of your fingers. And when it cools, it's

like glass and cuts like it, too. If you like, add a pinch of cayenne pepper—so little you can barely see it. It adds a nice warmth.

CLASSIC CHANTILLY AND HOT CHOCOLATE SAUCE

Filling: Start with a cold bowl, 2 cups (500 ml) cold whipping cream (35 percent butterfat), and a cold whisk, a whip attachment for a stand mixer, or cold beaters and a handheld mixer. Pour the cold cream into the cold bowl and start beating.

When the cream starts fluffing, add ¼ cup (50 g) sugar and 1 teaspoon vanilla extract and continue beating. When the peaks are soft, add another ¼ cup (50 g) sugar and continue to beat until the cream looks and tastes like whipped cream.

Topping: The sauce is served hot and poured at the table. Finely chop 12 ounces (340 g) dark chocolate (above 65 percent cacao) and place in a bowl. In a saucepan, bring 2 cups (500 ml) half-and-half (15 percent

butterfat) to a boil and pour over the chocolate. Let sit for 2 minutes, then whisk until the chocolate is melted and the sauce is smooth. Serve immediately or keep warm until serving.

MERVEILLEUX

Serves 4

My mom use to take me and my brother to a pastry shop in a weird apartment building in Ottawa, and it had the best pastries. She would always choose the *merveilleux*. A meringue dessert is the best thing to make when you want to use up egg whites, after, say, an eggnog party! We make it every few weeks at the restaurant and pour hot chocolate sauce over the top at tableside. Everyone digs it.

MERINGUE

5 egg whites

¼ teaspoon distilled white vinegar

Scant 2 cups (180 g) powdered sugar, sifted

CREAM

2 cups (500 ml) whipping cream (35 percent butterfat)

Scant ½ cup (90 g) granulated sugar

1 tablespoon rum

3½ ounces (100 g) dark chocolate (70 percent cacao), finely grated

TOPPING

3½ ounces (100 g) dark chocolate (70 percent cacao)

Hot chocolate sauce (see Classic Chantilly and Hot Chocolate Sauce variation for Éclairs, page 269)

1. Preheat the oven to 275°F (135°C). Cut a sheet of parchment paper large enough to line a large rimmed baking sheet, and place dull side up on a work surface. Place a circular object the size of a 45 rpm record on one end of the paper, and trace the outer edge with a pencil. Repeat twice more on the other end of the paper. Flip the paper over and put it on a baking sheet.

2. To make the meringue, in a stand mixer fitted with the whip attachment, whip the egg whites and vinegar on high speed until stiff peaks form, adding the sugar in three shots, the beginning, the middle, and toward the end. The whole process should take about 6 minutes.

3. Spoon the whites mixture into a pastry bag fitted with a round, plain tip (an Ateco no. 807, about ½ inch/ 12 mm in diameter, is ideal). First, pipe a tiny dab under each corner of the parchment to hold it in place while you pipe the disks. They will also prevent a fly out if you use a convection oven (imagine those old game shows where contestants had to grab money blowing around inside an air tube and you'll understand). Now, pipe the meringue onto one of the parchment templates in a spiral design, starting just inside the traced line and working toward the center in a continuous motion. Repeat on the two additional templates to make a total of three disks. If you have a little room and a little meringue left, make little dots here and there.

4. Bake for 30 minutes, then lower the oven temperature to 225°F (110°C) and continue to bake for another 2 hours, keeping the oven door ajar, if possible (a pair of metal tongs sometimes works). The meringues are ready when they are light beige and the surface is crisp but the middle is still soft.

5. Let the meringues cool on the pan before transferring them to a wire rack or a large platter. Don't worry if they break. They will be covered with cream and sauce.

6. To make the cream, in a bowl, by hand or with a mixer, whip the cream, gradually adding the sugar and rum, until stiff peaks form. Be careful to stop before it turns into butter. Using a rubber spatula, fold in the chocolate, distributing it evenly.

7. Put a little blotch of the cream on the center of a serving plate, and place a meringue disk on top (the cream will anchor it). Spread one-third of the chocolate cream evenly over the disk and place the second disk on top. Cover with another one-third of the cream and place the third disk on top. Cover with the remaining cream, press the disks to-gether slightly so the cream squishes out the sides. With a clean spatula, smooth the cream over the top and sides.

8. Finely grate the chocolate for the topping and blow it all over the cake. Cover and refrigerate for 1 hour before serving. (While you are wait-ing, you can munch on any little meringues that rode along with the big disks.)

9. Just before serving the meringue, make the chocolate sauce. To cut the meringue, dip a serrated knife blade in cold water before each cut, and wipe clean after each cut. Pass the hot chocolate sauce at the table.

THE DESSERT CHARIOT

CHAUD FROID DE PAMPLEMOUSSE au ROMARIN

Serves 4

Here is another great dish from the repertoire of Nicolas Jongleux. We used to scoff at people who said they knew how to make a great dessert that wasn't too sweet. But as you get older and the espresso and the social cigarillos have started to erode your taste buds, you find yourself liking bourbon, lemon, and dandelion. This is a perfect little dessert in that fashion. It's zingy and alive. We burn it with a blowtorch. If you don't have one, just use your broiler. Heat it to the max and put whatever is holding the grapefruit right under it. Don't forget dry rags or oven mitts and an ovenproof vessel.

CURD

½ cup (100 g) sugar
1½ teaspoons cornstarch
6 tablespoons (90 ml) fresh lemon juice
1 egg, separated
1 whole egg
Grated zest of 1 lemon
¼ cup (55 g) unsalted butter, diced

SYRUP

¼ cup (50 g) sugar
2½ tablespoons water
1½ teaspoons chopped fresh rosemary

4 pink or white grapefruits

1. To make the curd, in a bowl, stir together the sugar and cornstarch. Whisk in the lemon juice, egg yolk, and whole egg, mixing well. (Reserve the egg white for later.) Strain through a sieve into a bowl. Stir in the lemon zest and butter.

2. Pour the mixture into a thick-bottomed saucepan and place over medium heat. Heat, stirring constantly, including into the corners of the pot—until the mixture reaches 185°F (84°C). You will notice it starting to bubble along the sides of the pan. When you see the bubbles, immediately transfer it to a bowl and refrigerate it.

3. Rinse the saucepan so you can use it for the syrup. Add the sugar and water, stir once, and bring to a boil over medium heat. Remove from the heat, add the rosemary, and allow to infuse for 5 minutes. Strain the syrup through a sieve and set aside.

4. Peel the grapefruits, keeping the segments whole and tidy (Google for a video, but you already know this). Drain off the excess juice and drink it with gin and a dash of the rosemary syrup.

5. In a small bowl, whisk the reserved egg white until stiff peaks form. Set aside.

6. Get out your blowtorch, or preheat your broiler. Set out 4 broilerproof plates or individual gratin dishes. Put a grapefruit's worth of segments on each plate, arranging them side by side. Drizzle 1 tablespoon of the rosemary syrup over each portion of grapefruit segments. Gently fold the egg white into the curd, then spoon the curd evenly over the grapefruit portions.

7. Run the torch over the curd topping until nice and caramelized, or put the plates or dishes on a rimmed baking sheet and slip under the broiler for a minute or two. Remember the top should be hot but not the bottom. That's *chaud froid*! Serve right away.

THE ISLES OF CHEESE:

ÎLES-DE-LA-MADELEINE (THE MAGDALEN ISLANDS) AND L'ISLE-AUX-GRUES (THE ISLAND OF CRANES)

THE MAGDALEN ISLANDS ARE an archipelago of nine major islands off the coast of Prince Edward Island (PEI) in the Gulf of Saint Lawrence. Cartier was there, Champlain was there (both after the natives, of course), but the climate always scared off most would-be inhabitants, including any early French settlers. These islands make PEI look tropical and urban. L'Isle-aux-Grues is part of an archipelago as well, but sits in the middle of the Saint Lawrence River, about halfway between Quebec City and La Pocatiére.

The majority of the early inhabitants arrived via shipwreck, which also explains the islands' iconic symbol: the lighthouse. Even today, only twelve to thirteen thousand people live on all nine islands combined, and although the islands are closer to the Maritimes, they remain a part of Quebec. We have always wanted to make a trip there, yet in the back of our minds we have felt we have the best of the isles right around the corner at the gilded Fromagerie Atwater.

The northern setting of the islands reminds us so much of Winslow Homer and the romanticism of the Hudson River School of painters that in each cheese we taste passion, salt air, and madness. It's like tasting geography. The cheeses have been made the same way for centuries and are worth trying if you can find them where you live. They are best tasted in summer and fall when the pastures are good for grazing.

RIOPELLE, L'ISLE-AUX-GRUES

Named after Quebec's famous recluse painter who died on the Isle-aux-Grues. Smells of goose hunting, buckshot, and damp sweaters. Tastes like genius, feels like a long night in a cottage by the water with a single naked lightbulb.

PIED-DE-VENT, HAVRE-AUX-MAISONS

Probably the most famous of the Magdalen cheeses. Soft and in a washed rind, it is delicious in a Nordic-wind, ice-canoeing type way.

TOMME DE GROSSE-ÎLE, L'ISLE-AUX-GRUES

Thousands of Irish immigrants are buried on Grosse-Île, the southernmost island in L'Isle-aux-Grues archipelago, and this cheese commemorates the dead. This is a musky "mushroom" cheese with an edible rind. Classic Quebec cheese.

LA TOMME DES DEMOISELLE, HAVRE-AUX-MAISONS

Similar to Pied-de-Vent, but aged six months and has more pronounced smoky flavors. This cheese makes us think of Winslow Homer smoking a pipe and painting in knee-high waders. We love the idea of men smoking pipes and reciting poetry to one another. Painting watercolors and fishing. A basket with a piece of cheese wrapped in a clean cloth hankie. We want to grow old like this: sipping homemade brandy in hunting tweed suits and only eating things we kill or raise ourselves.

LE MI-CARÊME, L'ISLE-AUX-GRUES

Soft, mixed rind (meaning it has been washed then left to ripen and develop its typical flora) made with thermalized cow's milk. A delicious cheese, but we could do without the scary clown drawing.

Although it is not from the Magdalens or the Cranes, PEI's Avonlea Clothbound Cheddar is too good not to mention. It smells of grass, mashed potatoes, and clam brine. There is nothing else like it on earth. It's made by COWS Creamery and is available at the Fromagerie Atwater in Montreal (as well as in other Canadian cities). A creamy Cheddar, it comes in a big ten-kilogram wheel and crumbles when sliced. It is a must for dessert—or anytime really.

For a good source on Canadian cheeses, see www.ourcheeses.com/directory. If you want to find cheese purveyors who handle Canadian cheeses, check out *Canadian Cheese: A Pocket Guide*, by Kathy Guidi (MacArthur and Company, 2010).

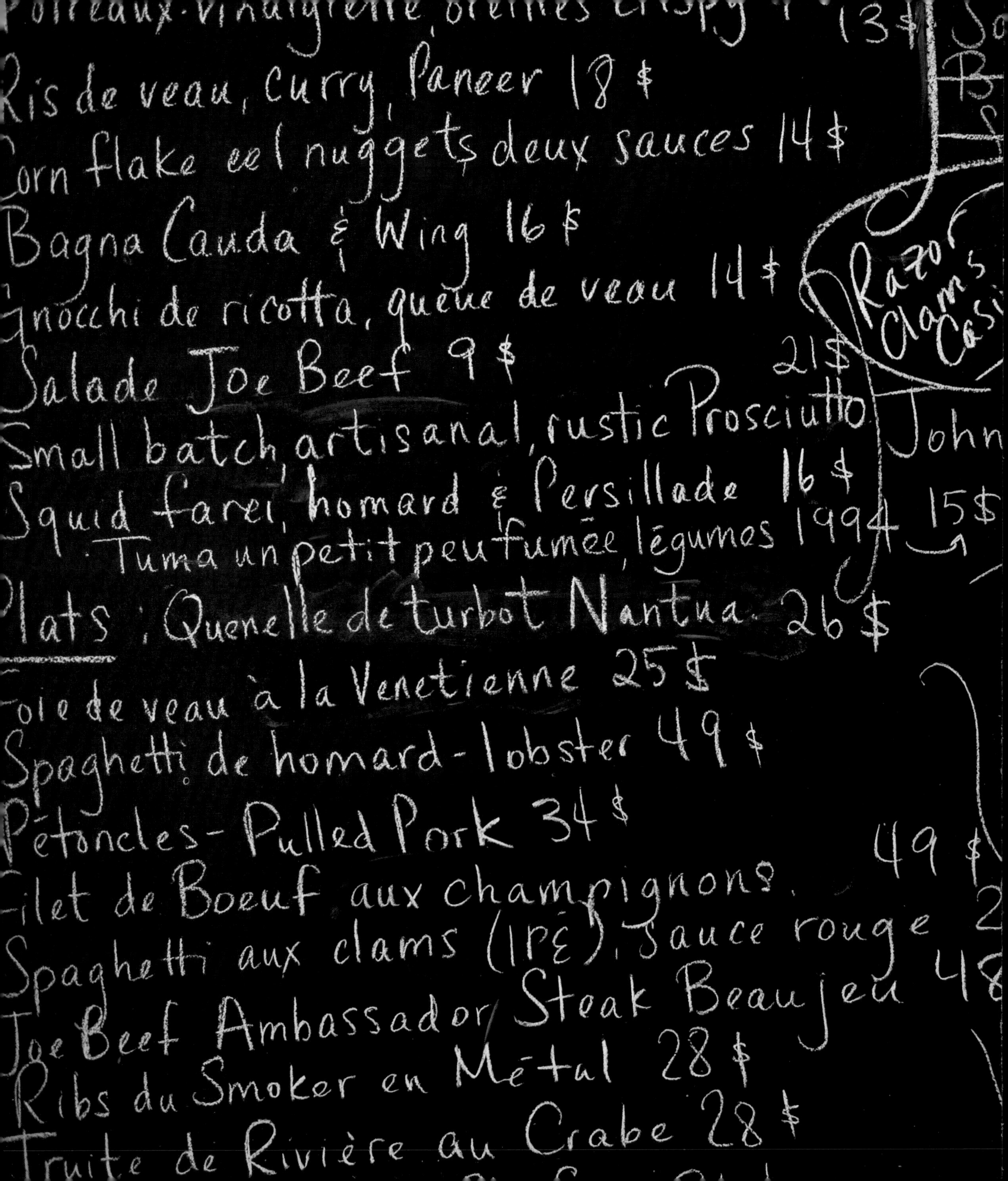

...reaux vinaigrette oreilles crispy + 13 $

Ris de veau, curry, Paneer 18 $

Corn flake eel nuggets deux sauces 14 $

Bagna Cauda & Wing 16 $

Gnocchi de ricotta, queue de veau 14 $

Salade Joe Beef 9 $ 21$

Small batch, artisanal, rustic Prosciutto

Squid farei, homard & Persillade 16 $ 15$

Tuma un petit peu fumée, légumes 1994

Plats ; Quenelle de turbot Nantua 26 $

Foie de veau à la Venetienne 25 $

Spaghetti de homard - lobster 49 $

Pétoncles - Pulled Pork 34 $ 49 $

Filet de Boeuf aux champignons.

Spaghetti aux clams (IPE), sauce rouge

Joe Beef Ambassador Steak Beaujeu

Ribs du Smoker en Métal 28 $

Truite de Rivière au Crabe 28 $

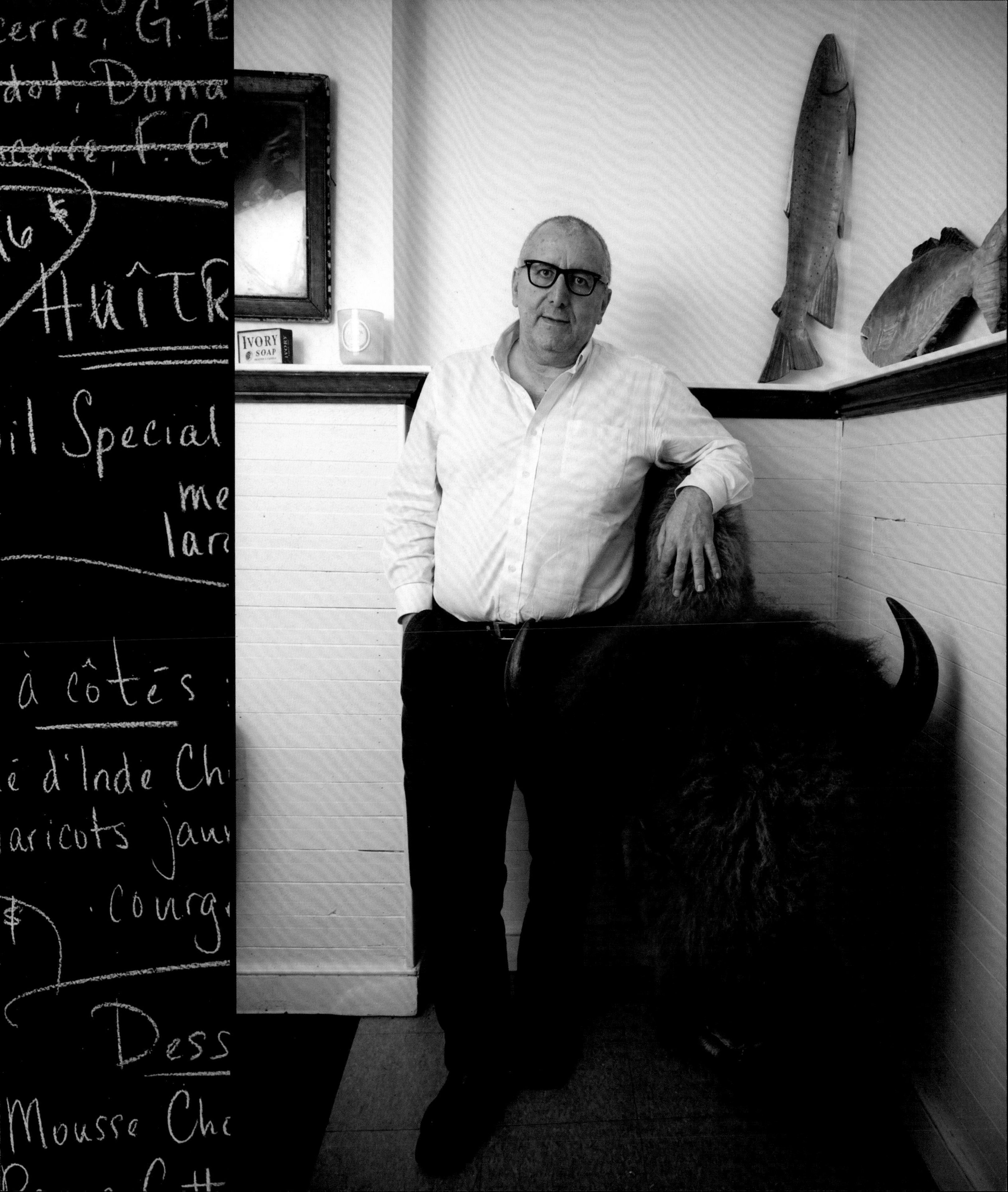
IVORY SOAP
Special
à côtés
Mousse

MONTREAL IN TWO DAYS

EVERY WEEK, PEOPLE CALL to make reservations and to chat about their upcoming weekend in Montreal. "Great," we say, "what else are you planning to do while visiting?" And then they begin (self-consciously) listing off a complete mess of a weekend. You know just by speaking with them, there are certain things that won't make them happy. It's like when you tell a trusted friend who lives in that city that you're going to X for dinner, and he folds his arms and says "Huh." In retrospect, he's always right.

When we are traveling, we count on local merchants and friends to help us navigate where to stay, where to eat, and what to do. The Trip Advisors of the world only make us panic. So we've included a sample itinerary showing what David recommends you do with two days in Montreal, whatever the season.

This itinerary is based on the things that my friends and I do every week. If you choose any of the places listed in our address book on pages 280–281, you won't go wrong. Everyone on this list is a likeminded colleague or friend, and they all want to make your trip to Montreal memorable.

DAY 1

The Antonopoulos family owns several hotels in Old Montreal. I like the Nelligan the best; it's hip, central, and busy, and offers a decent rate. From Old Montreal everything is more or less a short cab ride away, and if you're a walker, it's heaven.

Upon waking, coffee and food is in order. From the Nelligan, venture about five blocks west to Olive + Gourmando. Our friends Éric and Dyan—great people, truly!—own this Old Port gem, which has wonderful décor and delicious coffee, *viennoiseries*, salads, and sandwiches.

After breakfast, walk south toward the water. There are tons of odd and interesting shops on *rues* Saint Antoine, Saint Paul, Notre Dame, and de la Commune; have a nice walk!

For lunch, hail a cab at the hotel around 11:30 A.M. and go to L'Express. L'Express is a Montreal classic and the closest you'll get to France without taking a plane. Check out their inexpensive and unreal wine program (and ask to see the second "inventory" wine list; it's paradise!). Make sure you visit Arthur Quentin's kitchen and tableware shop across the street and Carré Blanc for fine bedding next door. This is a great boutique shopping area to kill a couple of hours.

After lunch, walk south from L'Express to Roy Street and then west for a few blocks until you can go no further to Saint Laurent. This is a great street full of history and delicious food. Walking north from the corner of Roy, check out the Euro grocery called La Vieille Europe. The smell of this shop is ambrosial, it's like all of my favorite foods rolled into one: cheese, smoked meats, pickles, tea, and sauerkraut. Since I figure it's around 3 P.M. now, it's a perfect time to get a smoked meat sandwich at Schwartz's, which is just a couple of shops north of La Vieille Europe. Go in, sit at the counter, and enjoy. Then write me a letter and tell me about it; this is a magical place.

From Schwartz's, walk south all the way down the Main back to Old Montreal. You will pass by our old stomping grounds at Buona Notte and Globe, through Chinatown, and back to the hotel to have a nap.

Fred and I are nostalgic guys and we get a little bored sometimes with all the cool, hip restaurants around the city. Since we both love going to old classic restaurants—although not many are left—I suggest you make a reservation at Le Mas des Oliviers for dinner. This is Mordecai Richler's old haunt. Ask Quentin, the maître d', if you can sit at Richler's old table. Le Mas, as regulars call it, is *pâté de campagne*, snails, fresh fish prepared simply, sirloin steak frites, Bordeaux, Calvados, Armagnac, a little teasing, a little hair pulling, you know what I mean.

It's still early and you're not done. Hail a cab and go to Pullman Wine Bar, sit at the bar or near it, and have more wine. The owner, Bruno Braën, is usually holding court, drinking grappa with artists and journalists. This is a fun place and you're in good hands.

When you can't take anymore, go back to the hotel, drink some water, and go to bed. You did good today!

DAY 2

Wake up, jump in a cab, and head to Café Myriade for breakfast and some of the city's best coffee.

From there, head north on Bishop to Sherbrooke Street, where you'll find several galleries, the Beaux Arts, and cool shops. Holt Renfrew is a great store and has some of Canada's best fashion shopping. A short walk from Holt's is Ogilvy for more amazing shopping.

From Sherbrooke Street, walk a couple of blocks south and meander down Saint Catherine East to Metcalfe and find the Dominion Square Tavern. This is a jewel of a restaurant that has been in its location forever and has recently undergone a meticulous restoration.

Have lunch here; it's very good and the place is eye candy. When you finish lunch, call and make your dinner reservation: Au Pied de Cochon, DNA, Brasserie T, Lawrence, Le Filet, Le Club Chasse et Pêche—the choice is yours, but these are the places where I would want to eat.

After lunch, jump in another cab and head west to the venerable Atwater Market. There are two levels, both brimming with a dozen or so 2,500-square-foot stalls. The lower level has gems like Les Douceurs du Marche (a space that used to be two stores—one carrying Caribbean specialties and the other Italian imports—that fused into one shop carrying the best Caritalian? Italobbean? goods. Of course, right down the row is our favorite cheese shop, Fromagerie Atwater. On the upper level is where the butchers are. All of them are good, but some are better at terrines and pâtés, and others are better at sausages. The competition is fierce! We use Boucherie de Tours, a haphazard bunch it seems, yet they are eager to please and quite funny to observe at work. At the top of the Tours chain is Yves, a French butcher who looks like an old French bulldog in his trademark red beret. Yves offers the best of Quebec, you won't be disappointed. After you leave the market, stroll along the Lachine Canal, in and around Notre Dame Street. If it's not too late in the day, you may even have time for a glass of wine and a bite at McKiernan.

By this time you've decided to head back east and eat at Au Pied de Cochon (PDC), and it's a smart choice. I strongly believe that everyone who visits Montreal should have a francophone experience. The French language is our treasure, our culture, and our strength. Preserving it and our traditions are of the utmost importance to those of us who love Quebec. Au Pied de Cochon is a must visit on my itinerary as they are one of our strongest ambassadors. Upon finishing dinner at PDC, we always like to hit Whiskey Café or any of the great little bars on Saint Laurent north for a few de-clogging glasses of brown booze.

THE JOE BEEF ADDRESS BOOK

B&B

Bed and Breakfast Downtown Montreal, 3458 Avenue Laval, Montreal, QC, H2X 3C8, (800) 267-5180, www.bbmontreal.ca

Casa Bianca, 4351 Avenue de L'Esplanade, Montreal, QC, H2W 1T2, (514) 312-3837, www.casabianca.ca

GingerBread Manor, 3445 Avenue Laval, Montreal, QC, H2X 3C7, (514) 597-2804, www.gingerbreadmanor.com

Les Passants du Sans Soucy, 171 Rue Saint Paul West, Montreal, QC, H2Y 1Z5, (514) 842-2634, www.lesanssoucy.com

Hotels

Antonopoulos Group: www.oldmontreal hotels.com/antonopoulos_group.htm

The Antonopoulos family are true Montrealers. Mr. Antonopoulos started as a short-order fry cook and saved enough to buy real estate in the decrepit, bombed-out-looking Old Montreal in the 1970s. Now, he's a hotel magnate with five stunning Montreal hotels. A homegrown phenomenon.

Auberge du Vieux Port, 97 Rue de la Commune East, Montreal, QC, H2Y 1J1, (514) 876-0081, www.aubergeduvieuxport.com

Hotel Nelligan, 106 Rue Saint Paul West, Montreal, QC, H2Y 1Z3, (514) 788-2040, www.hotelnelligan.com

Le Petit Hotel, 168 Rue Saint Paul West, Montreal, QC, H2Y 1Z7, (514) 940-0360, www.petithotelmontreal.com

Le Place d'Armes, 55 Rue Saint Jacques, Montreal, QC, H2Y 3X2, (514) 842-1887, www.hotelplacedarmes.com

Lofts du Vieux Port, 97 Rue de la Commune East, Montreal, QC, H2Y 1J1, (514) 876-0081, www.aubergeduvieuxport.com

Neighborhoods, Restaurants, and Shops of Note

LAURIER AND PARK AVENUE

Baldwin Barmacie (pharmacy turned bar), 115 Avenue Laurier West, Montreal, QC, H2T 2N6, (514) 276-4282

Buvette chez Simone (wine bar), 4869 Avenue du Parc, Montreal, QC, H2V 4E7, (514) 750-6577

Cafè in Gamba (coffee), 5263 Avenue du Parc, Montreal, QC, H2V 4G9, (514) 656-6852

Cocoa Locale (cake shop), 4807 Avenue du Parc, Montreal, QC, H2V 4E7, (514) 271-7162

Dieu de Ciel (brewpub), 29 Avenue Laurier West, Montreal, QC, H2T 2N2, (514) 490-9555

Henriette (fashion), 1031 Avenue Laurier West, Outremont, QC H2V 2L1, (514) 277-3426

Juni Sushi (restaurant), 156 Avenue Laurier West, Montreal, QC, H2T 2N7, (514) 276-5864

Lemeac (restaurant), 1045 Avenue Laurier West, Outremont, QC, H2V 2L1, (514) 270-0999

Lyla (lingerie), 400 Avenue Laurier West, Outremont, QC, H1V 2K7, (514) 271-0763

Malabar (novelty and costumes), 5121 Avenue du Parc, Montreal, QC, H2V 4G3, (514) 279-3223

Milos (restaurant), 5357 Avenue du Parc, Montreal, QC, H2V 4G9, (514) 272-3522

Orbite (hair salon), 221 Avenue Laurier West, Montreal, QC, H2T 2N9, (514) 271-6333

Touilleurs (kitchenware), 152 Avenue Laurier West, Montreal, QC, H2T 2N7, (514) 278-0008

LE PLATEAU MONT-ROYAL, SAINT DENIS, AND DULUTH

Arthur Quentin (kitchenware), 3960 Rue Saint Denis, Montreal, QC, H2W 2M2, (514) 843-7513

Au Pied de Cochon (restaurant), 536 Avenue Duluth East, Montreal, QC, H2L 1A9, (514) 281-1114

Bistro Cocagne (restaurant), 3842 Rue Saint Denis, Montreal, QC, H2W 2M2, (514) 286-0700

Café Neve (coffee), 151 Rue Rachel East, Montreal, QC, H2W 1E1, (514) 903-9294

Carre Blanc (French bedding), 3999 Rue Saint Denis, Montreal, QC, H2W 2M4, (514) 847-0729

Le Filet (restaurant), 219 Mont Royal Ouest, Montréal, QC, H2T 2Y6, (514) 360-6060

L'Express (restaurant), 3929 Rue Saint Denis, Montreal, QC, H2W 2M4, (514) 845-5333

Romados (restaurant), 115 Rue Rachel East, Montreal, QC, H2W 1C8, (514) 849-1803

DOWNTOWN

Brasserie T (restaurant), 1425 Rue Jeanne-Mance, Montreal, QC, H2X 2J4, (514) 282-0808

Café Ferreira (restaurant), 1446 Peel, Montreal, QC, H3A 1S8, (514) 848-0988

Café Myriade (coffee), 1432 Rue Mackay, Montreal, QC, H3G 2H7, (514) 939-1717

Dominion Square Tavern (restaurant), 1243 Rue Metcalfe, Montreal, QC, H3B 2V5, (514) 564-5056

Holt Renfrew (fashion), 1300 Rue Sherbrooke West, Montreal, QC, H3G 1H9, (514) 842-5111

Kitchenette (restaurant), 1351 Boulevard René Lévesque East, Montreal, QC, H2L 2M1, (514) 527-1016

Le Mas des Oliviers (restaurant), 1216 Rue Bishop, Montreal, QC, H3G 2E3, (514) 861-6733

Les Createurs (fashion), 1444 Rue Sherbrooke West, Montreal, QC, H3G 1K4, (514) 284-2102

Matt Bailey (jewelry and timepieces), 1427 Rue Crescent, Montreal, QC, H3G 2B2, (514) 845-8878

MBRG (restaurant), 2025 Rue Drummond, Montreal, QC, H3G 1W6, (514) 906-2747

McCord Museum (museum), 690 Rue Sherbrooke West, Montreal, QC, H3A 1E9, (514) 398-7100

Ogilvy (fashion), 1307 Rue Sainte Catherine West, Montreal, QC, H3G 1P7, (514) 842-7711

Pullman (wine bar), 3424 Avenue du Parc, Montreal, QC, H2X 2H5, (514) 288-7779

Queue de Cheval (steak house), 1222 René Lévesque West, Montreal, QC, H3G 1T1, (514) 390-0090

WESTMOUNT: SHERBROOKE WEST AND VICTORIA

Appetite for Books (cookbooks), 388 Avenue Victoria, Westmount, QC, H3Z 2N4, (514) 369-2002

Ben & Tournesol (gifts and stuff), 4915 Rue Sherbrooke West, Westmount, QC, H3Z 1H2, (514) 481-5050

James (fashion), 4910 Rue Sherbrooke West, Westmount, QC, H3Z 1H3, (514) 369-0700

Lola & Emily (fashion), 4920 Rue Sherbrooke West, Westmount, QC, H3Z 1H3, (514) 483-4040

Mimi & Coco (fashion), 4927 Rue Sherbrooke West, Westmount, QC, H3Z 1H2, (514) 482-6362

THE ART OF LIVING ACCORDING TO JOE BEEF

Pretty Ballerina (footwear), 392 Avenue Victoria, Westmount, QC, H3Z 2N4, (514) 489-3030

VicPark (health food and coffee), 376 Avenue Victoria, Montreal, QC, H3Z 1C3, (514) 488-7722

Wilfrid & Adrien (kitchenware), 4919B Rue Sherbrooke West, Westmount, QC, H3Z 1H2, (514) 481-5850

WESTMOUNT: SHERBROOKE WEST AND GREENE

Bleu Marine (fashion), 1383 Avenue Greene, Westmount, QC, H3Z 2A5, (514) 935-9825

Galerie Bellefeuille (art), 1367 Avenue Greene, Westmount, QC, H3Z 2A8, (514) 933-4406

Kaizen (restaurant), 4075 Rue Sainte Catherine West, Westmount, QC, H3Z 3J8, (514) 707-8744

Nicholas Hoare (books), 1366 Avenue Greene, Westmount, QC, H3Z 2B1, (514) 934-6046

Premium (fashion), 1385 Avenue Greene, Westmount, QC, H3Z 2A5, (514) 937-3627

Tavern on the Square (restaurant), 1 Westmount Square, Westmount, QC, H3B 2V5, (514) 989-9779

TNT (fashion), 4100 Rue Sainte Catherine West, Westmount, QC, H3Z 1P2, (514) 935-1588

OLD MONTREAL

Club Chasse & Peche (restaurant), 423 Rue Saint Claude, Montreal, QC, H2Y 3B6, (514) 861-1112

DNA (restaurant), 355 Rue Marguerite d'Youville, Montreal, QC, H2Y 2C4, (514) 287-3362

Galerie Orange (art), 81 Rue Saint Paul East, Montreal, QC, H2Y 3R1, (514) 396-6670

Garde Manger (restaurant), 408 Rue St-Francois Xavier, Montreal, QC, H2Y 2S9, (514) 678-5044

Gibbys (restaurant), 298 Place d'Youville, Montreal, QC, H2Y 2B6, (514) 282-1837

L'Orignal (restaurant), 479 Rue Saint Alexis, Montreal, QC, H2Y 2S1, (514) 303-0479

Olive + Gourmando (restaurant), 351 Rue Saint Paul West, Montreal, QC, H2Y 2A7, (514) 350-1083

Reborn (fashion), 231 Rue Saint Paul West, Montreal, QC, H2Y 2A2, (514) 499-8549

Rooney (fashion), 395 Rue Notre Dame West, Montreal, QC, H2Y 1V2, (514) 543-6234

THE MAIN AND MILE END

Barros Lucos (restaurant), 5201 Rue Saint Urbain, Montreal, QC, H2T 2W8, (514) 273-7203

Battat Contemporary (art), 7245 Rue Alexandra, Montreal, QC, H2R 2Y9, (514) 750-9566

Bottega (restaurant), 65 Rue Saint Zotique East, Montreal, QC, H2S 1K6, (514) 277-8104

Café Olympico (coffee), 124 Rue Saint-Viateur West, Montréal, QC, H2M 2T6, (514) 495-0746

Deppaneur Le Pick-Up (restaurant), 7032 Rue Waverly, Montreal, QC, H2S 3J2, (514) 271-8011

Galerie Simon Blais (art), 5420 Boulevard Saint Laurent, Montreal, QC, H2T 1S1, (514) 849-1165

La Vieille Europe (grocery), 3855 Boulevard Saint Laurent, Montreal, QC, H2W 1X9, (514) 842-5773

Lawrence (restaurant), 5201 Boulevard Saint Laurent, Montreal, QC, H2T 1S5, (514) 503-1070

Moishes (restaurant), 3961 Boulevard Saint Laurent, Montreal, QC, H2W 1Y4, (514) 845-3509

Nouveau Palais (restaurant), 281 Rue Bernard, Montreal, QC, H2V 4K8, (514) 273-1180

Schwartz's (restaurant), 3895 Boulevard Saint Laurent, Montreal, QC, H2W 1X9, (514) 842-4813

Sparrow (restaurant and bar), 5322 Boulevard Saint Laurent, Montreal, QC, H2T 1S5, (514) 690-3964

U & I (fashion), 3650 Boulevard Saint Laurent, Montreal, QC, H2X 2V4, (514) 844-8788

Wilensky (restaurant), 34 Avenue Fairmount West, Montreal, QC, H2T 2L9, (514) 271-0247

LITTLE BURGUNDY, GRIFFINTOWN, AND SAINT HENRI

Atwater Market (food), 138 Avenue Atwater, Montreal, QC, H3J 2J4, (514) 937-7754

Beige (housewares), 2475 Rue Notre Dame West, Montreal, QC, H3J 1N6, (514) 989-8585

Burgundy Lion (English pub), 2496 Rue Notre Dame West, Montreal, QC, H3J 1N5, (514) 934-0888

Dilallo (hamburgers), 2523 Rue Notre Dame West, Montreal, QC, H3J 1N6 (514) 934-0818

Fait Ici (only made in Quebec), 2519 Rue Notre Dame West, Montreal, QC, H3J 1N6, (514) 439-3888

Geppetto (restaurant), 2504 Rue Notre Dame West, Montreal, QC, H3J 1N5, (514) 903-3737

Grand Central (antiques), 2448 Rue Notre Dame West, Montreal, QC, H3J 1N5, (514) 935-1467

The Greene Spot (hot dogs), 3041 Rue Notre Dame West, Montreal, QC, H3C 1N9, (514) 931-6473

Griffintown Café (restaurant), 1378 Rue Notre Dame West, Montreal, QC, H3C 1K8, (514) 931-5299

Itsy Bitsy (cupcakes), 2621 Rue Notre Dame West, Montreal, QC, H3J 1N6, (514) 509-3926

Jane (restaurant), 2515 Rue Notre Dame West, Montreal, QC, H3C 1K8, (514) 932-8961

Joe Beef (restaurant), 2491 Rue Notre Dame West, Montreal, QC, H3J 1N6, (514) 935-6504

Lilly & Oli (coffee), 2515 Rue Notre Dame West, Montreal, QC, H3J 1N6, (514) 932-8961

Liverpool House (restaurant), 2501 Rue Notre Dame West, Montreal, QC, H3J 1N6, (514) 313-6049

Madame Cash (antiques), 2470 Rue Notre Dame West, Montreal, QC, H3J 1N6,

McKiernan (restaurant), 2485 Rue Notre Dame West, Montreal, QC, H3J 1N6, (514) 759-6677

Retro Ville (antiques), 2652 Rue Notre Dame West, Montreal, QC, H3J 1N7, (514) 939-2007

Rona (best hardware store ever), 2371 Rue Notre Dame West, Montreal, QC, H3J 1N3, (514) 932-5616

Surface Jalouse (art), 2652 Rue Notre Dame West, Montreal, QC, H3J 1N7, (514) 939-2007

Tavern Capri (tavern), 2172 Rue Saint Patrick, Montreal, QC, H3K 1B1, (514) 935-0228

Tuck Shop (restaurant), 4662 Rue Notre Dame West, Montreal, QC, H4C 1S6, (514) 439-7432

Uniform St-Henri (uniforms), 2671 Rue Notre Dame West, Montreal, QC, HC3 1N6, (514) 933-2989

ACKNOWLEDGMENTS

FRÉDÉRIC MORIN

A note for Allison: If you have ever worked for a business that's on bad terms with its suppliers, you know the eerie feeling. I would like to thank her for being there, for sixteen hours in the office deciphering my petty purchase bills, for calming down a fuming, frustrated customer (even though I made the mistake), and for honoring the kitchen's work. And for stopping me before I kicked the fridge door.

You rock.

Love to Allison, Henry, and Ivan.

To David, actually my best friend, best man, and best at playlists.

To Meredith, for getting shit done.

To my sweet mother, my *patenteux* dad, my grandparents, my brother Benoit, his wife, and Ed.

To Jean-Marie, both the plant one and the rock one. The families.

To Dave Lisbona, Jeff Bakonbitz, and Ronnie Steinberg, for an office to sleep in.

To the kitchens of Joe Beef, McKiernan, and Liverpool House, past and present, come and gone, and other places I worked (for the patience).

To everyone who has helped me build, including Antoine and Max.

To Frank, Marco, Emma, Jackie, Manu, Kaunteya, Donna, Pelo, Curtis, Pier Luc, and Mark.

Thank you to Boucherie de Tours, Fromagerie Atwater, Pépinière Jasmin, the Maachis.

To the floor people, Ryan, Vanya, and the team.

To the dishwashers, who raise families with two jobs and never come up with excuses.

To Pierre Chaumard, Marcel Kretz, Phillipe Belleteste, Normand Laprise, Claude Barnabe, Josée di Stasio, Nick Malgieri, Riad Nasr, David Chang, and Peter Meehan.

To John Bil, Michelle at Appetite for Books, Birri et Frères, Martin Picard, Wally, Mathieu, and the Hoff.

To Francois Reno, Melanie Dunea, Leigh, Omar, Pelo, Thomas, Osman, and Kholitha.

To Joshua and Jessica and everyone at Fleishers, Cole Snell from Provincial Cheese, Guillaume L'emouleur, Bonnie Stern, John at La Mer, Frank Castronovo and Falcinelli, the Big Gay Ice Cream Truck, Krissy Longtin, Twitter, Elvio Gallaso, Phillipe Poitras, ice cream, Gold Bond, Peter "Spiro" the plumber, trains, Roy Bar, Avi, Luc, Nial, and Doris.

To Adam for the train ride, Paul and Dominique Anne at LCC and Charles the brother, the tradesmen, Stephen Alexander, Paul Bocuse, Larousse, and Time-Life, Jean and Mark, Mathieu Gaudet, Cousin François, The Swifts, VIA Rail (please go back to real food), the cottage in PEI, and Phyllis Carr. To Rita Assouline and Mike at beige.

Thanks to Kim Witherspoon, Julie Bennett, Katy Brown, Aaron Wehner, and, of course, Jennifer May.

And to our customers.

DAVID MCMILLAN

Thanks to my Julie and my lovely girls, Dylan and Lola. I love you very much!

To my mother and father for enduring me, and to all of our friends who dine with us in our home. I value your friendship and support.

To my business partner Allison, for making sure everything is always all good. You're a great captain and I appreciate very much the solitary work you do.

To my brother Fred—it's been a great dozen years. You inspire us all with your drive and mild insanity; you're the king bud and a great father.

To Meredith, for putting this book together and managing not to lose your cool ever. I owe you forever.

To my friends—you're a sorry bunch! Hoffer, Ryan Gray, Lisa, Vanya, Samia, P. L., JC, Primeau, Veronica, Steve-O, Wally, and Baikowitz and company. Phil Price, you're a degenerate. To Chucky, Timmy, Kyle, John Bil, Mike and Kenny, Cass and Marley, the Cardarelli family, Moose, Trav, Monica, Kitchenette Nick and family, and, of course, the Royal Battat family.

To my friends and customers: To Jeff's and Lenny's families, Brian and Amber, Eric C, Hollywood, Jeff at the Drake, Barb, Nicholas Metivier, Jane Dixon, Glen G, the Tedeschi family, the Bensadoun family, the Rubenstein family, Bobby Sontag, the Schwartz family, the Mikulas, J. F. Sauvé, Master Paul Raymond, the Rodrigue brothers, the Blacks, Kelly Yee, Avi, and, of course, the Goineau family. Hubert and Claude, Greenspoon, Bagel, the Niro family, the Lavigne family, and the Faitas.

To Anna Maria, the Habs, Mike Griffon and kids, Dany Lavy, the Schiller family, the Isenberg family, the Cohen family, the Hill family, the best-dressed Vito Salvaggio, and the Baronessa Couture.

To the Takefman family, the Coffin family, the Bamberas, Huge Galdones, and the Schwam family.

To Dan and Caroline and to Billy Brownstein and family. To Mathieu Gaudet, Jean Paul Riopelle, Simon Blais, the Medalcy family, and the Grateful Dead.

To Martin and the PDC gang.

To David Chang, Mark Ibold, Pete Meehan, Riad Nasr, and Michel Ross and family. To Zack and the people at Lucille's. To the Burgundy Lion, where I've finished way too many nights—thank you Toby, Paul, Jean Michel, and Will.

To Vintageframescompany.com, Gabe at Fedora and Joseph Leonard, www.domainedemontille.com, Chris and Incanto crew, family Occhipinti, B.G.L., Billy Brownstein, Petzicoulis, Adam Sachs, Adam Gollner, McCord Museum, Village de Kamouraska, Martin Spaulding, M Wells Restaurant, Rowan Jacobsen, and Joe Dressner.

To the crew at DNA and Bottega. To Roberto Pesut, Massimo, Angelo Leone, Daniel Schandelmayer, Jean Paul Thibert, Jean Pierre Clerc, Nicolas Jongleux, the crew of the Sooke Harbour house, and the Dominion crew.

To Stephen and Claudine Bronfman, Diamantis crew, Wisemans, Mme McNicol, Francis and Gilles Martin, Dom Allnutt, Rezin, Geoff and Kate Molson, Stewart and Claire Webster, Kim Côté, Pullman crew, Michael's Genuine crew, Ruben Fogel, The Riddles, Sallenave Fam, Wine Bill Zak, M. Tailleferre, Paul Macot, Hal and Anne Gill, Dara Galinger, Normand and Charles Antoine at Toqué!, Hagen, Dr. Bombay, Notkins, Marc Emond, A. Hopkins, Dave Janecek, Marier & Bros., Kirk Muller, Angry Kevin, Sean O'Donnell and Pops, "Maitre" Steve Kelley, The real P. K., Mashaals, Pelo, "Young Master Cundill," Lesley Chesterman, Griffintown Café crew, and Molson Melanie.

To the people who make it happen: the Joe Beef, Liverpool House, and McKiernan staffs. All of my gratitude.

To Kim Witherspoon of Inkwell and Julie Bennett, Katy Brown, and Aaron Wehner of Ten Speed Press.

To Jennifer May, thank you.

Thank you to my high-school math teacher who told me that I might want to work with my hands, as my "brain isn't wired like a normal person's."

Sorry to those I've forgotten. You know where to find me.

I sincerely thank you all for being part of this.

MEREDITH ERICKSON

To Fred and Dave, brothers from different mothers. Who would have thought that five years of working together would have culminated into this? You're like family.

To the Joe Beef crew in its entirety. Yes, Liverpool and McKiernan (the island of misfit toys), I mean you, too. Without you, none of this would be possible, from start to finish. You've all been as fun to work with on the outside as you were on the inside. I know service is hard enough without my shit. But look, I'm gone!

Special thanks in particular goes out to Frank "the Tank" Côté. I promise you'll never hear "Frank, um, I have a question" again. Also to Marco, whose enthusiasm to help wherever possible kept me going. To Vanya Filipovic and Ryan Gray, your booze knowledge and (moreover) intake truly astound me. To Pier Luc Dallaire, for constantly testing, cooking, and helping in any way possible. You've got the good stuff.

Big thanks to Allison Cunningham, for letting us destroy your kitchen for weekends at a time, and to Julie Sanchez, an ever-present ally.

To Peter Meehan, who has been not only a great friend, but also my

sensei since day one. A deep thanks to you, Pete. Maybe next time we go out for dinner, you'll stay awake.

To Mark Ibold, whose sunny insight and recipe comments always made me smile. You're right, obscure recipes are kind of like rare B-sides.

To Jennifer May, my teammate and bunk buddy. Thanks for the (beautiful) proof that this actually happened.

To Kim Witherspoon—our first conversation was truly a great moment for me. Big thanks to Julie Schilder and Allison Hunter.

To the Ten Speed crew, in particular, Aaron Wehner, for plucking up nerds like us, and to Julie Bennett, for your patience and ever-thoughtful comments. A big thank you to Katy Brown, for understanding our nonsensical art direction.

To John Bil and all the islanders for hooking us up.

To Theo, Paul Coffin, and the Montreal wine contingent.

To VIA Rail, for the train tickets. And to Josée Vallerand from Exporail, for her patience and rail knowledge.

To Peter Delottinville, for the words and inspiration.

To David Chang, Riad Nasr, and Josée di Stasio. Your good words have never hurt.

To all the testers, in particular Veronique Dryden, Sybille Sasse, and Patrick McEntyre.

To my parents, all four of you, who are probably the most excited about this book. To my grandparents, who are the second most excited.

To my friends, who supported me through the chaos. Thanks for listening.

To Oliver Sasse—you kept me on the right, when I could have easily gone on the wrong.

ABOUT THE AUTHORS & PHOTOGRAPHER

FRÉDÉRIC MORIN is the co-owner/ chef of Joe Beef, Liverpool House, and McKiernan Luncheonette. Destined for craftsmanship, Fred, at only twelve, would wake up at 6:30 A.M. to work in his backyard, a compound of sorts. When he turned thirteen, his grandfather gave him a smoker. He attended L'École Hôtelière des Laurentides, where he remembers (among other things) classes being held at a vacated steak house named "Pep," as the school was under renovation. Pastry classes were held in the coat check. After graduation, he worked at the ebullient Jean-Talon Market selling peppers and onions.

Notably, Fred served as garde-manger at the distinguished Toqué! before becoming the chef de cuisine at Globe. He worked there for seven years before opening Joe Beef.

When not gardening, building in his workshop, or at the restaurants, he can be found at home nearby, with Allison (his wife and a third partner of the restaurants) and sons.

DAVID MCMILLAN is the co-owner/ chef of Joe Beef, Liverpool House, and McKiernan Luncheonette. Born and raised in Quebec City, David grew up playing hockey, digging holes in snowbanks, and watching *Wok with Yan.*

Inspired by the French school, David has worked in many classic restaurants in Montreal. He credits Nicolas Jongleux as his prime mentor and still practices the *cuisine Bourgeoise* approach taught to him by Nicolas and which he learned simply through his time spent in Burgundy. He also considers the venerable Sooke Harbour House on Vancouver Island as a life-changing work experience.

David has been holding court in the restaurant business for close to twenty years. When not at the restaurants, he can be found painting at his studio in Saint Henri or with his wife and daughters at their cottage in Kamouraska, Quebec.

One of the original Joe Beefers, MEREDITH ERICKSON has written for various magazines, newspapers, and television series. Currently collaborating on several books, Meredith splits her time between Montreal and London.

JENNIFER MAY is a photographer specializing in food, location, and portraits. Her work has appeared in books published by Clarkson Potter and Stewart, Tabori & Chang, and she is a frequent contributor to the *New York Times.* A west coast Canadian, she is now based in Woodstock, New York, where she lives with her husband, the artist Chris Metze.

INDEX

Text copyright © 2011 by Meredith Erickson,
    Frédéric Morin, and David McMillan
Foreword copyright © 2011 by David Chang
Photographs copyright © 2011 by Jennifer May
Illustrations copyright © 2011 by Frédéric Morin

Grateful acknowledgment is made to *Labour/Le Travailleur* for permission to use an excerpt from *Joe Beef of Montreal: Working Class Culture and the Tavern, 1869–1889* by Peter DeLottinville (*Labour/Le Travailleur*, 8/9, Autumn/Spring, 1981–1982, 9–40). Reprinted by permission of *Labour/Le Travailleur*.

Grateful acknowledgment is made to the following for permission to reprint previously published material:

Exporail, the Canadian Railway Museum: train illustrations, pages 80-81; dining car menus, page 89; and Canadian Pacific logo, page 282. Reprinted by permission of Exporail, the Canadian Railway Museum. McCord Museum: photographs and maps of Joe Beef's Canteen (M995X.5.35.4), pages 6 and 53; Joe Beef of Montreal (UAPT5014), page 7; City of Montreal (M4824), page 46; Molson's Brewery beer cart (VIEW-8753), page 82; and A New Map of the Province of Quebec (M3683), page 110. Reprinted by permission of the McCord Museum.

All photographs are by Jennifer May with the exception of those noted here: page 12 (left), 13 (left), 47, 49 (row 1 center and right, row 2 left and center, row 3 left, row 4 left and center), page 72, and page 214 by David McMillan; page 15 (left) by Meredith Erickson; page 48 by Marie-Claude St-Pierre; page 50 by Doris McMillan; pages 137 and 223 by Chris Snow; page 173 by Frédéric Morin; page 177 by Melanie Henault-Tessier; page 215 by Eric Deguire; and end sheets from a painting by Peter Hoffer.

Library of Congress Cataloging-in-Publication Data is on file with the publisher.

ISBN 978-1-60774-014-8

Printed in China

Design by Katy Brown

10 9 8 7 6 5 4 3

First Edition

MAR __ - 2013